Colonial Capitalism and the Dilemmas of Liberalism

Colonial Capitalism and the Dilemmas of Liberalism

ONUR ULAS INCE

OXFORD
UNIVERSITY PRESS

OXFORD

UNIVERSITY PRESS

Oxford University Press is a department of the University of Oxford. It furthers
the University's objective of excellence in research, scholarship, and education
by publishing worldwide. Oxford is a registered trade mark of Oxford University
Press in the UK and certain other countries.

Published in the United States of America by Oxford University Press
198 Madison Avenue, New York, NY 10016, United States of America.

© Oxford University Press 2018

First issued as an Oxford University Press paperback, 2020

CIP data is on file at the Library of Congress
ISBN 978–0–19–063729–3 (hardcover) | ISBN 978–0–19–7506400 (paperback)

To my parents, Hülya İnce and Nedim İnce.

Annem Hülya İnce ve Babam Nedim İnce'ye.

CONTENTS

ACKNOWLEDGMENTS

It takes a village to write a book. I have incurred many debts over the ten years that it took to chisel an intuition into a question, an argument, and eventually a book. Of those debts, heavy are those owed to Susan Buck-Morss, Isaac Kramnick, Richard Bensel, Jason Frank, and Diane Rubenstein, mentors who evinced an exemplary combination of encouragement of unorthodox thinking and demand for scholarly rigor. I am grateful for the unwavering support and exacting standards of Jeanne Morefield, who, as a friend, interlocutor, and outstanding scholar of liberalism and empire, has read and commented on my written work more than anybody else. I hold the privilege of having Andrew Sartori, Siraj Ahmed, Aziz Rana, and William Clare Roberts read and commented on the entire manuscript. The argument of the book stands much clearer and sharper thanks to their extensive and trenchant criticisms. The remaining faults, of course, are mine.

I have found intellectual inspiration and a rare generosity of spirit in James Tully, Barbara Arneil, Karuna Mantena, and Daniel O'Neill—all pioneers in the study of political theory and empire—who provided feedback on various sections of the manuscript. Robert Nichols has been a kindred mind and an astute critic of my work in our shared endeavor of bringing the study of colonialism and capitalism within the fold of political theory. J. G. A. Pocock awed and humbled me by taking the time to read the monstrously long first draft of the chapter on E. G. Wakefield and mail me his comments. The chapter on Edmund Burke benefited greatly from Robert Travers's expert advice. Adom Getachew and Sayres Rudy have my thanks for their incisive commentary on the framing chapter of the book. My exchanges with Alex Gourevitch and Burke Hendrix on capitalism, primitive accumulation, and liberalism were a kind of intellectual calisthenics that kept my thinking in shape. I have to commend Murad Idris's professionalism in helping me to clarify the book's stakes. Dear friend and indomitable critic Ayça Çubukçu has my thanks for her relentless probing into the assumptions, commitments, and limits of the book as well as for her warm hospitality in Cambridge, Massachusetts. Long and intense conversations with Anthony Reed and Carl Gelderloos, extending into the early hours of many a morning, proved formative of my ideas in more ways that I can identify.

Some of the insights central to this project emerged from several institutional involvements during my time at Cornell University. Beyond the Department of Government, I found an intellectual home at the Institute for Comparative Modernities that invited a wealth of transdisciplinary and heterodox research. I will always be thankful to Barry Maxwell for pulling me into the institute as soon as it got off the ground and involving me with its lecture series, conferences, and reading groups. I was also fortunate enough to be part of the New Enclosures Research Working Group at Cornell, which pushed my research horizons beyond political theory and intellectual history, and gave me the opportunity to discuss parts of the project with James Scott, Silvia Federici, and George Caffentzis. Of the founding members of the Working Group, the formidable Charles Geisler has my special thanks and admiration. Harvard Law School's Institute for Global Law and Policy provided an ecumenical venue for intellectual exchange with critical legal scholars on questions central to the project. I would like to thank Sundhya Pahuja, Zoran Oklopcic, and Matthew Craven for their close engagement with the first chapter of the manuscript at the 2013 workshop. I also found the chance to present the arguments of the book at the Cornell Political Theory Workshop, Politics of Land Conference at the University of Alberta, Law and History Workshop at Tel Aviv University, and the Institute for Global Law and Policy. The organizers and the audiences have my thanks.

It was a pleasure to work with David McBride at Oxford University Press. I heavily relied on the patient and able support of Emily Mackenzie and Janani Thiruvalluvar in preparing the manuscript for publication. Ginny Faber has my heartfelt thanks for the invisible yet invaluable labor of copyediting.

Elements of this book have appeared in previous journal articles. I am grateful to the editors of *The Review of Politics, Polity*, Cambridge University Press, and Springer for the permission to revise published material.

The greatest debt is due to my life companion, better half, and fellow scholar, Sinja Graf. From the inception to the conclusion of the book, which stretched over a decade, two intercontinental moves, three jobs, and plenty of rough patches, she has not lost her patience and acumen in listening to my reflections and reading every piece of writing that I have sent her way. My debt to her is one that I hope will keep accruing for the decades to come.

This book is dedicated to my parents, Hülya and Nedim Ince.

Colonial Capitalism and the Dilemmas of Liberalism

Introduction

Liberalism and Empire in a New Key

In his magnum opus of political economy, Adam Smith described the discovery of America and the circumnavigation of the Cape of Good Hope as "the two greatest and most important events in the history of mankind." His estimation of the consequences of these oceanic expeditions, however, was less than sanguine.

> By uniting, in some measure, the most distant parts of the world, by enabling them to relieve one another's wants, to increase one another's enjoyments, and to encourage one another's industry, their general tendency would seem to be beneficial. To the natives, however, both of the East and West Indies, all the commercial benefits which can have resulted from those events have been sunk and lost in the dreadful misfortunes which they have occasioned.[1]

In the brief span of a passage, Smith encapsulated a key contradiction of the global political economic order that had been taking shape since the sixteenth century. Smith's world was a world of transoceanic trade, an emergent international division of labor, and growing prosperity and social refinement in Europe. It was also a world of colonial empires replete with territorial conquest, demographic extirpation, and enslavement in the West, and militarized trading, commercial monopolies, and tribute extraction in the East. For Smith and his fellow Enlightenment thinkers, modern Europe had witnessed the birth of a historically unique form of human society, one that promised a new model of peace, opulence, and liberty. The same Europe also presided over a violent network of colonial economies that forcibly harnessed the West and the East into a world market. This paradox—a liberal, commercial society incubating in a world of illiberal, colonial empires—was at the root of Smith's ultimately ambivalent assessment of global commerce.[2]

This book is a study of the constitutive and contradictory relationship between capitalism, liberalism, and empire. It argues that British political and economic

thought, both before and after Smith, was marked by a tension between the illiberal origins of global capitalist relations and the theoretical attempts to envision
these capitalist relations in liberal terms. It examines the theoretical efforts of
liberal thinkers to explain, navigate, and justify the coercion inherent in colonial
economic relations and connects these efforts to the liberal ideology of capitalism as an economic system of market freedom and equality. I maintain that
this tension flared most vividly at those moments when the colonial land expropriation, slavery, and resource extraction that were central to the formation of
global capitalism appeared too cruel, rapacious, and tyrannical when judged by
the liberal political economic principles that were taking shape in Britain. At the
heart of my analysis is the curious (and curiously persistent) imagination of the
British Empire as a liberal empire of commerce, in spite of the violent record
of dispossession, servitude, and depredation that typified its economy, most
blatantly in the colonies. I contend that the Britons could extol their empire as
the empire of liberty and the harbinger of a peaceful, civilized, and prosperous
global order only on the condition that the violence that undergirded colonial
economic structures was ideologically contained. I further argue that such ideological containment owed a great deal to the theoretical efforts of liberal intellectuals, specifically John Locke, Edmund Burke, and Edward G. Wakefield,
who strove to mediate between the illiberality of British colonial capitalism
and the liberal British self-image. The study elucidates this ideological problem
around the political-economic debates between the mid-seventeenth and mid-
nineteenth centuries over the status of property, trade, and labor relations within
the empire. By the end of the period examined here, the British political and
intellectual opinion could applaud the British Empire as the standard-bearer
of private property, free trade, and free labor, thanks to the successive disavow-
als of the territorial conquest, commercial pillage, and labor bondage that built
Britain's imperial economy across North Atlantic, South Asia, and Australasia.

Liberalism, Capitalism, and Empire

The gulf between the self-professed liberalism of the British Empire and the illib-
eralism of its actual history has been a major leitmotif in the recent "imperial turn"
in the field of political theory.[3] In the words of two influential theorists, a guiding
premise of studying political thought in the imperial fold is that "European constitutional states, as state empires, developed within global systems of imperial
and colonial law from the beginning,"[4] and consequently, "[e]ven when practical
and administrative issues were to the fore, the discussion of what we can broadly
call colonial government encompassed disputes over universality, sovereignty,
freedom, democracy, property, and justice."[5] Groundbreaking works in this

vein first appeared with the discovery that canonical liberal thinkers like John Locke and John Stuart Mill were personally and professionally invested in the imperial enterprise.[6] Intellectual historians and political theorists expanded on those efforts, adopting imperial history as a critical vantage point for revisionist appraisals of these and other eminent members of the European political theory pantheon. Clustering around the British Empire, such reappraisals evinced a palpable anti-Whiggism in exposing the philosophies of subordination that authorized and justified its systematic violence against non-Europeans. For a growing number of scholars, the juxtaposition of "liberalism and empire" has since come to denote both a specific area of study and its central problematic, that is, a contradictory assemblage that comprised, on the one hand, principles of moral equality, subjective rights, the rule of law, representative government, and ethical pluralism, and on the other, practices of domination, foreign rule, naked coercion, untrammeled power, disenfranchisement, and exclusion.

This book sets out to challenge a notable disposition that stamps this scholarship—namely, the penchant to frame the connection between liberalism and empire primarily as a problem of the politics of representation, culture, or identity. Notwithstanding differences of textual interpretation, historical studies in this field frequently concentrate on liberal thinkers' perceptions of and normative judgments about the colonized peoples, which these studies then construe as an index of liberalism's relationship to imperial rule. Although the exact nature of the liberalism-empire nexus remains controversial,[7] the controversy remains noticeably unified in its occupation with questions of universalism and difference, its heavily intratextual approach, and its attention to the linguistic over the material contexts of the liberal ideas under study.[8]

By itself, this methodological preference is not problematic. As with any other interpretive lens, it brings into focus certain features of liberalism's interface with empire, leaving others outside the depth of field. The problem is that among the dimensions that are left blurry is the socioeconomic and institutional materiality of empire, which in turn limits the capacity of this scholarship to analyze and critique liberal imperialism. As I detail in the next chapter, on the critical front, a culturalist focus on universalism and difference commands little firepower against the presentist vindications of the British Empire as the historic protagonist of economic globalization.[9] On the analytic side, a blanket politics of universalism cannot adequately elucidate how liberal thinkers parsed and ordered the range of cultural differences between Europeans and non-Europeans, and why they emphasized certain differences over others as being more relevant for imperial justification or anti-imperial critique.

This book attempts to address these limits by "rematerializing" the relationship between liberalism and empire. The task involves complementing an account of the semantic context of liberal ideas with an analysis of the socioeconomic context, that is, paying as much attention to the institutional structures and economic practices that constituted the fabric of empire as to the political languages and vocabularies in which liberal intellectuals articulated their assessment of it. There are no doubt multiple ways of rematerializing the imperial context (e.g., gender, ecology, technology, law, governance), each of which would highlight a different aspect of empire's formative impact on liberal thought. I propose viewing the materiality of empire specifically through the lens of "colonial capitalism," a notion inspired by critical social theory and colonial political economy. As an analytic framework, colonial capitalism rests on the fundamental premise that capitalism has historically emerged within the juridico-political framework of the "colonial empire" rather than the "nation-state." It grasps capitalist relations as having developed in and through colonial networks of commodities, peoples, ideas, and practices, which formed a planetary web of value chains connecting multiple and heterogeneous sites of production across oceanic distances.

A major corollary of the colonial perspective on capitalism is to underscore the constitutive role of extra-economic coercion in effecting capitalist social transformations. Within this picture, colonial land grabs, plantation slavery, and the forced deindustrialization of imperial dependencies configure as crucial moments in the global formation of capitalism.[10] Borrowing a key concept from Marx's account of the origins of capitalism, I employ the term *colonial primitive accumulation* to theorize the forcible transformation and uneven integration of colonial land, labor, and resources into global networks of capital.[11] My focus falls on colonial sites, not because primitive accumulation did not also transpire in Europe, but because it played out much more brutally at the imperial frontiers, called for different frameworks of justification, and exercised liberal metropolitan minds with more vexing questions.

The principal contribution of this framework to the study of liberalism is to highlight the economic undertakings of colonial entrepreneurs as a type of colonial anomaly that had to be accounted for by the liberal standards of metropolitan thought. The optic of colonial capitalism redefines empire's challenge to liberalism by shifting the focus from who the colonized *are* to what the colonizers *do*, that is, from the cultural difference of the subject populations to the deeds of imperial agents themselves. In charting a new map of the liberalism-empire nexus, I mainly follow metropolitan reflections on territorial conquest, indigenous dispossession, bonded labor, and armed trading, rather than judgments about the rational capacity or civilizational status of the non-Europeans. For sharpening the contours of this problem, the study capitalizes on the peculiarity of the British imperial ideology. Although the British matched and eventually surpassed their European rivals in the capacity and readiness for imperial warfare, conquest, and brutality, they stubbornly believed themselves to be, in David Armitage's classic formulation, a "Protestant, commercial, maritime, and free" people.[12] The clash of this commercial, pacific, and free self-image with the ruthless expropriation and despotic coercion of colonial economies offers a window onto the tension between the liberal conceptions of capitalism and its illiberal conditions of emergence and possibility.

Cognizant of the notoriously protean character of the term "liberalism," I purposely restrict the investigation of liberalism to its instantiations in metropolitan theories of capitalism rather than taking on the entire range of family resemblances associated with the term.[13] I identify the primal norms of contractual freedom and juridical equality as the ideational core of the liberal conception of capitalism. While freedom and equality as normative values are most commonly associated with liberal political theory, they were also, and perhaps more systematically, elaborated and enshrined in the language of classical political economy. Originating in the seventeenth century, political economy as a field of knowledge evolved in tandem with global capitalism, and its practitioners often proclaimed it to be the appropriate medium for explaining the dynamics of commerce and capital, as well as for charting an enlightened course of domestic and imperial policy.[14] By concentrating on political economy, this book therefore anchors core tenets of liberalism in a sphere of reflection that adopted capitalist social forms and their global variegation as its principal object of inquiry.

I dissect the entangled histories of liberalism, capitalism, and empire around three critical moments of imperial expansion and controversy in which the theoretical parameters of liberalism were articulated. The first of these is the seventeenth-century colonial land appropriation in the Americas that enabled the formation of Atlantic colonial capitalism and ignited momentous European debates over legitimate claims to property in the New World. The second moment centers on the East India Company's ascendancy in Bengal and British merchant capital's intrusion into the Indian economy, which triggered a public storm about the nature of Anglo-Indian trade. The third and final moment concerns nineteenth-century schemes of imperial labor allocation that aimed to promote colonial emigration and settler capitalism in Australasia, which threw into question the legal and economic boundaries between free and bonded labor. "Property," "exchange," and "labor" thereby constitute a triadic constellation at the core of liberal political economy's encounter with colonial capitalism. Extralegal appropriation of land in America, militarized trading in India, and elaborate schemes of dependent labor in Australasia each represents a vital moment in the development of global capital networks *and* a challenge to narrating this development as the triumph of private property, market exchange, and free labor.

Corresponding to the central questions of property, exchange, and labor, I analyze the theoretical attempts of Locke, Burke, and Wakefield to reconcile the essentially liberal image of Britain's capitalist economy with the illiberal institutional arrangements and practices on which it stood. My specific focus on these three intellectuals stems from their simultaneous commitment to a modern capitalist economy, to imperial expansion as an instrument of economic prosperity and political power, and to the primal liberal norms of contractual freedom and juridical equality. These multiple and often incongruent theoretical commitments render their writings privileged ground for detecting the frictions between liberalism, capitalism, and empire and their negotiation in the register of political economy. Compounding this rationale is the active involvement of the three thinkers in Britain's imperial politics: Locke as Secretary to the Council of Trade and Plantations and later a member of the Board of Trade; Burke as a member of the Parliamentary Select Committee on India; Wakefield as a pro-colonization publicist, lobbyist, and the intellectual leader of the Colonial Reform Movement. Their shared institutional and intellectual investments in the colonial capitalist enterprise and the empire of liberty furnishes the overarching framework within which a comparison of these otherwise dissimilar thinkers can generate unexpected insights into the liaisons between liberalism and empire.

The following chapters demonstrate that when compared to the twenty-first-century reclamations of British imperialism as the vanguard of economic globalization, Locke, Burke, and Wakefield were ironically less self-assured about the coercive interventions that went into making Britain's imperial economy. Their disquiet about the illiberality of empire was reflected in their strategies of "disavowal." Crucially, none of them denied the fact of indigenous dispossession, unequal exchange, and labor bondage that pervaded colonial economies. Instead of joining contemporary critics in denouncing the imperial system, however, they resorted to theoretical maneuvers, rhetorical strategies, fictions, and myths that insulated the liberal image of Britain's commercial economy from the enormities of colonial ventures. These theoretical innovations include Locke's myth of mankind's "universal consent" to the use of money, which ultimately blamed Native Americans for their own expropriation; Burke's fantasy of "imperial commerce" that promised equitable economic dealings between the British and their conquered Indian subjects; and Wakefield's fictive "settler contract" whereby poor colonial immigrants acceded to work as wage laborers rather than become independent landowners. Such efforts at reconciliation also set these three thinkers apart from other political economists, like Adam Smith and David Hume, for whom the empire, particularly in its territorial and extractive variety, was nigh irredeemable from a liberal economic perspective. When the liberal British self-image traveled overseas, it crashed against the violent shores of colonial capitalism. It fell to the liberal intellectuals of the empire, such as the three examined here, to brace the hull.

Structure of the Book

I advance the main argument of the book in four chapters. Chapter 1 elaborates the analytic framework of colonial capitalism for reconstructing the relationship between liberalism and empire. I offer a more detailed engagement with the extant literature and outline a social theory of the imperial context as a promising way forward. Drawing on critical political economy, social and economic history, and postcolonial theory, I construct an account of the heterogeneous and globally networked property structures, exchange systems, and labor regimes that comprised Britain's imperial economy. Against this background, I delineate the dilemmas of liberalism that materialized in the effort to reconcile the liberal British self-image with the violence of the empire. In crafting the hermeneutic key for interpreting the works of Locke, Burke, and Wakefield, I also clarify this study's stance on methodological questions about contextualization, textual interpretation, and the risks of reductionism and anachronism.

Chapter 2 offers an analysis of Locke's theory of property in the context of Atlantic colonial capitalism. Political theorists and intellectual historians have extensively documented Locke's professional involvement in English colonialism and explored its implications for his political thought.[15] What has gone unnoticed, however, is the centrality of Locke's theory of money to the liberal justification of English colonization in America. The prevailing research agenda revolves around Locke's labor theory of appropriation as the linchpin of his justification of indigenous dispossession. Recasting this problematic in the light of Atlantic colonial capitalism, I trace the shifting terms of Locke's theory of property from labor to monetization as the grounds for adjudicating rightful property claims in the state of nature. This alternative account brings into conversation the colonial interpretations of Locke with the earlier Locke scholarship on natural law, morality, possessive individualism, and capitalism. I contend that Locke predicated labor and improvement on the use of money and construed the absence of monetization in America as a sign that the continent remained in the natural common and thereby open to nonconsensual appropriation. The ingenuity of Locke's theoretical construction lay in conjuring up a myth of mankind's universal tacit consent to the use of money and positioning Native Americans at once inside and outside such consent. The fiction of universal consent enabled Locke to hold Native Americans responsible for the natural common status of America and thereby sutured the rift between his liberal theory of private property and extralegal land appropriations in the New World.

Chapter 3 turns to Edmund Burke's intervention in eighteenth-century debates on global commerce and empire as refracted through the East India Company's rule in Bengal. Burke has been a major figure of investigation in the recent literature on empire by virtue of his fervent effort to impeach Warren Hastings and champion the cause of the Indians against British oppression and misrule. Some scholars have interpreted Burke's crusade as the expression of his peculiar and untimely cosmopolitanism; others have chalked it up to his conservative defense of empire or his anxieties about the revival of an atavistic spirit of conquest.[16] The chapter expands the terrain of analysis by bringing Burke's political economic writings to bear on his arguments for maintaining the empire while reforming its illiberal economic policies. I maintain that Burke's diatribe against the Company rule was that it systematically violated the liberal economic principles that he believed defined the British national character. Holding onto both the empire and its liberal image required Burke to denounce the politicization of commerce in India and distance it from what he conceived to be Britain's properly commercial—that is, peaceful and equitable—economic system. His condemnation of the Company's system of tribute extraction can therefore be understood as an attempt to shore up the frayed boundaries between civilized commerce and unabashed pillage, between enlightened self-interest and unbridled rapacity, and between the "imperial commerce" that a reformed empire promised and the "imperious commerce" that had been destroying India.

Chapter 4 examines the writings of Edward Gibbon Wakefield, an unduly neglected and only recently rediscovered figure in the intellectual history of empire.[17] At the center of my analysis is Wakefield's theory of "systematic colonization" as a solution to the problems of overpopulation in Britain and labor shortage in its colonies. Historians of the British Empire and political economy have noted the remarkable success of Wakefield's theory in converting the British public and political opinion to a pro-colonization position. I argue in this chapter that systematic colonization was not simply a strategy for imperial labor allocation but also an attempt to protect capitalist civilization from the dangers of "barbarization" both at home in the colonies. In Britain, proletarianization, unemployment, and pauperization stoked labor militancy and threatened social revolution. Relieving the population pressure by pauper relocation was not only economically ineffectual but also bred a repugnant species of frontier barbarism in the colonies by turning British emigrants into poor and rude smallholding farmers. Wakefield proposed to solve both problems at once by imposing preemptive crown rights and artificially inflated prices on colonial lands, which would compel emigrants to work for colonial capitalists. This strategy of state-led, preemptive proletarianization was aimed at rendering laborers structurally dependent on capitalists without formally abridging their civil liberties. Well aware that his plan contravened the laissez-faire orthodoxy of his time and foisted "wage slavery" on colonial settlers, Wakefield took refuge in utilitarian myths of contractual dispossession. He represented the imposition of colonial wage labor by the hand of the imperial state as nothing other than the enforcement of a fictional "settler compact" whereby colonial emigrants had voluntarily agreed to divide themselves into capitalists and wage laborers for the sake of capitalist civilization.

Ways Forward

My overall purpose is to critically augment the existing scholarship on the political theory of empire by casting a number of key research questions in new theoretical light. Colonial capitalism opens the way to studying liberalism as a historically mediated language of politics that was worked out precisely in and through the political economic debates around the contested meanings of private property, market exchange, and free labor. The proposed interpretation does not abandon the engagement with the politics of universalism that revolves around metropolitan judgments about non-Europeans' rationality, level of civilization, and capacity for autonomy or progress. Rather, it demonstrates how such normative judgments were mediated by liberal thinkers' perceptions of the colonial dispossession, exploitation, and extraction that belonged to the history of global capitalism. Without attending to the contradictions of the imperial economy as a source of doubt, anxiety, and endogenous critique for liberal intellectuals, these mediations remain out of sight, leaving one with a blanket politics of universalism that hinges on the exogenous binary between the colonizer and the colonized.

Blanket conceptions of universalism run into difficulties in the attempts to explain why *certain* historically specific practices and not others were deemed to be universal; or why *certain* cultural differences were translated into deficits and braided into civilizational hierarchies, while others were considered irrelevant for purposes of colonial rule, dispossession, and exploitation. To name a few such questions that arise in the course of this book: Why did John Locke decisively put monetization before monotheism in America for deciding whether the New World was terra nullius and therefore open to English colonization? On what basis did Edmund Burke differentiate between Britain's imperial subjects, defending Indians against British oppression, prescribing a despotic discipline for Africans, and envisioning the total extermination of Native Americans? How to explain that the enclosing and improving settler, who embodied the civilizing mission of the British Empire in the seventeenth century, was scorned by Edward Gibbon Wakefield, John Stuart Mill, and other Philosophic Radicals in the nineteenth century as the incarnation of civilizational degeneration?

The contextual variation in these questions is paralleled by the theoretical cross-pollinations displayed by the historical mutations of British liberal thought. Recent scholarship has generated an impressive inventory of the instances in which liberal thinkers, when confronted with specific problems of colonial rule, enlisted as diverse and even conflicting political discourses as universal human progress, cosmopolitan pluralism, and insurmountable cultural difference.[18] This book conjectures that such cross-pollinations emerged partly from intellectual efforts to suture the rift opened up in the universal claims of liberalism by the manifest unfreedom and inequality that characterized Britain's colonial economies. Using the framework of colonial capitalism, we can take a step beyond the historicist reconstruction of liberalism's collusion with other political languages and delineate the historical patterns that such collusions assumed in concrete contexts of imperial political economy. I hazard some reflections in this direction in the conclusion of this study.

The implications of my analysis extend beyond the study of liberalism's relationship to empire. As I dwell on in some length in the next chapter, connecting liberal ideas to a social analysis of institutions and ideologies of capitalism discloses historical continuities that elude the purview of the linguistic contextualist approach to intellectual history. This book presents both a preliminary excursion, as well as an invitation for further inquiry, into the longer genealogy of the liberal imaginations of capitalism that have persisted down to our present. Conceiving of liberalism as a historically circumscribed and polyphonous political language, which is too convoluted to fit generalizing frameworks of social analysis, risks obscuring its status as the dominant ideology of the Anglo-American-centered capitalist world order in the past century and a half. One is reminded of Charles Maier's astute observation about the prevailing approach to the intellectual history of empire:

> What remains remarkable from the viewpoint of intellectual history was the general unwillingness to admit that markets might have a connection with empire. During the long period of Marxist challenge and Cold War, attributing any underlying socioeconomic causation gave most intellectuals in the West great discomfort, and those who offered such theories were dismissed as fundamentally unsound. Better to affirm the obvious point that imperialism and empire are phenomena too complex to reduce to a uniform underlying causality. Multicausality became and remains the last refuge of historians.[19]

The current insistence on treating liberalism as an idiom that strictly exists in and travels through discrete semantic contexts similarly takes refuge in complexity, contingency, and discontinuity—the battle cries of the cultural turn in its assault on the totalizing frameworks of social analysis, mainstream and critical alike.

Questioning this proclivity does not amount to rejecting the plurality and variance of discursive modes in which the liberal ideology of capitalism finds articulation. Witness, for instance, Niall Ferguson's glowing historiography applauding the British Empire for fashioning a liberal capitalist international order and Michael Ignatieff's plea for an "empire lite" to protect the same from its illiberal enemies.[20] Consider, on the other hand, Douglass North and Barry Weingast's hugely influential institutionalist tribute to the Glorious Revolution for establishing the constitutional commitments necessary for capital accumulation to take off, and James Robinson and Daron Acemoglu's narrative of the rise of capitalism on the bedrock of liberal, inclusive, and ostensibly anti-imperial institutions.[21] As important as the attention to the specific vocabularies and argumentative protocols of these discourses is the attentiveness to their resonance and the staying power of the fundamental worldview that they project. The former offers an indispensable historical inventory of the liberal and essentially Euro-American conceptions of capitalism, but by itself cannot explain the resilience of this liberal image and its capacity to reinvent itself across different historical contexts. As I discuss in chapter 1, this is where "critical history," which incorporates a social theory of the socioeconomic context and a notion of ideology, enters (or ought to enter) the picture.

A final conclusion of this book concerns the parameters of political theory as a distinct scholarly mode of reflection. One crucial upshot of extending the framework of political inquiry to problems of imperial rule is to theorize problems of dispossession and exploitation as political questions, which political theorists have for the most part preferred to relegate to the province of political economy or social theory. The historical elaboration of the liberal norms of freedom and equality through controversies on property, exchange, and labor offers a cautionary corrective against the current penchant to sequester the domain of "the political" from the putative field of "the economy" (a sequestration evocatively captured in Hannah Arendt's resolute distancing of politics from the "social question"). Confining political theory of empire to problems of freedom and domination, consent and legitimacy, inclusion and exclusion, and universalism and pluralism amounts to a sociospatial expansion of the objects of political inquiry that stops short of revising the conceptual framework with which such inquiry is practiced. If the principal benefit of placing the history of political thought in an imperial context is simply to enrich those central problems that are already well entrenched and recognizable to political theorists, then "empire" ultimately remains an exogenous and contingent addendum. In contrast, a crucial trajectory of conceptual innovation promised by political theory's encounter with empire is to undo the boundaries between the political and the social.[22] This requires that we understand colonial empires not only as structures of political domination and subordination but, equally importantly, as economic systems of dispossession and exploitation. The necessary correlate of Ann Laura Stoler and Frederick Cooper's celebrated call to place the metropole and the colony in the same analytic field is to integrate political and economic analysis in a more capacious conceptual terrain, and treat political economy as a species of political theory.[23]

The discovery that cardinal categories of reflection in Western political thought were forged in the crucible of colonial empires has been vastly rewarding for the field of political theory. It would be equally rewarding to leverage the framework of colonial capitalism and imperial economy for expanding the conceptual boundaries of political inquiry.

Colonial Capitalism and the Dilemmas of Liberalism

Framing an Inquiry

In the colonies the truth stood naked, but the citizens of the mother country preferred it with clothes on.

—Jean-Paul Sartre

The field of political theory is now home to a veritable cottage industry in the study of liberalism and empire. The purpose of this chapter is to trace the contours of this literature, identify the limitations, and propose a new interpretive framework for studying liberal ideas that will complement the current state of the art. Put summarily, I argue that the fine-grained textual analysis of liberal ideas in imperial contexts has not been matched by a clear socioeconomic analysis of imperial relations themselves. As a result, an overly culturalist and discursive orientation undermines the analytical power and critical commitments of scholarship on liberalism and empire. Although I broadly share the critical impulse animating the major works in this field, I believe this impulse must extend to examining the ways in which capitalist relations mediated between liberal ideas and imperial practices in the early modern British Empire.

I elaborate an alternative approach to interpreting liberal ideas in imperial contexts, one that centers on the notions of "colonial capitalism" and the "primitive accumulation of capital." The principal contribution of this perspective is to disclose the contradictions between, on the one hand, liberal market conceptions of capitalist relations as articulated in British metropolitan political economy and, on the other, the violent methods and coercive processes that gave rise to capitalist forms in the colonies. Through the lens of colonial capitalism, we can delineate the violent capitalist transformations in British colonies as an ideological problem for a self-avowedly liberal and commercial polity, which proudly contrasted itself to the despotic and imperialist spirit that it imputed to its Continental rivals. By the same token, we can analyze how British liberal thinkers, canonical or otherwise, struggled to navigate this problem in ways that proved formative of liberalism as a political language in the early modern period.

I begin with a brief assessment of the current trends in the study of liberalism and empire. I contend that what is eschewed in this scholarship is a social theory of the imperial context, as is reflected in the dominant predilection to restrict analysis to the level of cultural representations of the colonized or the linguistic conventions that delimit metropolitan political discourse. In addressing this lacuna, I turn to critical social theory and imperial economic history to develop the notion of colonial capitalism as an interpretive framework that enables a new appraisal of liberalism's relationship to empire. I go on to distinguish the ideological difficulties generated by the illiberality of colonial capitalism and highlight the role of "disavowal" as a strategy of confronting and mitigating their potentially corrosive effects on the British self-image. I also lay out the methodological premises that I follow in my reappraisal of the history of liberal ideas and address possible objections regarding contextualization and textual interpretation. I conclude with some reflections on the need to compound historical contextualism with a "stereoscopic view of history" for a *critical* study of liberalism in conjunction with capitalism and imperialism.

Because my primary aim is to construct an interpretive framework and delineate the theoretical problematic to be pursued in the rest of the book, my discussion of colonial capitalism is limited to the extent that it brings to light dilemmas of liberalism that are largely bypassed in the existing literature. I therefore do not delve into long-standing controversies on the capitalist transition and world-system, nor do I dwell in much detail on the recently revived debates on primitive accumulation and the violence of capital. I have devoted sustained attention to these questions elsewhere.[1] Here I draw on the theoretical tenets and conclusions that are germane to the intellectual history of liberalism this book offers.

Liberalism and Empire: Rematerializing a Field

Since the early 1990s, growing numbers of scholars have done an impressive job of reinterpreting liberal ideas by situating them in imperial contexts. Not surprisingly, a focus on the English and, later, the British Empire has pervaded this scholarship owing to Britain's status, as one commentator recently put it, as "the crucible of liberal political thinking and the most extensive imperial formation in history."[2] Without going into a comprehensive overview of this literature, I would like to identify two of its broadly shared dispositions that are relevant to my argument.[3] The first of these is a critical attitude toward the British Empire as an instrument of subjugation, exclusion, and domination. This condemnatory outlook has drawn inspiration from the kindred fields of postcolonial studies and the "new imperial history," which have sought to upend Whig narratives that depict the Anglo-American hegemonic project as the harbinger of a liberal, democratic world order.[4] Exceptions to this trend, such as Niall Ferguson's brash defense of the British Empire as the avatar of "Anglobalization" and his endorsement of the United States' open interventionism, have only carried grist to the mill of anti-imperial critique.[5]

Second, and more importantly, there has been a marked penchant to organize these critical studies around ideologies of universalism and cosmopolitanism and conceptions of culture and difference.[6] This predilection has been in marked contrast to the early twentieth-century analyses of European imperialism and colonialism in terms of geopolitical and economic priorities, wherein the problem of capitalism and its crises loomed large.[7] Inflected by the cultural and linguistic turns in the social sciences and the humanities, political theorists and new imperial historians have trained their attention primarily on the identities, perceptions, and cultural representations of the imperial self and the colonial other.[8] Uday Mehta's acclaimed *Liberalism and Empire* (1999) in particular proved extremely influential in setting the terms of the debate in this culturalist key. Pioneering works have variously explored, for instance, how European thinkers "analyzed and judged unfamiliar societies," their "philosophical claims about human unity and diversity," or the "importance of *difference*" in the formation of imperial "subject-positions."[9]

Once the problem of imperial domination was posited in terms of the symbolic exclusion of colonial subjects from the ambit of freedom and equality accorded to metropolitan citizens, the question of "liberalism and empire" became a question of whether liberal arguments were mobilized to elaborate and justify such exclusion or to denounce and challenge it. Researchers accordingly turned their attention to liberal thinkers, from John Locke to John Stuart Mill and beyond, and explored the extent to which these thinkers had discovered in colonial difference a reason to question Eurocentric cultural assumptions or instead mapped such difference onto evolutionary civilizational hierarchies that privileged the Europeans. These opposing modes of grappling with colonial difference could translate into, at the one extreme, a precocious cosmopolitanism that censured imperial arrogance and respected non-European polities and, at the other, a renewed confidence in imperial tutelage that perpetually withheld from the colonized the dignity and autonomy promised by liberalism.[10]

The eschewal of social analysis in the new theories and histories of empire stems in part from the justifiable skepticism of reductive teleology associated with Marxism, which, as one critic puts it, has "displaced [colonialism] into the inexorable logics of modernization and world capitalism."[11] The unfortunate outcome of such skepticism, however, has been to dematerialize the study of empire by adopting a heavily culturalist focus and intratextual approach, which, I argue, blunts the critical edge of recent scholarship. In these studies, as Andrew Sartori observes, "the representational order always takes precedence in the analytical sequence" over the concrete relations of force, coercion, and exploitation that formed the materiality of imperial rule.[12] Richard Drayton strikes a similar chord when he writes, "A focus on subjectivity displaced examination of practical and material experience . . . Historians appeared to be more bothered by 'epistemic violence' than the real thing."[13] This oversight becomes particularly pronounced when faced with the sort of Whig imperial apologetics elaborated by Ferguson, which vindicate the British imperial record on institutional-economic grounds, extolling the empire for disseminating private property, free trade, and the rule of law across the globe. If, as Frederick Cooper reminds us, "for friend or foe alike, the ideological framework of globalization is liberalism—arguments for free trade and free movement of capital," then representing the British Empire as the prime mover of globalization scores a powerful ideological point.[14] On this account, exclusion, subjugation, and even violence and the human costs imperial expansion entails are conceded with disarming frankness and then emplotted as unfortunate yet *incidental* anomalies to the essentially liberal character and mission of the empire.[15] Against such institutional-economic "balance sheet" arguments in support of liberal imperialism, culturalist critiques of empire command little traction.

In addition to diminished critical capacity, bracketing the socioeconomic and institutional dimensions of empire also undermines analytic power. Even when critical scholars emphasize imperial violence and economic exploitation in order to expose Whig narratives, their efforts stop short of a systematic explication of these two elements, their various configurations, and how these configurations inflected imperial ideology and metropolitan thought in specific ways. It is true, as Jennifer Pitts writes against Ferguson's apologetics, that the history of the British Empire is a history of "massive resource extraction, establishment of catastrophic systems of bonded labor, deindustrialization, entrenchment of 'traditional' structures of authority, and insertion of subsistence farmers into often wildly unstable global markets . . . proletarianization, emiseration, chaos, and misrule."[16] One can likewise hardly disagree with Duncan Bell's rebuttal of John Darwin's crypto-Whiggism on the grounds that "extra-judicial killing, sexual cruelty, indentured labour, coercive displacement, the annihilation or radical disruption of existing traditions, institutions, and ways of life, even mass murder and genocide" were all integral to what made the British Empire.[17] However, short of a theoretical account of how these different forms and moments physical coercion, economic exploitation, and social destruction are structurally interconnected, this ignominious record congeals into an undifferentiated mass of "imperial violence" that liberal thinkers then rationalize or criticize. The result is an abstract politics of universalism that has little to say about how colonial differences are parsed, why they are differentially evaluated synchronously and over time, and which ones are conscripted into imperial ideologies of rule, dispossession, and domination. In other words, although the current scholarship does a commendable job of interpreting liberal texts in imperial contexts, much remains to be done to relate these interpretations to a social theory of imperial contexts.

The eschewal of capitalism and, more generally, social history has been even more pronounced in the field of intellectual history, where the bane of reductionism is joined by the bugbear of anachronism.[18] "Linguistic contextualism" is the broad moniker of the methodological effort to banish these fallacies from the practice of intellectual history, originating in J. G. A. Pocock and Quentin Skinner's thunderous rejoinders to C. B. Macpherson's portrayal of a number of early modern thinkers as "bourgeois" political philosophers and thereby defenders of capitalism.[19] As the dominant disciplinary stricture currently governing what counts as bona fide intellectual history, linguistic contextualism turns on the premise that the proper contexts of the history of ideas consist in conventions of language and political discourses, as opposed to economic structures and social practices.[20] On the one hand, linguistic contextualism disputes the validity of textual interpretations that rest on longue durée assumptions about social structure and economic change.[21] The allusion to the "rise of capitalism" represents perhaps the most suspicious of the incursions of "the social" into the perimeter of intellectual history. As Istvan Hont astutely observes, when scholars of eighteenth-century intellectual history cannot avoid speaking of the economic relations of the period, they "use terms like 'commercial society' to get away from Marxist language and categories of sociology. Terms like 'capitalism,' 'bourgeois society,' and 'inorganic society' now seem to be both loaded and disturbingly sloppy as categories."[22] At the same time, linguistic contextualism functions as a "strategy of containment" against the plumbing of the past for consistent and linear intellectual traditions.[23] On this account, invoking "liberalism" in the seventeenth century amounts to thrusting certain notions back in time and upon thinkers who would be at a loss recognize themselves as "liberal."[24] The prescribed path for avoiding these cardinal sins of intellectual history is to embed historical texts in strictly bounded linguistic contexts, wherein one can, as accurately as possible, reconstruct what the author intended his utterance to mean in the light of his immediate interlocutors and the semantic universe available to him.[25]

There is no reason to dispute that careful attention to historical context and to the specific vocabularies, idioms, and terms of debate is indispensable to a study of liberalism and empire. However, linguistic contextualism proves inadequate for an investigation that aspires not only to reconstruct past arguments but also to build explanations of why certain paradigms of thought and modes of argumentation proved more tractable and durable than others. The critical task of delineating historical continuities in imperial ideologies necessitates a retrospective gaze that detects their transmutation over time and translates past vocabularies into present ones, not only on the basis of their shared semantic content, but also with attention to the political and legal institutions in which they instantiate and the socioeconomic power relations they underwrite. This critical retrospective gaze appears unsound when judged by linguistic contextualism's author-centered and forward-looking approach to the history of political ideas and its default suspicion of intellectual history motivated by critical agendas rooted in the present. I elaborate my position on this score in more detail at the end of this chapter, once I have outlined the interpretive framework that informs my inquiry into liberalism and empire.

The particular reappraisal of liberal thought I propose in this study places capitalism and, specifically, coercive capitalist transformation in the colonies, at the heart of the relationship between liberalism and empire. The conceptual pivot of my analysis, colonial capitalism, addresses the manifold processes of territorial expropriation, social displacement, resource extraction, and bonded labor that typified British imperial expansion and played an essential role in the formation of capital circuits connecting the Americas, Europe, Africa, and Asia. Colonial capitalism can offer a theoretical account of the imperial context that is largely absent in the extant analyses of liberalism and empire by bringing into focus the political economic dynamics that propelled, shaped, and delimited the course of imperial expansion. Although colonial capitalism is by no means the definitive standpoint for an imperial account of liberalism, it has the merit of highlighting two key characteristics of the imperial context. First, Britain's imperial economy emerges as a totality of heterogeneous yet interdependent socioeconomic forms consisting of, for instance, Caribbean plantations, English manufactories, Asian and African trading posts, and North American smallholding farms.[26] Second, the violent methods by which these forms were established, such as indigenous dispossession, enclosure of common lands, chattel slavery, and militarized trading, present us with an imperial formation in which the entwinement of political force and economic transformation was not incidental but followed the logic of capitalist expansion.

The analytic of colonial capitalism enables us to disaggregate "imperial violence" by identifying the political and economic priorities behind it, strategies and vectors of its exercise, and, most importantly, how these priorities and strategies shaped the specific terms in which liberal arguments about empire were articulated. In the context of the early modern British Empire, such arguments revolved around totalizing visions of an imperial-commercial order in which the twin objectives of capital accumulation and state-building entered conscious reflection. Political economy increasingly furnished the main medium in which the English and, later, the British political and intellectual classes expressed their views on the governance of the empire, direction of its force, and significance of its consequences.[27] Political economy is therefore the principal site this study excavates to unearth liberal responses to coercive capitalist transformations in the colonies and to reconstruct the attempts to reconcile colonial capitalism with the pacific and commercial self-image of Britain.

I contend that the notion of the "primitive accumulation of capital" that Marx elaborated in *Capital* presents a particularly fruitful way of theorizing the coercion and heterogeneity characteristic of capitalist networks in the early modern period.[28] Marx coined the term "primitive accumulation" with sardonic reference to Adam Smith's origin story of capital as the result of hard work and frugality. Marx maintained that capitalist relations had instead sprung up from the violent separation of direct producers from their means of production and subsistence, most importantly, from the expropriation of agricultural producers.[29] Marx designated the English enclosures and the Highland Clearances as the "classic" case of primitive accumulation, which created a mass of dispossessed proletarians, who, in a repressive regime of vagrancy laws, criminal codes, and workhouses, would later be disciplined into the first waged working class in history.

Perhaps more importantly, Marx extended the notion of primitive accumulation beyond England and Scotland to cover a range of violent economic ventures of global scope and imperial nature. He wrote, in a frequently quoted passage:

> The discovery of gold and silver in America, the extirpation, enslavement, and entombment in mines of the indigenous population of that continent, the beginnings of the conquest and plunder of India, and the conversion of Africa into a preserve for the commercial hunting of blackskins, are all things that characterize the dawn of the era of capitalist production. These idyllic proceedings are the chief moments of primitive accumulation.[30]

If the atrocities listed in this passage sound familiar, it is because we have encountered roughly the same record in Pitts's and Bell's renditions of the British Empire's history of violence. The major difference, however, is that when viewed from a Marxian perspective, these violent acts appear to be more than just moral wrongs, the "systemic injuries" (Pitts) or the "original sin" (Bell) of the empire. The moral valence and liberal assessment of imperial violence is compounded and mediated by its formative role in the global inceptions of capitalism, generating the sort of tensions we saw Smith grappling with in the opening of this book. This is not to suggest replacing empire with capitalism as the relevant context of liberal thought but to conceptualize it more precisely as "colonial empire," understood as the politico-legal framework in which capitalist relations historically developed and liberal thought found its conditions of possibility.[31]

Social historians of imperial and transoceanic connections have long underscored the historical symbiosis between imperialism and capitalist expansion. Robin Blackburn, in his magisterial history of the New World slavery, describes the seventeenth- and eighteenth-century Atlantic as the stage of "pioneering capitalist industrialization." Commercial wars, territorial conquests, slave trade, and the union of extra-economic coercion and export-oriented production in slave plantations placed these activities "entirely within that sphere of primitive accumulation about which Marx wrote . . . force as an economic power."[32] Turning from the West to the East Indies, we find an aggressive form of what Jairus Banaji calls "company capitalism." This species of mercantile capitalism, prominent in the seventeenth and eighteenth centuries, combined militarized trading by chartered companies in the Indian Ocean with their forcible intrusion into the organization of agriculture and manufacturing in South Asia, especially after the British military and political ascendancy on the subcontinent.[33] Cautioning against overemphasizing commercial imperialism, the recent revival in the area of settler colonial studies has alerted us to the cascades of displacement and depopulation that passed over North America and Australasia in the eighteenth and nineteenth centuries, supplying the "ghost acres" that proved essential to capitalist expansion.[34] Finally, Sven Beckert's recent reconstruction of the Industrial Revolution weaves together these strands of imperial violence, planetary economic reorganization, and institutional innovation into an account of "war capitalism" that rampaged between the seventeenth and nineteenth centuries. Although Beckert rarely invokes Marx, his story of war capitalism is almost entirely coextensive with Marx's story of primitive accumulation,[35] above all in its focus on the "transformative powers of a union of capital and state power" as the propulsive force behind "imperial expansion, expropriation, and slavery [that] became central to forging a new global economic order and eventually the rise of capitalism."[36]

There are two reasons for adopting the concept of primitive accumulation in the study of colonial capitalism and liberalism. The first is the pivotal role it assigns to extra-economic coercion in the creation and maintenance of the institutional background conditions of capitalism.[37] As a number of theorists have recently pointed out, capitalism is much more than simply an economic system of production, circulation, and consumption. It consists of an entire "institutionalized social order," a historically determinate mode of imagining, organizing, and practicing human beings' relationship to one another and to the nonhuman world, which encompasses social, ecological, and political dimensions at both the macro-level of institutional-ideological complexes and the micro-level of subjectivities.[38] That being said, the perceived autonomy of the "economic" relations institutionalized via self-regulating markets is critical for the liberal imagination of capitalism. As I will dwell on in more detail, liberal theories of capitalism normatively exclude nonmarket coercion from economic dealings between legally free and equal property-owning individuals, even as they consign such coercion to the enforcement of property rights and contracts. To this extent, capitalism can be extolled as the economic system of freedom par excellence, an identification that finds vernacular expression in the phrase "free market economy" in today's parlance, and whose genealogy can be traced at least back to Smith's idea of the "system of perfect liberty."[39] By contrast, Marx, in his discussion of primitive accumulation, stressed that the *creation* of capitalist relations hinged on the employment of "the power of the state, the concentrated and organized force of society."[40] Rosa Luxemburg expanded on this by observing extra-economic force to be a "permanent weapon" of capital at every moment of its history, on the grounds that it "is an illusion to hope that capitalism will ever be content with the means of production which it can acquire by commodity exchange."[41]

The main vector of coercive capitalist transformation, according to the Marx-Luxemburg line, is "expropriation," which sets the conditions of capitalist "exploitation" by instituting capitalist private property, a dispossessed labor force, and a market in productive inputs and wage goods. Expropriation in this sense is not a simple transfer of resources or "stockpiling." It denotes a structural transformation, or the "capitalization of social reproduction," which makes laborers' access to conditions of labor and means of subsistence contingent on producing a surplus that can be privately appropriated and accumulated as capital.[42] Nancy Fraser captures this point well when she writes that the move "from the front-story of exploitation to the back-story of expropriation constitutes a major epistemic shift" by directing our attention beyond the market (sphere of circulation) and the workplace (sphere of production) to the "political conditions of possibility of capitalism" (sphere of institution).[43] Chief among these political conditions is the role of public authority in suppressing the "resistance to the expropriations through which capitalist property relations were originated and sustained."[44] This emphasis on the constitutive violence of primitive accumulation is not intended to displace or occlude other illiberal forms of power and force that are internal to the general law of capitalist accumulation, the most important of which is what Marx famously called the "despotism of the workplace." Instead, one can fruitfully construe the despotism of the workplace as resting on the institutionalized structural inequality and unfreedom created by primitive accumulation. If the accumulation of capital, as Marx argued, depends on the subjection of social reproduction to the law of value—that is, the generalization of commodity form and the domination of abstract labor in the satisfaction of social needs—then the law of value itself presupposes, in Werner Bonefeld's words, "the law of private property that primitive accumulation established."[45]

It is important to note that abstract labor and the law of value that it subtends are always already organized through historically specific and varying forms instead of manifesting themselves in a singular and uniform social configuration.[46] Historically, the entwinement of political power and capital accumulation occasioned different property institutions, exchange systems, and labor regimes in the imperial metropole and in the colonies. In the former, institutionalized political power assumed the form of an interventionist "fiscal-military state" that secured capitalist private property, safeguarded returns to investment, enforced contracts, and protected domestic industries from foreign competition.[47] Elsewhere, it functioned as a "colonial state" that upheld titles to expropriated land and enslaved labor, lent military and financial support to chartered companies, reined in unruly subjects overseas, and, of course, waged imperial wars against European and non-European rivals.[48] If one follows the thread that runs through the Atlantic slave-plantation complex, the deindustrialization and agrarianization of India, and the opening up of the Chinese markets, one eventually arrives at the imperial state, whose sovereign power circulated, grew, and ramified in an imperial constitution that connected the metropole and its colonial officials to chartered companies, trading factories, settler societies, and plantocracies.[49]

Secondly, the Marxian notion of primitive accumulation enables us to conceive of violent socioeconomic transformations in the colonies as *capitalist* transformations, rather than developments that are anomalous or incidental to the history of global capitalism.[50] The dismissal of the relevance of colonialism to a theory of capitalism has come in many disciplinary shapes and colors, yet in one way or another, they all flow into the metanarrative of endogenous capitalist development in Europe and the rise of the West.[51] Those who call this Eurocentric standpoint into question have linked colonialism to global capitalism in its capacity to "confiscate and conscript" land and labor into circuits of capital, thereby overcoming resource constraints that might have stifled capitalist expansion.[52] Perhaps more importantly than this crude material aspect, colonial economic spaces also functioned as spaces for imagining and implementing new ways of organizing social production for profit, at times by means so brutal that they would have been difficult to imagine and let alone attempt in Europe— genocidal expropriation of native populations and chattel slavery being the most obvious examples. In the words of two Atlantic historians, "[C]olonization itself was an experiment in economics on a transoceanic scale . . . it did act as a crucible in which economic, social, and political experimentation with new ideas and approaches, both imported from the old world and spawned in the new, were allowed to flourish, often unfettered."[53]

This last point is also the reason this study devotes more attention to colonial capitalist transformations than to metropolitan ones. Primitive accumulation and capitalist innovation flourished "unfettered" in the colonies because they were located "beyond the line" of *jus publicum Europeaum*, that is, beyond the laws, customs, and conventions that limited the use of force and fraud in economic competition, social struggle, and political conflict in Europe[54]:

> The "inside" encompassed the laws, institutions, and customs of the mother country . . . The "outside," by contrast, was characterized by imperial domination, the expropriation of vast territories, decimation of indigenous peoples, theft of their resources, enslavement, and the domination of vast tracts of land by private capitalists . . . In these imperial dependencies, the rules of the inside did not apply . . . violence defied the law, and bold physical coercion by private actors remade markets.[55]

It is tempting to perceive in this description an international order bifurcated between the norm-bound spaces of Europe and exceptional spaces of the colonies. Yet, as Antony Anghie has compellingly shown, far from existing in a legal void untouched by European international public law, colonial spaces were constituted as unbound by norms through a hierarchical differentiation *within* the one and same sphere of international law.[56] Molding colonial territories into the peripheries of the capitalist world economy turned in great measure on defining them as "exceptional zones of armed expropriation" and designating their inhabitants as "expropriable subjects . . . shorn of political protection, ripe and ready for confiscation."[57] Furthermore, as Nikhil Singh correctly observes, the colonies were

> domains not only for enacting plunder, that is, primitive accumulation (or accumulation by dispossession), but also for developing cutting-edge procedures, logics of calculation, circulation, abstraction, and infrastructure—the slaver's management of human cargo, the camp, the prison, the forward military base—innovations that can proceed insofar as they are unfettered by legally protected human beings advancing new prejudices, built upon the old.[58]

Liberated from political, legal, or customary limits to expropriation, enslavement, and plunder, colonial entrepreneurs, such as planters, slave traders, merchants, and chartered company agents, found a much freer hand in in reshaping local systems of production and exchange wherever they managed to secure political or military predominance. Consequently, although various forms of coerced dispossession and bondage dotted the European landscape in the early modern period, the union of political power and capital birthed much more violent and much "primitive" methods of accumulation beyond the "civilized" pale of Europe. Brutal forms of economic extraction and exploitation in the colonies represented the "systemic edges" of capitalist expansion in the early modern period, where the scale and nature of the deep social transformations central to the birth of the global capitalist order fell into sharper relief.[59]

New Dilemmas of Liberalism

The primitive accumulation of capital was therefore "primitive" in two respects. In the first, structural sense, it marked the "originary" (*ursprünglich*) and coercive transformations that gave rise to capitalist relations and drove their subsequent expansion by subsuming noncapitalist relations. In the second, normative sense, it signified the uncivilized, barbaric, and brutish means by which the conditions of capital accumulation were instituted and maintained. At the dawn of global capitalism, in Beckert's words, "not secure private property rights but a wave of expropriation of labor and land characterized this moment, testifying to capitalism's illiberal origins."[60] Yet in what sense and by what standard were these origins "illiberal"? By the standard, I argue, of a liberal conception of capitalism that imagined it as an economic system based on the sanctity of exclusive private property, voluntary market exchange between juridical equals, and the freedom to dispose of one's labor without subjection to the arbitrary will of another. Marx himself conceded this much when he took classical political economy at its word and described the realm of the market, the sphere of capitalist circulation, as the realm of "Freedom, Equality, Property, and Bentham."[61] As the silent compulsion of economic relations qua threat of destitution replaced the overt coercion of primitive accumulation, capital's despotism retreated to the "hidden abode of production," leaving the sphere of circulation as the domain of freedom and equality, where the owners of the means of production and the owners of labor power entered into voluntary and self-interested agreements.

If we boil down these institutional arrangements and their structuring principles to their normative core, we arrive at *contractual freedom* and *juridical equality* as two primal norms of liberalism. This is certainly a rarefied, abstract formulation, but it is useful for clearly delimiting the scope of inquiry into such a notoriously polysemic concept as "liberalism." First, restricting focus on contractual freedom and juridical equality helps us avoid entanglement in the whole range of family resemblances (such representative government, natural rights, consent of the governed) that have been associated with the term. The argument advanced here specifically concerns the centrality of juridical equality and contractual freedom to the liberal metropolitan imaginings of capitalism, rather than claiming to have discovered, in Bell's words, the "ineliminable core" of liberalism tout court.[62] We can thus dial in, for example, on Locke's defense of private property in the context of English occupation in the Atlantic or Edmund Burke's advocacy of free trade in the face of British depredations in India, without getting mired in the dispute over whether we can speak of "liberalism" in the seventeenth and eighteenth centuries.[63]

Secondly, and relatedly, a focus on these two primal norms situates our analysis in the idiom of political economy, which, as a political language and self-styled science of society, was born of the intellectual attempts to comprehend the emergent global capitalist order.[64] The latter included, as we have seen, the commercialization and newfound prosperity of European societies but also the imperial expansion and war capitalism that made it possible. Political economy therefore constitutes a particularly propitious discursive terrain in which to trace the formulation and evolution of contractual freedom and juridical equality in connection with "the violent nature of capitalist expansion, . . . the convulsive developments that tore up the globe even as they started integrating it."[65] In this field we find theses about security of property, the rule of law, division of labor, mobility of capital, and market expansion to be closely entangled with debates over claims to conquered territories, the colonial drain of wealth, the (dis)advantages of slave labor, and despotic rule over subjugated populations.

It is my contention that from the last third of the seventeenth century onward, contractual freedom and juridical equality, through their varied yet persistent reiterations across different contexts and controversies, calcified into the backbone of a liberal understanding of capitalism in the early modern period. As the following chapters demonstrate, these norms displayed striking historical continuity in their conceptual intension, relative geographic indifference in their claims, and a remarkable compatibility with otherwise quite dissimilar political languages, including natural jurisprudence, ancient constitutionalism, conjectural history, and utilitarianism. As modular premises, they circulated less as strictly specified codes of conduct than as "a set of characteristic dispositions" that were "articulated in universal terms and entertained universal ambitions," yet always already negotiated against various circumstances.[66] Although it is not possible to exhaust their normative essence in any one of their historical expressions, these primal norms are recognizable as animating principles behind a range of discourses that can be grouped under a liberal understanding of capitalist relations.

In the early modern period, the term that constituted the semantic pivot of liberal political economy was "commerce," a term that was simultaneously descriptive-particularistic and normative-universal. "Commerce" at once referred to the historically determinate capitalist socioeconomic relations obtaining in the seventeenth and eighteenth centuries *and* christened these relations with a cosmopolitan morality and civilizational superiority under the sign of "commercial society."[67] Moral philosophy and political economy converged around this term, as disputes over the reason of state and the common good of the people, disagreements over how to govern colonies and imperial dependencies, and philosophical conjectures over the natural course of societal development increasingly partook of a new lexicon of social theory centered on commerce.[68]

English, and later British, political economists were both precocious and influential in articulating a liberal dialect within this new idiom. David Armitage remarks that in late seventeenth-century England, political economy functioned not just as a technical language of administration but also as a "political and constitutional argument" for imagining a novel polity that comprised the composite monarchy of the Three Kingdoms and its colonial possessions in the Atlantic.[69] The expansion of English trade in the mid-seventeenth century, argues Steve Pincus, was critical to "creating for the first time a truly self-conscious commercial society" and with it "a new ideology applicable to a commercial society [which is] better understood as liberalism."[70] Although the British were not alone in increasingly relying on political economy for framing problems of imperial governance,[71] they were peculiar in insinuating a liberal variant of political economy into the imagination of the British Empire as an "empire of trade." In the British political and public opinion, this empire of trade and liberty united its metropolitan and colonial constituents by an ethos of material and moral improvement, bonds of mutual benefit, and the civilizing power of commerce. This liberal self-image was further galvanized by systematically contrasting its essentially maritime, free, and commercial character with the land-based despotism and territorial aspirations of Spain and France. "The virtues of an expanding commerce," P. J. Marshall observes, "were widely extolled in Britain and in the colonies. . . . The freedom generated by commerce was assumed to be the distinguishing feature of Britain's relations with her colonies by comparison with the oppressive empires of other European powers."[72] Even Smith in his acerbic critique of the mercantile system conceded that the British Empire, for all its faults and follies, was "less illiberal and oppressive" than its continental rivals.[73]

Most importantly, this commercial self-conception meant that liberal thinkers in Britain would apply the same normative standards to judging the economics of the empire. It is at this point that the liberal thrust of political economy in fashioning the British self-image came up against the accelerating processes of colonial conquest, military extortion, and enslavement on which Britain's imperial economy rose. As Chris Bayly summarizes, the imperialist drive to "retain and enhance control over land and labour" in the colonies "clashed with judicial and administrative philosophy of contemporary Britain which was imbued with ideas of freedom of contract, freedom of trade and free title to land."[74] The idea of a maritime and commercial people implied a belief in the fairness of the voluntary exchange of commodities and experiences between parties whose moral right to pursue their interests was respected, in other words, a vision of "free exchange as the model of human interrelations."[75] At the same time, it was no secret that the making of Britain's overseas commercial ties, and consequently the seed-bed of the modern economy and material prosperity, followed a course of imperial violence to pursue economic objectives.[76] Consequently, while metropolitan condemnations of the abuses of empire "did not prevent imperial governments and settlers from being brutal and exploitative, it did ensure that scandals would be a periodic feature of imperial governance . . . over slavery, massacres, colonial wars, forced labor and poverty."[77] Containing these scandals in Britain was critical to straddling the simultaneous embrace of its commercial self-image and the imperial foundation of its power and prosperity.

An uncompromising way out of this conundrum would be either to radically overhaul Britain's imperial structure along liberal principles or to abandon any pretense of upholding these principles as a matter of British character. The first option, most famously proposed by Smith's advocacy of decolonization or imperial federation, would spell the end of the British Empire as the Britons knew it. Liberal critique of empire failed to resonate with the majority of the British political and economic elite (merchants, planters, manufacturers, statesmen), who dismissed it as little more than abstract philosophical speculation.[78] In a context of interstate rivalry, with the Dutch in the seventeenth century and the French in the eighteenth, contemporaries held that empire, especially for an island country like Britain, secured the wealth and prosperity that was vital for domestic peace and national survival.[79] "Nearly everyone at this time perceived that economic progress, national security, and the integration of the kingdom might well come from sustained levels of investment in global commerce, naval power, and, whenever necessary, the acquisition of bases and territories overseas."[80] Mercantilism or the "old colonial system," which hinged on the deployment of the organized power of the state for economic expansion and consolidation, was not considered an aberrant political intervention in what would otherwise be global free trade. Far from being an obstacle to economic globalization, the colonial empire provided the political framework in which transoceanic linkages of commerce could emerge as a historical reality and an object of contemplation in the first place.[81]

The second option, of resolving this contradiction by jettisoning liberal commitments, likewise failed to find adherents among the advocates of empire, who remained wedded to what Karuna Mantena has labeled "ethical imperialism," an ideology that rationalized imperial expansion as the instrument of "liberal, utilitarian, and evangelical reforms to transform, civilize, and emancipate the native."[82] The British imperial ideology obstinately remained "peculiar," in Partha Chatterjee's words, in its "reconciliation of a critique of Continental empires as land-based absolutist tyrannies with its own possession of overseas territories."[83]

Despite widespread awareness of colonial slavery in the West Indies, economic extortion in the East Indies, and territorial aggrandizement in both, the regard for the British Empire as the "empire of liberty" carried the day, though certainly not without recurrent ambiguities and anxieties.

We are thus confronted by the puzzling obduracy of the liberal conception of Britain's imperial economy in the face of the endemic violence of colonial capitalism. I argue that such obduracy can be explained by the discursive strategies of disavowal that circulated in the discursive space of the "imperial commons" and shaped the British political opinion on empire.[84] Borrowing from Sybille Fischer, "disavowal," in contradistinction to "denial," involved the recognition of the disturbing realities of colonial coercion, expropriation, and exploitation. Instead of suppressing the disturbance by passing over it in silence, disavowal was a rather verbose strategy, a sort of incitement to discourse, that worked volubly and productively through "stories, screens, fantasies, that hide from view what is to be seen."[85] These strategies were particularly pronounced and deftly executed in the works of intellectuals of empire such as Locke, Burke, and Edward Gibbon Wakefield, who were at once earnestly committed to the liberal values enshrined in metropolitan political economy *and* to Britain's colonial capitalist economy that undergirded her national prosperity and power. Such intellectuals provided the British political elite with the theoretical resources for furnishing an undeniably imperial political economic order with an ultimately liberal character. I say "ultimately" because in simultaneously defending British colonial capitalism and its liberal image, they neither ignored colonial violence nor cynically admitted it as the trademark of empire. Instead, they wove together a series of discursive strategies, rhetorical maneuvers, and literary fictions to demonstrate that the British imperial economy and the British polity remained at heart wedded to liberal values without denying the violence that checkered its career in the colonies.

The argument from disavowal differs from the existing explanations of the resilience of liberal imperialism. For some, such resilience can be traced to an upsurge of imperial confidence in British public opinion at the turn of the nineteenth century.[86] The difficulty with this argument is that the impact of public opinion on the course of imperial policy was, at best, questionable between the 1780s and 1830s, which saw a combination of proconsular imperialism abroad and political conservatism at home.[87] The alternative account locates the key to the puzzle in the pervasive cynicism of the British political elite and treats imperial ideology as a perennial "exercise in lofty denial."[88] While I concur that the elite consciousness is where we should look for ideological tensions—not least because it harbors more unambiguous expressions of such tensions as compared to popular consciousness—the explanation from cynicism remains facile. Despite its tempting simplicity, collapsing the tension between liberalism and empire to the logic of duplicity is hard to sustain, if only because, as Bernard Porter notes, the British political classes may have been ideologically gullible, but they were not hypocrites.[89] Imputations of a conscious instrumentality to liberalism as an imperial ideology forget that such ideologies were the "opiates of the elite" and that their various iterations "primarily targeted their fellow Europeans. It was, above all, their own countrymen and political leaders that colonists had to convince of the legitimacy of their actions, not indigenous peoples."[90]

Liberal imperialism, as Bell argues, shared with other ideologies of justification a common "imperial imaginary" structured by the metaconcept of "civilization," in which the world was "envisioned as a space of inequality and radical difference" and "peoples and societies are arrayed in a hierarchical manner."[91] Crucially, the thinkers who openly criticized imperial institutions and practices that were regnant in their time, thinkers who have been hailed as the representatives of anti-imperial Enlightenment, also broadly subscribed to the civilizational hierarchies of the imperial imaginary, though certainly with different normative inflections and conclusions. The liberal strand in British imperial ideology proved to be rather resourceful and adaptive, to the point of co-opting fragments of anti-imperial critique to use in renewed justifications of expansion and control.[92] Consequently, the claim that "the conflict between the domestic and the foreign regime proved too contradictory to bridge" is at best greatly overstated.[93]

In breaking with culturalist interpretations and "rematerializing" liberalism's relationship to empire, we are not simply inverting the lexical order between ideation and materiality but, rather, restoring materiality back to the circuit of imperial ideology and practice. Expressed another way, we are *not* reducing liberalism to an ideological handmaiden of capitalism but positing a reciprocal and contradictory relationship between the two. Liberalism is better understood as a mode of theoretical reflection and a value system that found its social conditions of possibility in the historically situated capitalist institutional forms but could not normatively accommodate the violent processes that engendered them. Processes of enclosure, commodification, and dispossession originating in the seventeenth century gave birth to "private property," "market exchange," and "free labor" as concrete social relations on which theoretical reflection could fasten and around which liberal tenets such as "the private," "consent," "contract," and "self-ownership" could germinate and crystallize. At the same time, however, these very conditions of possibility saddled liberalism with contradictions inasmuch as these conditions came into existence through the forcible obliteration of the "strange multiplicity" of alternative modes of life, in Europe but more dramatically in the colonies.[94] The enthronement of private property as the natural and universally beneficial mode of appropriating and exploiting the earth's resources depended on the forcible marginalization of competing property systems, which was accomplished on a colossal scale by the land appropriations in the New World. The ascendancy of free trade involved the coerced assimilation or the subordination of nonmarket forms of distribution to the logic of self-interested market exchange, which, for instance, made agricultural exports possible during famines in India and Ireland.[95] Finally, the triumph of free labor over serfdom and slavery was at the same time the triumph of an agenda of forcing individuals to "freely" contract their labor power on the market by cutting their access to alternative means of social reproduction, a logic that vividly played out, first in England and later in its settler colonies in North America and Australasia.

The upshot of this reasoning is condensed by Bonefeld, who writes, "The violence of capital's original beginning is the formative content of the civilized forms of equality, liberty, freedom, and utility."[96] At the same time as primitive accumulation established the social conditions of capitalist exploitation on a global scale, it also engendered the institutional forms that would become the hallmarks of liberal political economy in Europe. However, the element of violence in the capitalist appropriation and conscription of land, labor, and resources overseas could always become too intense, offensive, and thus unacceptable to liberal sensibilities in the British metropole. For the colonial capitalist ventures to be carried out by private agents, endorsed by public authorities, and condoned by public opinion, these ventures needed to be recognized—or more accurately, *misrecognized*—as being on the whole "British," that is, commercial, pacific, and free. If we situate liberal thought in a framework of "ideology," then the critical role of British imperial ideology in this period was to uphold the *necessary misrecognition* of colonial capitalism as an essentially liberal market phenomenon.[97]

The relationship between liberalism and capitalism can therefore be grasped as one of contradictory co-constitution, wherein capitalist transformations created the institutional conditions of the possibility and tractability of the primal norms of liberalism, while liberal misrecognition of capitalism endowed the inequalities and power effects generated by such transformations with normative validity and legitimacy. "Slavery, colonial rule, and white domination all depended on long-distance connections and on ocean-crossing ideological constructs: on the sense of normality and entitlement of colonial planters, settlers, and officials, and on publics in Europe accepting such arrangements as legitimate parts of an imperial polity, a global economy, and Western civilization."[98] The conviction that the British Empire was a global engine of liberty, property, civility, and law not only supplied post hoc justification of colonial violence; it also lent ideological force to renewed authorizations of further waves of coercive expropriation, secure in the faith that the empire project remained liberal at heart.

The staying power of this article of faith in the liberality of empire, and therefore the reproduction of this necessary misrecognition, owed in no small part to the efforts of metropolitan intellectuals to disavow the illiberal underpinnings of

Britain's imperial economy. Locke, Burke, and Wakefield were three such intellectuals whose works present privileged grounds for observing liberal strategies of disavowal. First, these three figures evinced a bona fide dedication to a secular conception of progress and civilization that was shaped by Britain's capitalist economy.[99] A central theme in their writings was the material benefits to be reaped by humanity from increased economic productivity, finding expression in such tropes as the "common stock of mankind" (Locke), "universal opulence" (Burke), and "accumulation of capital" (Wakefield). Second, they saw in the British imperial project an avatar of commercial civilization with a world-historical purpose as much an instrument for ensuring Britain's survival as a great power. Furthermore, all three men were actively involved in Britain's imperial politics: Locke, in his capacity as a colonial administrator on the Board of Trade; Burke, as a parliamentary member of the Select Committee on India; and Wakefield, as a colonial reformer who had a coterie of followers in Parliament. Third, they were all "liberal" political economists in that they made contractual freedom and juridical equality the keystone of their appraisal of capitalist relations, be it in Locke's global theory of private property, Burke's ideal of imperial commerce, or Wakefield's plans for colonial free labor. Finally, all three belonged to what contemporaries called the "middling sorts" who offered their talents to the British political elite whose patronage they sought. Being excluded from the direct exercise of political power, their principal means for exerting influence on imperial policy was the theoretical cogency and appeal of their writings on the political economy and morality of the empire, which they variously addressed to Parliament, the government, and the Colonial Office. By virtue of this peculiar status, the works of such intellectuals displayed an unusual attention to the contemporary universe of political discourse, keen engagement with the major debates, and a pronounced and even self-avowed concern with theoretical consistency.

Such shared institutional, intellectual, and professional investments constitute the overarching framework in which a comparison of these otherwise dissimilar thinkers can generate unexpected insights into the liaisons between liberalism and empire. At once animated and constrained by these commitments, Locke, Burke, and Wakefield made remarkable attempts to navigate the aporias attendant on professing liberal political economic principles at home while endorsing illiberal economic practices in colonial peripheries. Their conception of British capitalism as an essentially commercial and pacific system rested on representing the expropriation, extortion, and exploitation of the empire as something *incidental* to British capitalism instead of its historical *modus operandi*. Their emphatic endorsement of empire also set them apart from other liberal political economists, such as David Hume or Smith, who similarly diagnosed the conflicting commitments of liberalism and imperialism but sided with liberal commitments against empire. The intellectual efforts Locke, Burke, and Wakefield registered those moments in which the cardinal premises of liberalism were forced into an open confrontation and negotiation with their historical conditions of possibility.

Having outlined the theoretical problem, historical scope, and the interpretive approach of the study, we can now return to the question of method broached earlier. From a rigorous linguistic contextualist perspective, the interpretive apparatus of colonial capitalism appears suspect because neither "liberalism" as a self-conscious doctrine nor "capitalism" as a descriptive concept existed in British political discourse in the period under study. As I have suggested, this is a matter of the register of analysis. The fact that seventeenth-century thinkers did not invoke liberalism and capitalism *eo nomine* does not mean that the *practices* and *principles* that we now recognize and analyze under these rubrics did not exist at the time.[100] Secondly, and equally importantly, designating the relevant context at the level of institutional practices and ideological principles rather than linguistic conventions and discursive protocols does not render the analysis less contextual. The framework of colonial capitalism does not dislodge texts from their historical conditions of articulation, but it does carve out of historical relations and temporalities a different type of context in which liberal arguments can be subjected to questions—in this case, social contradictions, theoretical conundrums, and ideological tensions—that are different from those available to linguistic contextualism.

As a number of commentators have recently observed, the contextualist suspicion of the social and the longue durée in the study of political ideas is conditioned by a rather narrow understanding of what "context" is.[101] Perhaps most importantly, there exists no ultimate a priori standard by which to adjudicate between the validity of discursive/linguistic and practical/socioeconomic contexts, and as social theorists have not ceased to remind us, the division itself is highly dubious and unsustainable except by disciplinary strictures.[102] The important question is not so much whether the proposed textual interpretation adopts the "correct type" of context as whether it contains a coherent theory of the relationship between ideation and practice and an account of why the contexts it demarcates are relevant for investigating the questions it sets for itself. For instance, the argument that the commodification of agriculture in Bengal is as relevant to the history of liberalism as the British debates on commercial society would be anathema to linguistic-contextualist sensibilities, as would be a study of liberal imperialism that proceeds by comparing the widely disparate contexts of early twentieth-century Britain and early twenty-first-century United States. Yet recent books by Andrew Sartori and Jeanne Morefield accomplish precisely these feats, demonstrating the rich interpretive possibilities activated by expanding one's scope to other "logics of history" beyond the linguistic and to other temporalities beyond the provincial.[103]

The interpretation of liberalism undertaken in these pages is animated by a kindred impulse to "embed the conceptual structure of liberal thought in the sociohistorical contexts of its articulation."[104] While I pay due attention to historical detail and the specificity of the political languages in which liberal ideas on property, exchange, and labor were articulated, my interpretation directs liberal arguments beyond the self-enclosed domain of textual circulation. Liberal ideas and the dilemmas they embody assume their significance (that is, both meaning and import) in this study with reference to concrete colonial capitalist forms and the challenge of their manifest illiberality.

I follow two premises in mooring the works of Locke, Burke, and Wakefield in their respective contexts of territorial dispossession, unequal exchange, and unfree labor. The first is the capacity of these authors "to articulate a (relatively) coherent formulation of specific modes of social reflection and ethico-political argument that had either emerged or would soon emerge to prominence."[105] The significance of the writings of Locke, Burke, and Wakefield resides not in their immediate illocutionary force, but in their status as elaborate condensation points of social forces, political and economic priorities, and imperial agendas. Viewed under the light of colonial capitalism, their writings shine as surfaces on which we find inscribed the social and ideological contradictions that were internal to Britain's imperial economy. These contradictions were of interest to their contemporaries and their future readers, and to the extent that they provide a window on the contradictory co-constitution of capitalism and liberalism that persists in our present, they should be of interest to us.

The persistence of the past in the present, in other words, is arguably more pronounced in practical and ideological contexts than in strictly linguistic ones, but it is also this persistence that renders historically distant utterances on the common ground of liberalism, capitalism, and imperialism commensurable. In this sense, a theory of colonial capitalism, as Dipesh Chakrabarty puts it in a moment of exceptional lucidity, can be adopted "as not so much . . . a teleology of history as . . . a perspectival point from which to read the archives."[106] Such a reading is enabled by a retrospective gaze that pierces through multiple historical contexts, which, in turn, necessitates parting ways with the strict linguistic contextualism that "helps in identifying particular idioms of speech within historical political discourse, but it is less productive when naming key concepts that transcend linguistic fashion."[107] To argue this much is not to suggest that contextual contingencies that shaped the circulation and reception of the ideas studied here are irrelevant; only that an exclusive focus on the temporality of contingencies occludes from view the significance of ideas in the temporality of capitalism.

Secondly, I consider each author to be writing in the very thick of the problems of imperial political economy and governance rather than in clearly isolable periods (for instance, the "first" empire or the "second" empire or Pax

Britannica) each having its settled issues and agendas of government. Their contexts were marked by flux, when extant modes of political and economic thought had revealed their limits in comprehending the novel world-historical phenomena emerging within the networks of Britain's imperial formation. As Ellen Meiksins Wood succinctly puts it, "[L]ong-term developments in social relations, property-forms and state-formation do episodically erupt into specific political-ideological controversies."[108] At its most immediate, the debates examined in the following chapters concerned whether the English were rightfully occupying vacant lands rather than usurping them from Native Americans by force, whether Britain's trade with its Eastern empire could be restored to its true commercial foundation or was irredeemably corrupt, and whether it was possible to compel British emigrants to work for capitalist farmers in the colonies without abridging their civil liberties. At stake in these debates, however, were the broader ideological questions about the nature of Britain's imperial economy; the means by which it ought to be promoted and regulated; and the implications of these imperial strategies, institutions, and practices for imagining the British polity and national character. One can find these comprehensive ideological stakes reflected in the writings of Locke, Burke, and Wakefield, who not only directed their arguments to their contemporaries but also advanced their claims in expressly universal terms with an indication to speak beyond their immediate context and communicate enduring verities to imagined future audiences. If we further widen the analytic aperture from the history of the British Empire to its intersection with the history of global capitalism, we can identify the significance of their reflections for the liberal imagination of capitalism understood as a problem of political theory. From this vantage point, we can see their ruminations on the naturalness of private property, the justice of the market, and the utility of free labor cutting across the history of global capitalism, classical political economy, and problems of imperial governance.

This is why in studying the history of liberalism in the context of empire, one ought not to rest content with questions of culture and language, of universalism and difference, as important as these questions are. If we are to gain analytic purchase on the cardinal liberal institutions of private property, free exchange, and free labor, as well as the primal norms of contractual freedom and juridical equality they incorporate, in Geoff Kennedy's emphatic call, "we *do* need a conceptualization of capitalist development as the relevant social context."[109]

Conclusion: Stereoscopic View of History

In his essay "Theses on the Philosophy of History," Walter Benjamin wrote, "Every image of the past that is not recognized by the present as one of its own concerns threatens to disappear irretrievably."[110] The historical articulation of the past for Benjamin emphatically did not mean to reconstruct it as accurately as possible. Instead, his historical pedagogy aimed at training the faculty of seeing "dimensionally, stereoscopically, into the depths of the historical shade."[111] The expression is rather aphoristic and allegorical, but it gestures at a potentially productive, critical orientation to history that often gets brushed aside as methodologically unsound. The three-dimensionality implied in the stereoscopic view is of the same order as Benjamin's more famous call to "blast open the continuum of history" and release fragments of the past to restore their relevance to our present. A relevant fragment could be something that is fragile and threatens to vanish from the historical record altogether—abandoned attempts or quashed possibilities of different ways of organizing human communities, such as indigenous systems of social reproduction, nonstate forms of political organization, or moral economies of commoning, which, though defeated by the alliance of the modern state and capital, reminds one that the present could have been, and can perhaps still be, otherwise. By contrast, a relevant fragment could also be something that is robust and persists in the present but eludes our recognition by its ubiquity—a dominant social principle or historical logic, which, precisely because it is not recognized as historical, pervades the present as timeless common sense, such as the assumption that all property is essentially individual private property, the state is a necessary evil, and human beings are hardwired utility maximizers.[112]

By linguistic-contextualist reasoning, if the early modern political period is circumscribed by political idioms in which liberalism and capitalism are conceptually absent, then there is little to be attained by delving into this period for sharpening our understanding of either liberalism or capitalism in general. The past remains a foreign country. By contrast, a *critical* history, in Martti Koskenniemi's words, "should not dispose of materials from other chronological moments," and at times, the spark of critical insight arises precisely from the juxtaposition of fragments from disparate historical contexts. Consider, for instance, the following two passages that are separated by more than three centuries:

> God gave the World to Men in Common; but since he gave it them for their benefit, and the greatest Conveniencies of Life they were capable to draw from it, it cannot be supposed he meant it should always remain common and uncultivated. He gave it to the use of the Industrious and Rational, (and *Labour* was to be *his Title* to it); not to the Fancy or Covetousness of the Quarrelsom and Contentious.[113]
>
> Development knowledge is part of the "global commons": it belongs to everyone, and everyone should benefit from it. But a global

partnership is required to cultivate and disseminate it. The Bank Group's relationships with governments and institutions all over the world and our unique reservoir of development experience across sectors and countries, position us to play a leading role in this new global knowledge partnership.[114]

The first of these is by John Locke, in the *Second Treatise of Government*; the second is by the former World Bank president John Wolfensohn, in his 1996 inaugural address. One could either dismiss the resonance between the two as mere imagistic analogy and reassert their incommensurability or, alternatively, investigate the shared logics of history and specific temporalities that render them resonant despite their different historical circumstances, immediate concerns, and political vocabularies.

One such explanation (admittedly at a level of abstraction that may make historians uncomfortable) is the persistence in Western political thought of the "notion that states, and indeed humanity itself, could only preserve themselves through the exploitation of the earth's resources to which all people had a common right, but to which particular people gained superior and particular rights through their acts of exploitation or occupation."[115] The book from which this quote is taken, Andrew Fitzmaurice's survey of the Western "doctrine of occupation" over five centuries, suggests that longue durée studies in intellectual history do not have to end up in positing unbroken, evolutionary continuities from pristine ideational origins, or what Michel Foucault called "pedigree" in contrast to "genealogy."[116] Rather, I contend that obtaining a stereoscopic view of history involves parsing different historical logics and temporalities to identify what persists in the present. This in turn necessitates an alertness to historical fragments that can provide us with clues about continuities and discontinuities and about disappearance and resurgence, instead of a methodological probity that safely ensconces each fragment in its historically proper place.

Stereoscopic view of history is therefore, to borrow from David Armitage, "transtemporal" but not "transhistorical."[117] Returning to the problem of theorizing the imperial context, however, the historical configuration in which we find Locke's late seventeenth-century proto-liberalism and Wolfensohn's late twentieth-century neoliberalism does not immediately present itself to us. Discerning it requires the mediation of a specific theoretical vantage point, one attuned to the continuities between the institutional-ideological structures and social imaginaries of European colonialism, the Mandate System, and the postwar development regime, through which the nineteenth-century binary of civilized and barbarian mutated into that of developed and underdeveloped.[118] Similarly, dissecting the amoebic resilience of the "rise of the West" metanarrative, which has reinvented itself over the last century and a half through a host of different idioms (evolutionary biology, sociology, political science, history, and, most recently, institutional economics), necessarily points beyond the specific languages in which it has instantiated and toward a theory that incorporates their nondiscursive connections.[119] To use a celestial metaphor favored by Benjamin, gazing at the writings of Locke, Burke, and Wakefield through the looking glass of colonial capitalism aligns them in a historical "constellation" that discloses the constitutive dilemmas of liberalism in its fraught relationship with capitalism and empire.[120]

In the Beginning, All the World Was America

John Locke's Global Theory of Property

Thus in the beginning all the World was *America*, and more so than that is now; for no such thing as *money* was any where known.

—John Locke

The imperial turn in political theory began when a number of commentators took John Locke's famous pronouncement on America as more than simply a metaphorical appendage to a hypothetical state of nature. Cast in the light of Locke's personal and professional involvement in English colonialism, Locke's direct and indirect allusions to overseas colonies in his manuscripts, notebooks, and correspondence laid the groundwork for a new interpretive perspective that placed his thought in a decisively Atlantic context. Colonial interpretations of Locke have reframed his theory of property and civil government as much as a commentary on occupation and conquest in the New World as a protoliberal theory of political sovereignty and limited government in England. These efforts have not only spawned an ongoing debate on Locke's status as an imperial ideologue; perhaps more importantly, they sparked the germinal interest that has since animated the studies on liberalism and empire.[1]

Unfortunately, the colonial turn in Locke scholarship bears the imprint of the culturalist disregard for the socioeconomic context, as outlined in chapter 1, even when the controversy centers on Locke's theory of property. Highly emblematic of this predilection, the profuse invocation of "thus in the beginning all the World was *America*" has not been matched by a sustained explication of "and more so than that is now; for no such thing as *money* was any where known" (II. 49).[2] This relative neglect is all the more striking given that there already exists a rich scholarly debate over the social and economic coordinates of Locke's political thought that precedes the colonial appraisals by at least a generation, wherein questions of capital accumulation, commodification, and proletarianization occupy a pivotal position.[3]

I contend that one can decode Locke's strange pronouncement on money and America by contextualizing it in seventeenth-century Atlantic colonial capitalism. This necessitates complicating the terms of the colonial interpretation by detecting the capitalist parameters of Locke's view of England's overseas possessions. The analysis advanced here consists of three interlocking parts. First, I hold that Locke's theory of private property expressed a specifically *capitalistic* worldview that centered on the productive capacities of labor for transforming inert nature into an ever-expanding domain of value. Second, natural jurisprudence constituted the moral language in which Locke articulated the *liberal* economic premises of freedom, equality, consent, and contract. Third, the juridico-economic valences of Locke's theory of property were embedded in the English *imperial* ambitions in America, not least because the early-modern languages of political economy and natural jurisprudence both took shape against the background of European incursion in the New World.

I maintain that Locke's arguments about money, its origins, and its implications constitute the linchpin of this theoretical configuration, where capitalism, liberalism, and colonialism intersect. Locke's peculiar conceptualization of money plays a twofold role in his theory of property. First, it undergirds his articulation of an accumulative worldview of "possessive universalism" imbued with a universal moral force.[4] Locke's theory justifies European land appropriations in the New World by sanctioning a distinctly private, productive, and accumulative mode of appropriation as the morally superior basis of property. The function of money here is to store the value produced by human labor, thereby unleashing its productive powers in a drive to increase "the common stock of mankind" on a global scale. Second, the same notion of money helps Locke reconcile the nonconsensual appropriation of land and indigenous displacement in America with the liberal values of juridical equality and freedom enshrined in his theory of property. Locke performs this theoretical maneuver through a fiction of "universal tacit consent" that he ascribes to money's genesis, yet from which he excludes Native Americans. This fiction of a universally binding agreement to the use of money enables Locke to represent Native Americans as responsible for the status of land in America as natural common and thus open to unilateral appropriation by labor.

The chapter begins with a brief description of the colonial capitalist configuration of the seventeenth-century Atlantic in which Locke was deeply involved as an official and intellectual functionary of England. The thread that connects Locke to Atlantic colonial capitalism are the early modern debates spurred by the wave of land seizures in the Americas, the rise of a commercial plantation system that reoriented the economies of the three continents, and the consequent transformation of interstate rivalries and conceptions of political government in Europe. I then turn to a discussion of the socioeconomic fundamentals of Locke's political thought that are often glossed over in colonial interpretations, in particular, the place of capital and accumulation in Locke's political economy. I contend that Locke's theory of property formulates a universal and distinctly liberal language of progress in which the theological-moral injunctions of natural law map onto a transatlantic capitalist agenda. This theoretical feat hinges on Locke's idiosyncratic notion of money, which inhabits a conceptual zone of indistinction between the moral absolutes of natural law and the historical contingencies of human convention. I extend this analysis into the question of Native American title to land, whereby I argue that money's conceptual ambiguity enables Locke to furnish a liberal self-image for the English capitalism in the face of its structural connection to colonial land appropriation and native dispossession. I also illustrate how the existing colonial interpretations of Locke, most notably James Tully's account of constitutional parochialism and Uday Mehta's thesis of liberal exclusion as well as David Armitage's recent objection to them, stand to benefit from an analysis of Atlantic colonial capitalism and England's imperial economy.

Locke and the Atlantic

That Locke conceived his theory of property with Atlantic colonies in mind is by now a clearly established argument.[5] What needs further elaboration is, first, a socioeconomic account of "the Atlantic" as a network of people, commodities, and ideas, and second, the pivotal role of colonial land as one of the key productive assets (along with slave labor and merchant capital) that made possible this transoceanic formation.[6]

Following on the heels of Spain and Portugal, the English were latecomers to the Atlantic. Their initial exploits against the Iberian powers amounted to little more than "a little war of trade and plunder, a continuous exertion of economic and naval pressure by individuals acting for private gain."[7] This haphazard pattern changed dramatically when English colonization received a burst of energy from Oliver Cromwell's Western Design, which inaugurated the episode of territorial acquisitions.[8] The post-Restoration policy stayed the course of colonial expansion and sought to harness the colonies to the metropole demographically and institutionally via colonial migration, the Navigation Acts, and the recognition of the slave codes legislated by colonial assemblies.[9] Public-private collaborations in colonization thickened through military, diplomatic, and administrative channels presided over by the Council of Trade and Plantations, effectively coalescing into a discernible English imperial formation spanning the Atlantic by the third quarter of the century.[10] The commitment to overseas colonies was further consolidated by the commercial reorientation of the English political elite and the planter-merchant alliance behind the Whig imperial project, which carried the day with the Glorious Revolution and clinched the symbiosis between the politico-legal power of the English state and capitalist enterprise in the Atlantic.[11] The resultant ensemble of governmental techniques coalesced into what has been dubbed the "fiscal-military state."[12] Commonly referred to as "mercantilism," this political economic program went beyond a mindless fixation on the balance of trade and aimed more broadly at analyzing, promoting, and systematizing the *creation* of value, even if the ultimate target of obtaining "plenty" remained maximizing "power" in European interstate rivalry.[13] As a "peculiarly descriptive theory of imperial antagonism," mercantilism functioned as novel language in which "European expansion would be understood primarily in economic terms, as theories of *imperium* gave way to recognizably modern doctrines of imperialism."[14]

From the moment the English gained a territorial foothold in the Atlantic, plantation agriculture formed the economic backbone of the English colonial system, though this was less a reflection of a peaceful agriculturalist national character than the outcome of frustrated attempts to find precious metals or tributary vassals in America.[15] The commercial visions of Richard Hakluyt and other middle-class intellectuals notwithstanding, English colonies themselves were born of conquest and only gradually commercialized.[16] A key impetus was the discovery that tremendous profits were to be reaped from the cultivation of tropical cash crops. Portuguese sugar plantations in Brazil set the model, and the English followed suit, replicating this pattern for cultivating sugar in the Caribbean and tobacco in Virginia.[17] Against this background, the word "plantation" gradually assumed its singularly modern meaning, that is, "an overseas settlement producing a cash crop for export," established on land seized from Native Americans, worked by white indentured or black slave labor, financed by metropolitan merchant credit, and ruled by a slave-owning planter class.[18]

The significance of the Atlantic "slave-plantation complex" for the global inceptions of capital cannot be overstated. Plantation colonies stood in the crux of a massive reorganization of property, production, and exchange on an oceanic scale for the explicit purpose of profit. "[T]he invention of the Atlantic by early modern Europeans was driven primarily by the quest for financial gain, whether on the part of individual adventurers, or the monarchs (and later, governments) that backed them."[19] This public-private collusion of interest engendered in the New World private forms of land tenure much stronger than could be found in Europe, absolute commodification of men and women of African origin, and large-scale, capital-intensive forms of agricultural production that outstripped in its efficiency and exploitative brutality anything known in the Old World. As one social historian puts it, "[T]he commercial dynamic that was transforming England . . . in the new World found its most uncompromising form."[20] Global commodity chains that proliferated in and through the socioeconomic transformation of the Atlantic "were directly connected to institutional and organizational shifts, including financial trends that conditioned the very possibility for the global movement of capital."[21] Manufactured goods from England, slaves from Africa, foodstuffs and timber from the mainland colonies converged on the Caribbean, rendering it "the hub of empire" and "the primary location of capital accumulation in Americas."[22]

Crucially, as Jairus Banaji cautions, "the building of the Atlantic economy was not just a 'precondition' of the growth of capitalism in Europe or Eurasia, but *embodied the embrace of capital through its own forms of capital accumulation.*"[23] The plantation itself represented the capitalist enterprise par excellence, as it had the logic of capital accumulation inscribed in its design and operation since its genesis. On the one hand, the imperative to extract maximum labor from the workforce prompted planters to commission more efficient labor-saving technologies like sugar-mills, the "most advanced technical installations of the time."[24] On the other, the planter elite steadily preyed on smallholding settlers for commandeering their land and labor.[25] The trend was to consolidate operations into "large integrated units, with sufficient land and labour to justify their own mill and processing plant," which by the 1680s had replaced "dispersed production with large numbers of small-holders."[26]

The slave-plantation complex also stimulated the development of capitalist social forms and productive capacities in England through feedback loops, promoting tendencies toward mass production and consumption, economies of scale, innovations in the industrial processing of colonial imports and exports, new instruments of finance and trade, and investment in shipping and insurance.[27] After assessing comparative data on European economies in the seventeenth century, Steve Pincus arrives at the "conclusive implausibility of the internalist history" of English economic success.[28] "The key factor in explaining the differences in economic development, the key factor in accounting for English and Dutch prosperity in the face of crisis elsewhere in Europe, is the growth of long-distance trade and the development of overseas colonies . . . Atlantic trade provides the only plausible explanation for England's divergence from the European pattern."[29]

Colonial land was the origin, the linchpin, and the highest stake of the Atlantic economy in which European states tried to carve for themselves zones of imperial self-sufficiency.[30] As "the seizure and occupation of territory became the *sine qua non* of the overseas activity," the legitimate basis of land appropriation in America emerged as a vital question that preoccupied some of the foremost political intellects of sixteenth- and seventeenth-century Europe.[31] David Armitage remarks:

> The early-modern overseas empires of Spain, Portugal, France, Britain and Holland had to be justified, not only to their competitors but also to themselves, and their effects on the metropolitan nations as well as the native and later colonial populations had to be accounted for, understood and explained . . . [P]hilosophers shouldered the ideological task of justifying overseas enterprise, and political theory in particular would thereafter bear the marks of early-modern Europe's expanding world.[32]

After the swift obsolescence of the Papal Bulls and the Treaty of Tordesillas, principles of conquest, first occupation, and settlement furnished the terms in which rival European claims to America were debated.[33] The Roman legal tradition, from which these terms were derived, dictated that land appropriations be legitimated by appeal to some preexisting law. The situation was further complicated by the fact that the lands in question were patently inhabited by peoples thought to be outside the civic history of the Old World.[34] At this juncture, the idiom of natural jurisprudence presented itself as the proper idiom for adjudicating property claims of Native Americans and Europeans insofar as it enabled the formulation of a minimal yet universal normative core that would be "binding on all humankind no matter what their civil constitution might be."[35] James Tully neatly encapsulates the point:

> One of the leading problems of political theory from Hugo Grotius and Thomas Hobbes to Adam Smith and Immanuel Kant was to justify the establishment of European systems of property in North America in the face of the presence of "American Nations." Almost all the classic theorists advanced a solution to this problem justifying what was seen as one the of the most important and pivotal events of modern history . . . to justify European settlement on the one hand, and to justify the dispossession of the Aboriginal peoples of their property on the other.[36]

Theories of property thus became the principal means by which European colonizers legitimated their acts of appropriation before their European contenders, as well as the bar of their own conscience.[37] Debates over the foundations of property rights were more than a pastime for European intellectuals; these debates shaped the ideological resources available to public and private agents interested and invested in overseas colonization:

> Even if it weakly described actual systems of property-holding, the rhetoric of absolute private property was politically important. The idea that absolute private property was the best way incentivize owners and maximize productivity was used . . . to legitimate the taking of land from foreign peoples with different systems of property.[38]

The ideological problem was arguably more pronounced for the English, who neither shared the proselytizing zeal of the Spanish nor the readiness of the French to intermix with the natives. As had been the case in Ireland, "[f]or the English, the indigenes [in America] were always of secondary importance— persons who were to be displaced, not incorporated."[39] This outlook colored seventeenth-century English justifications of colonial expansion in America, which betrayed little, if any, intention for sustained interaction with Native Americans. Locke's theory of property was a particularly dramatic exemplar of the English colonial ideology because it articulated the colonial agenda of displacement in a protoliberal framework of natural law.

As the most illustrious intellectual of the post-Restoration Whigs and an official functionary of the English state, Locke was deeply enmeshed in the administrative webs of colonial capitalism and subscribed to the new political economy that developed in response to seventeenth-century transatlantic commercial economy.[40] The patronage of Anthony Ashley Cooper (1st Earl of Shaftesbury) secured him the position of the Secretary to the Council of Trade and Plantations (1673–1674) and, later, membership on the Board of Trade (1696–1700).[41] The massive volume of colonial reports, dispatches, and correspondence Locke had to process during his services made him "one of the two best-informed observers of the English Atlantic world of the late seventeenth century."[42] Shaftesbury also involved Locke in his designs to found a colony in Carolina, and Locke participated in the drafting of the *Fundamental Constitutions of Carolina* (1669).[43] Furthermore, Locke had economic investments in English colonialism. He held shares in the Royal African Company that traded in slaves, was one of the merchant adventurers to the Bahamas (1672–1676),[44] and through the agency of his cousin and financial manager Peter King, engaged in "stock-jobbing" in the East India Company bonds.[45] Taken together, these involvements have led one critical scholar to describe Locke as "the wise organic intellectual both of the seventeenth-century British elite and of future generations of the British ruling classes" and "a great philosopher of the developing world system which linked the old world with the new with ties of domination and subordination."[46]

Locke's experience in colonial affairs also honed his acumen in the emergent "science" of political economy.[47] His labor theory of property, clearly inflected by his engagement with colonial administration, captured the essence of the accumulative economic vision that triumphed with the Glorious Revolution.[48]

Locke upheld a Baconian view of "useful knowledge" that fused natural history with induction for generating knowledge that would improve the material liveli-hood of human beings.[49] This orientation was manifested most directly in his unrelenting advocacy of boosting agricultural productivity and his scorn for absentee landlords in England, which led one observer to label him a proponent of "agrarian capitalism."[50] Locke's concerns with agricultural "improvement" extended to England's colonies, as evidenced in his "agricultural espionage" in France in late 1670s "on Shaftesbury's behalf . . . for a practical economic future for Carolina in the business of Mediterranean import substitution."[51] On matters of commerce and finance, he figured among the champions and first sharehold-ers of the Bank of England, and the financial pamphlets Locke published during the Great Recoinage debates made an invaluable contribution to the revolution-ary cause.[52]

Locke's professional, personal, and intellectual investments in the English imperial economy were reflected most consequentially in his intervention in the European debates over colonial property rights. Building on an established pedigree of arguments from natural jurisprudence (articulated most notably by Hugo Grotius and Samuel Pufendorf), Locke's theses on property represented the pinnacle of the seventeenth-century English efforts to validate English claims to American territory.[53] His arguments simultaneously addressed rival theories of appropriation,[54] the Native American rights to land, and the homegrown skepticism of Englishmen, such as Robert Gray, who inquired, "[B]y what right or warrant we can enter into the land of these savages, take away their rightfull inheritance from them, and plant ourselves in their places, being unwronged or unprovoked by them?"[55] Locke's distinct contribution to the property disputes would reverberate far beyond the immediate context of its articulation, as he "gathered together many of the arguments of the early seventeenth century and his theory set the terms for many of the later theories that were used to justify the establishment of European property in America," effectively establishing "the unexamined conventions of many Western theories of property."[56]

The Atlantic focus on Locke has informed two principal lines of interpret-ing Lockean liberalism around the encounter between Europeans and non-Europeans. The first of these, a critique of the "agriculturalist argument," has argued that the sedentary, peaceful, and agrarian vision espoused in the fifth chapter of the *Second Treatise* aims to invalidate the alternative property claims of the nomadic Indian, the marauding Spanish, and the trading French. At the center of Locke's distinctly English assertion to occupy America stands the act of enclosing and improving the land by "mixing labor," which disqualifies aborigi-nal hunting and gathering practices as grounds of landed property.[57] Locke com-pounds his refusal of indigenous property (*dominium*) by insisting that Native Americans lack recognizable institutions of sovereign authority (*imperium*). The

absence of property and sovereignty renders America a vacant territory popu-
lated by private individuals and households, and therefore open to the appropriation by colonists.[58] The second line of interpretation, a more emphatically
postcolonial critique, has focused on the hidden civilizational hierarchies that
structure Locke's "liberal strategies of exclusion."[59] In this reading, the coexistence in Locke's philosophy of inclusive liberal values side by side with exclusionary impulses against non-Europeans reflects his uncritical universalization
of historically specific (English and gentlemanly) forms of subjectivity. The
implicit assumptions of calculating, utilitarian, and self-disciplinary rationality
built into Locke's abstract conception of personhood translate social difference
into civilizational deficit. Locke's liberalism inevitably infantilizes the colonial
Other by capturing her in narratives of historical development and the political
tutelage of the colonizing power.

Palpable in both accounts of colonial expropriation and denigration is a lack
of sensitivity to the specific socioeconomic parameters of Locke's historical conjuncture. In shifting the focus to the other side of the Atlantic, commentators
seem to have left behind questions of commercialization, accumulation, labor,
social rights and obligations, and modern and moral economies. To address this
shortcoming, I first investigate the possibility, limits, and morality of capitalist accumulation in Locke's theory of property, and then position the colonial
aspects of his political philosophy in relation to these economic and moral coordinates. Parting ways with the conventional preoccupation with "labor," I contend that the nexus between capitalism, colonialism, and liberalism in Locke's
thought falls into sharpest relief when one focuses on Locke's notion of money.
Locke's arguments on money are replete with paradoxical propositions that
enable him to uphold, in one and the same theory of property, the liberal principles of natural liberty and equality *and* the agenda of justifying colonial land
appropriations in the service of capital accumulation. The terms in which Locke
relates money to the precepts of natural law that govern appropriation, dispossession, and accumulation in the state of nature not only morally sanction the
accumulative vector of capitalism, but also wrap its expropriatory colonial thrust
in liberal myths of universal consent.

The main reason this point has eluded attention in Locke scholarship is arguably the assumption, pervasive in metropolitan and colonial interpretations alike,
that money is a contingent and second-order theoretical construct in Locke's
theory of property. When it is not construed as a duplicitous scheme to justify
inequality or dispossession, money is deemed irrelevant for understanding the
moral parameters of Locke's conception of property. I propose an alternative
explanation that has not been considered thus far. Money is a structurally necessary if conceptually ambiguous element that holds together the composite and
contradictory edifice of Locke's theory of property, which attempts to formulate

a universal defense of property rights against extralegal absolutist power in England, at the very same time it seeks to validate the expropriation of Native Americans by the extralegal imperial power of the English state. Locke's notion of money forms the thread that binds together "life, liberty, and property," the original mantra of political liberalism, and "thus in the beginning all the World was *America*," the signal for the primitive accumulation in the New World.

Money and Morality of Accumulation

At first glance,[60] the role of money in Locke's theory of property appears rather straightforward and can be summarized as follows. In the fifth chapter of the *Second Treatise*, Locke sets out to "shew how Men might come to have a *property* in several parts of that which God gave to mankind in common, and that without any express Compact of all the Commoners" (II. 25). Locke constructs this openly nonconsensual theory of appropriation around the idea that labor is an exclusive property in each person, expenditure of which on the natural common removes a portion of it from the common state and inscribes that person's private property in it (II. 27, 35). However, God, who bestows upon man the earth and the means to appropriate it, also places limits on appropriation (II. 31). Natural law is breached when appropriation overrides the "sufficiency limitation," which dictates that "enough and as good" should be left in common for others (II. 27, 33), or the "spoilage limitation," which prohibits one to engross more than one can mix his labor with, and make use of before it perishes (II. 31, 36, 38). This double circumscription restricts the amount of private property in the state of nature "to a very moderate Proportion" (II. 36). The invention of money and men's mutual consent to put a value on it instigate a drastic transformation of this egalitarian state of affairs by enabling one to "fairly possess more land than he himself could use the product of, by receiving, in exchange for the overplus, Gold and Silver, which may be hoarded up without injury to anyone" (II. 50), since the "*exceeding of the bounds of* just *Property*" lies not "in the largeness of his Possession, but the perishing of anything uselessly in it" (II. 46). By giving men with different degrees of industry the opportunity to continue to enlarge their property, money eventually introduces scarcity of land (II. 45). Yet this "disproportionate and unequal Possession of the Earth," does not violate the natural rights of the propertyless, for the universal consent conferred on the use of money amounts to universal consent to the inequality that it engenders (II. 50).

The question that stoked much controversy in the decades before the colonial turn was how to interpret this narrative: as a defense of capitalist accumulation or as an objection to it. Scholars adopting the former position have considered

Locke's understanding of property to be emblematic of the emergent bourgeois sensibility, with its central tenets of self-interest, individualism, utilitarianism, alienable wage labor, robust private property rights, natural inequality of wealth, and, above all, unlimited accumulation of wealth.[61] The detractors of this interpretation have located Locke's philosophy in the Thomistic natural law tradition and its moral economy, emphasizing instead the inherent purposefulness of God's design, moral odium and restrictions on acquisitive behavior, primacy of the common good, and enforceable charity claims over absolute private property rights.[62] In short, the dispute has revolved around morality and accumulation or, rather, the morality *of* accumulation in Locke's thought.

The analysis that I advance here provides a different picture, in which moral and capitalist premises in Locke's theory of property are not antithetical but necessarily enmeshed. In this account, the moral universals of natural law and historical practices of capital accumulation shade into each other and coalesce into a global theory of property that stakes its claims with equal force in the metropole and the colony. Locke's ingenuity resides in the particular way he sets the terms and the narrative structure of his account, which enables him to depart from God's command to make use of the earth for the benefit of mankind and arrive at the necessity of accumulation in a way that renders the seventeenth-century colonial capitalist practices not merely permissible but morally commendable. Locke's narrative, however, runs into two theoretical bottlenecks: first, the antinomy between the maximalist teleology and the moral limits of accumulation, and second, the potential illiberality of nonconsensual appropriation of land. Locke's construal of money as an area of indeterminacy between natural law and human convention helps him steer through these problems. As I discuss below, the morality of accumulation and the role of monetization as its enabling condition bear momentous implications for the justification of New World land appropriations within the liberal parameters of freedom, equality, and consent.

A theoretical constant based on "the architectonic importance of theology" in Locke's thought is the idea of the purposefulness of creation.[63] Men are created as innately equipped with the capacity for reason that is necessary for apprehending God's purpose or divine telos, which manifests itself in the form of three key obligations under natural law.[64] The first and most important moral obligation is the *preservation of mankind*, which Locke constantly reiterates in the *Two Treatises of Government*:

> God having made Man, and planted in him . . . a strong desire of Self-preservation and furnished the world things fit for Food and Rayment and other Necessaries of Life, *Subservient to his design*, that man should live and abide for some time upon the Face of the Earth, and not that so curious and wonderful a piece of Workmanship by its own Negligence,

or want of Necessaries, should perish again, presently after a few moments of continuance. (I. 86; emphasis added)[65]

God has intended men to "*Increase* and *Multiply*" (I. 41) and given them the means to realize this intention, though not without effort. The telos of self-preservation is yoked to the second obligation—that is, to *labor* on the earth in order to provide for human needs. Locke asserts in the chapter on property, "God, when he gave the World in common to all Mankind, commanded man also to labour, and the penury of his condition required it of him" (II. 32). "He gave it to the use of the Industrious and Rational (and *Labour* was to be *his* title to it)" (II. 34). "Laboring is not just something we happen to do to resources," remarks Jeremy Waldron, "it is the appropriate mode of helping oneself to the resources given what resources are *for.*"[66] Labor's status as divine injunction renders it a fundamentally *moral* act, whereby mixing one's labor entitles the laborer to private property not only on practical but also on moral terms.[67]

Labor at the service of the preservation of mankind is compounded by a third moral obligation, which directs it to the *improvement of the earth*. Initially contenting himself with property rights in the provisions "produced by the spontaneous hand of nature" (II. 26), Locke later proclaims the "*chief matter of Property*" to be the earth itself and contends, "God and Reason commanded him to subdue the Earth, i.e. improve it for the benefit of Life. As much *Land* as a Man Tills, Plants, Improves, Cultivates, and can use the Product of, so much is his property" (II. 32). As with the previous obligations, the improvement of land is not a mere technical expediency but the appropriate method for supporting livelihood. God has intended the uncultivated land lying in nature to be brought under the improving labor of man. "God gave the World to Men in Common; but since he gave it them for their benefit, and the greatest Conveniences of Life they were capable to draw from it, it cannot be supposed He meant it should always remain common and uncultivated" (II. 34).

At this juncture in the chapter on property, the terms of discussion change noticeably, and the binary of "value" and "waste," through which Locke articulates the *telos* of improvement, takes the foreground. Although all useful things owe the great part of their value to labor, none does more so than land, which is "of so little value, *without labor*." If not enclosed and improved by man, God's gift lies as "neglected, and consequently waste Land" (II. 36). In other words, enclosing and improving the waste of the earth is not only a more efficient way of producing the conveniences of life, it is also a moral duty because, by *rescuing* the land from waste, it more fully consummates the purpose for which God has bestowed the earth upon men.[68] As one commentator puts it, "Locke was deeply haunted by the idea of waste and wanted all the material potentialities of the earth to be fully realized."[69] Agricultural improvement is in marked contrast to hunting and gathering in the first stages of the state of nature, exemplified for Locke by Native Americans, which not only renders men "needy and wretched" for the want of labor and improvement (II. 37), but also falls short of following God's purpose by letting the resources that *could* be made use of waste.

At this point one begins to discern a progressive imaginary. As men rescue more land from waste by enclosing and cultivating it, as they labor and produce more necessities and conveniences for the benefit of life—in other words, as they transform greater parts of the world into *valuable* things—they better fulfill the obligations of natural law and more fully consummate God's purpose. As Andrew Fitzmaurice has recently argued, Locke's emphasis on economic "value" as a function of enclosing the common marks a crucial turning point in the history of the doctrine of occupation. By combining a labor theory of appropriation with a labor theory of value, Locke turns property into a juridico-economic compound, wherein the legal binary of common/property is amalgamated by the open-ended, ordinal continuum of economic progress. The crucial term Locke devises to substantiate this progressive imaginary is "common stock of mankind":

> To which let me add, that he who appropriates land to himself does not lessen but *increase the common stock of mankind*. For the provisions serving to support humane life, produced by one acre of inclosed and cultivated land, are (to speak much within compasse) ten times more, than those, which are yeilded by and acre of Land, of equal richnesse, lyeing wast in common. And therefore he, that incloses Land and has a greater plenty of the conveniencys of life from ten acres, than he could have from an hundred left to Nature, may truly be said, to give ninety acres to Mankind. (II. 37; emphasis added)

The increase in the common stock is not restricted to leaving more land available for others to enclose and improve but extends to the products of the earth, as the example of Spain testifies: "[T]he Inhabitants think themselves beholden to him, who, by his Industry on neglected, and consequently waste Land, *has increased the stock of Corn, which they wanted*" (II. 36; emphasis added).[70] Locke's comparison of America and England on this point is perhaps most exemplary because it assesses their respective contributions to the common stock of mankind in monetary terms:

> An Acre of Land, that bears here Twenty Bushels of Wheat, and another in *America*, which, with the same Husbandry, would do the like, are, without doubt, of the same natural, intrinsick Value. But yet *the Benefit Mankind receives* from the one, in a Year, is worth 5 *l.* and from the other possible not worth a Penny. (II. 43; emphasis added)

The notion of the common stock of mankind constitutes the privileged nexus in Locke's theory of property, around which the obligations to preserve, to labor, and to improve are interwoven and set in moral, teleological motion. God has furnished the earth with the material intended for not only the necessities but also the conveniences of life, which allow men to augment their livelihood beyond bare subsistence. The capacious and maximalist understanding of production in Locke's vision is evident: "[G]reat and primary blessing of God Almighty, *Be fruitful, and multiply, and replenish the earth* ... contains in it the improvement too of arts and sciences, and the conveniences of life" (I. 33). "Industry and accumulation" therefore are endowed with a teleological gravity as the medium in which men "discharge the duty to develop earth's resources and create a prosperous society."[71] The more mankind expands its common stock through the *improvement of land* by *labor* for the *preservation of mankind*, the more it approximates to fulfilling God's purpose.

Although Locke's account may at first appear to be a religious story of a divine design unfolding through human activity on earth, its fixation on the material development of society instead of the spiritual salvation of the individual betrays an "ethic productivity" as opposed to a "puritan ethic."[72] Augmentation of the common stock and the subjective dispositions and objective methods of achieving it become the index of historical advancement and moral rectitude, leading Tully to credit Locke with setting up the "background assumption of the 'stages view' of historical development" that would inspire "the four-stages theories of property in the Scottish and French Enlightenments, even when the theorists disagreed with Locke in other respects."[73]

The increase in the common stock, however, does not readily assume the form of accumulation. The moral precept that the fruits of the earth are intended for the *use* of mankind (spoilage limitation) restricts the extent of the common stock to what can be actually utilized by human beings before they perish. The point is obvious in the case of the individual producer for whom it is "a foolish thing, as well as dishonest, to hoard up more than he could make use of" (II. 46). One solution Locke proposes to spoliation limitation is gift or barter:

> If he gave away a part to anybody else, so that it perished not uselessly in his Possession, these he also made use of. And if he also bartered away Plumbs that would have rotten in a Week, for Nuts that would last good for his eating a whole Year, he did no injury; he wasted not the common Stock; destroyed no part of the portion of Good that belonged to others, so long as nothing perished uselessly in his hands. (II. 46)

The crucial point to note here is that while gift or barter overcomes the spoilage limitation for the individual producer, the same limitation remains in effect for mankind as a whole. That is to say, while saving the common stock from waste, barter circumscribes it with the immediate and concrete needs of mankind at a given moment. Subsistence or "hand-to-mouth existence," regardless of how much it is enriched by the conveniences, remains the paradigm of production and consumption. This might explain why though Locke was cognizant of the complex systems of barter and gift giving among Native Americans, he nonetheless dismissed these forms of exchange as irrelevant to the spoilage limitation.[74] The distinction between the paradigms of subsistence and accumulation is critical for delineating the precise vector of colonial dispossession in Locke's theory of property.

Because the moral restrictions on appropriation clash with the maximalist provisions of enclosing and improving the earth, Locke's interpretation of natural law reaches the first bottleneck and reveals an internal impasse. The industrious and rational, to whom God gave the earth, now face "an ethical dilemma."[75] They can avoid spoilage by limiting their labor to what can be used by themselves and others. This would entail enclosing and improving less than they *could* if the spoilage limitation did not exist, hence leaving most of God's gift wasting in the natural common. This is clearly at odds with God's intentions, for "it cannot be supposed He meant [the earth] should always remain common and uncultivated" (II. 34). Alternatively, they can enclose, improve, and rescue as much land from waste as their capacity to labor permits. This ultimately culminates in overproduction and the subsequent wasting of the fruits of labor. This is equally against God's purpose, for "if either the grass on his enclosure rotted on the ground, or the fruit of his planting perished without gathering, and laying up, this part of the Earth, notwithstanding his enclosure, was still to be looked on as waste" (II. 38). In short, the dilemma is between *letting waste* and *making waste*, or the loss of *potential value* and *actual value*.

The resolution of this theoretical impasse hinges on demonstrating that it is possible to unleash the full force of industry and labor in the service of God's purpose. There must be a way to labor and bring the entire waste of the earth under cultivation without violating the spoilage limitation, which means that there must be a way to store the *value* created by labor without letting it decay and return to the waste of the common. Consequently, there must be a way to *accumulate* if the dilemma of the industrious and rational is to be dispelled. That is to say, even though Locke does not include accumulation among the original precepts of natural law, the way he constructs his theory of property culminates in the necessity of accumulation for the consummation of divine purpose. Given the necessity of accumulation, there must be a medium in which economic value can be disentangled from the transience of the perishable goods and accumulated in abstract form for the satisfaction of anonymous future needs. The introduction of money, as the medium of accumulation par excellence, should be understood as Locke's attempt to navigate this paradox.

The primary function of money is the fulfillment of the spoilage limitation in a way that allows for accumulation.[76] Unlike the concrete products of labor, money would "keep without wasting or decay" (II. 37) and "may be hoarded up without injury to any one" (II. 50). One "might heap up as much of these durable things as he pleased; the *exceeding of his* just *Property* not lying in the largeness of his Possessions, but the perishing of any thing uselessly in it" (II. 46). The motive behind the accumulation of money is not "miser's reason" for hoarding for its own sake, but the possibility of converting the stored abstract value back into use-value: "And thus *came in the use of Money*, some lasting thing man might keep without spoiling, and that by mutual consent Men would take in exchange for the truly useful, but perishable Supports of Life" (II. 47).[77] While remaining anchored to the realm of use-value, money introduces an element of temporal freedom by making it possible in principle to postpone the moment of use *indefinitely*. In so doing, it liberates men from the "hand-to-mouth existence" of immediately consuming the products of labor and enables them to rationally orient their productive activities toward some perceived future good.[78]

The new element of temporal freedom harbors momentous implications for the binary of waste and value, and it is not coincidental that this binary makes its appearance in the very section where money is mentioned for the first time (II. 36). Monetization of surplus production resolves the dilemma between "letting waste" and "making waste" by suspending the latter, and frees men to focus their energies on enclosing and cultivating, not in accordance with their concrete immediate needs, but based on the extent of their capacity to labor. Consequently, insofar as the subjection of the earth through labor is among God's intentions for the world (II. 34-5), money proves indispensable for the consummation of the divine telos. Given this significance, it is hard to conceive of money as a contingent, practical expediency. This point finds support from several central passages in the chapter on property, which suggest that the invention of money ushers a whole new way of imagining mankind's relationship to the world:

> [Y]et there are *great tracts of Grounds* to be found, which (the Inhabitants thereof not having joined the rest of Mankind, in the consent of the Use of their common money) *lie waste*, and are more than the People, who dwell on it, do, or can make use of, and so still lie in common. Tho' this can scarce happen amongst that part of Mankind, that have consented to the Use of Money. (II. 45)

Note that in this passage, enclosure and improvement of land as grounds of entitlement are annexed to the logic of money, which is at once the condition and the substantiation of the drive to exhaust the earth through its transformation into value. Wherever money is used, the land ceases to be waste in principle, without regards to the actual state of land, as attested by the fact that Locke does not use the term "waste" to denote the land "left in common by compact" in England (II. 35). Locke effectively equates the presence of a progressive attitude that strives to put an end to the waste of the world with the presence of monetization:

> Where there is not something both lasting and scarce, and so valuable to be hoarded up, there Men will not be apt to enlarge their *Possessions of Land*, were it never so rich, never so free for them to take. For I ask, What would a Man value Ten Thousand, or an Hundred Thousand Acres of excellent *Land*, ready cultivated, and well stocked too with Cattle, in the middle of the in-land parts of *America*, where he had no hopes of Commerce with other Parts of the World, to draw *Money* to him by the Sale of the Product? *It would not be worth inclosing*, and we should see him give up again to the wild Common of Nature, whatever was more than would supply the Conveniences of Life to be had there for him and his Family. (II. 48; last emphasis added)

This last point can be more compellingly illustrated by tracing Locke's repeated and emphatic deployment of the term "waste" after he introduces the notion of money (II. 36–50). For an empiricist, as Locke is famed to be, nothing in nature would be "waste" as such. Nature is apprehended as "wasting" only when looked upon with a progressive and acquisitive gaze that perceives the world as a reservoir of potential value to be extracted and accumulated. This is not only reflected in Locke's monetary assessment of the comparative benefits mankind would derive from uncultivated American wastes and improved English farms (II. 43), but it also grants some clarity on Locke' famous announcement, "Thus in the beginning all the World was *America*, and more so than that is now; for no such thing as *Money* was any where known" (II. 49). The strange predication of the state of nature on the absence of money loses its mystery once we see that money inaugurates a paradigm shift from subsistence to accumulation. Whether a plot of land is "worth inclosing" and improving is conditional on whether it is possible to accumulate the value that is derived from it, which, in turn, hinges on the use of money. "Find out something that hath the *Use and Value of Money* amongst his Neighbours, you shall see the same Man will begin presently to *enlarge* his *Possessions*" (II. 49). As a result, money becomes the axis around which the religious teleology of subduing the earth and the practices geared toward the accumulation of value coalesce. From this perspective, the enlargement of possessions and the subsequent scarcity in land under a monetary economy is not to be lamented but rather celebrated as the sign of a fuller consummation of the moral purpose for which the earth was granted to mankind. True, such scarcity entails inequality in land ownership and even dispossession. Yet, this inequality is ameliorated by the expansion of value that feeds into the common stock of mankind, which renders a day laborer in England better fed, lodged, and clad than "the king of a large and fruitful territory [in America]" (II. 41). Hence monetization not only leaves intact the moral obligation to preserve all mankind; it also fulfills this obligation better than the more egalitarian yet more penurious pre-monetary system, barter and gift notwithstanding.[79] And to bring matters full circle, since the expansion of the common stock of mankind is intended by God, money, as the precondition of this expansion, evinces a kernel of moral import.

The stakes of Locke's theory thus appear to be far more expansive than Macpherson's "possessive individualism" thesis suggests. What is articulated here is indeed "unlimited accumulation," but at the global level whose scale is "mankind" or, to use George Caffentzis's excellent neologism, a theory of "possessive universalism."[80] The specific mediation that Locke establishes between the "common" and the "common stock of mankind" by way of privatization, monetization, and accumulation amounts to nothing short of a magnificent reversal of the conventional terms governing the reception and understanding of property relations and social justice. Locke renders "the private" as the door opening onto "the common good"; particularization of the common becomes the precondition for universal prosperity; dispossession paves the road to welfare (as in the case of the day laborer), while persistence in holding things in common (as do Native Americans) appears as virtual theft from the prospective wealth of mankind. Money functions as the linchpin of a global theory of property, a new moral economy that enlists a theological conception of moral and material progress to the service of primitive accumulation qua land enclosures on both shores of the seventeenth-century Atlantic.

Money, Possession, and Dispossession

Locke's notion of money thus navigates a contradiction between two components of his theory of property, each equally indispensable for the moral force of private appropriation. The first of these, the spoilage proviso, endows original appropriation with a moral force by linking it to the satisfaction of human needs, thereby restricting the domain of appropriation. The second, the injunction to subdue the earth, sanctions the universal enclosure and improvement of the earth's waste for increasing the common stock of mankind. Money resolves the conflicting implications of these moral principles by propelling mankind beyond the material immediacy of hand-to-mouth existence, making the perpetual development of productive forces and accumulation of value possible.

The implications of this argumentation for colonial land appropriations are clear: Native Americans will materially benefit if their territories are enclosed and improved by English colonists. "[T]he Aboriginal peoples are better off as a result of the establishment of the commercial system of private property," thanks to "not only finished products but also the opportunities to labor"; in short, they are "more than *compensated* for their loss."[81] The justification of appropriation by the common stock of mankind is a powerful one, for it stakes its claims in *universal* benefit, that is, in a catholic principle of nonexclusion. By itself, however, it does not amount to a *liberal* justification of appropriation, insofar as the argument from universal benefit can be easily coupled with a paternalistic notion of authority that rejects the liberal norms of juridical equality and consent. It was precisely this strand of paternalistic authority that Sir Robert Filmer had advocated in *Patriarcha* (1680), which Locke devoted the entirety of the *First Treatise of Government* to refuting.

A key stake of Locke's objection to Filmer is the definition and locus of extralegal power in the constitution of political society. The idea of extralegal power in Locke's political theory is most clearly articulated in his discussion of "prerogative" (II. 159–168). Prerogative refers to a residual executive power lingering from the state of nature, which is deployed by civil governments to respond to exigencies that cannot be foreseen by promulgated laws. To the extent that it is not answerable to positive law, prerogative is properly defined as *extralegal*, as opposed to *illegal*, power. Its abuse can only be decided on by the people as the ultimate sovereign who determine if and when the use of prerogative has breached the social contract. In other words, the extralegal constituent power of the people is the counterpart to the extralegal prerogative of the executive, and because there can be no earthly arbiter between the two, their clash ends in an "appeal to heaven"—that is, in armed rebellion, dissolution of civil government, and the resumption of the state of nature.[82] What is significant for our discussion is that insofar as Locke designates the Europeans and Native Americans as interacting in the state of nature (II. 14), and insofar as Native Americans are denied the status of commonwealths (which would render the colonial encounter one between sovereign states; II. 108), the force that the Englishmen deploy to expropriate Native Americans emerges as a species of untrammeled executive prerogative. This power is "untrammeled" because it is not wielded by a constituted government over subjects who have consented to it and who pose a political counterbalance through vigilance and the threat of revolution. If the exercise of such unaccountable power within the jurisdiction of a polity constitutes absolutism, then its exercise in territories beyond sovereign borders amounts to imperialism.[83] That is to say, notwithstanding Locke's discourse of natural equality colonial land appropriations betray an imperial juridico-political logic when judged by Locke's own standards.

This brings us to the second bottleneck in Locke's theory of property, which stems from the uneasy coexistence of two distinct agendas. The first is protecting private property in England from the encroachments of extralegal power propounded by Filmer's absolutism. The second is establishing private property in America precisely through the deployment of extralegal power. Locke advances the first agenda through the language of natural rights, departing from a "*state of perfect freedom*" and a "*state* of also *equality*" in which "all the power and jurisdiction is reciprocal, no one having more than another" (II. 4). His second agenda, however, cuts against the grain of this language inasmuch as it endeavors "to shew, how men might come to have a property in several parts of that which God gave to mankind in common, and that *without any express compact* of all the commoners" (II. 25; emphasis added). To appreciate the full significance of Locke's nonconsensual, unilateralist thesis of original appropriation, one has to bear in mind that it explicitly the targeted the compact theory of radical title elaborated by Samuel Pufendorf. While Pufendorf did not dismiss the link between labor, use, and property, he nonetheless held, in Fitzmaurice's words, that "it was not labour . . . that created property, as it would be for Locke, but the *agreement* to recognize the fruits of labor."[84] The crucial corollary of placing "agreement" at the origin of property was to relativize the terms of appropriating the common and to recognize different expedients of occupying the earth (for instance, hunting and gathering) as equally valid and sufficient grounds for property claims. If Locke had followed Pufendorf on this premise, then he would have found it much more difficult to construe indigenous practices of subsistence as being inadequate for claiming property in land. Consequently, "settlement in America without consent would have been unjust by his own criteria, for the land would have been owned, rather than unowned and common as the original appropriation argument requires."[85] In other words, had Locke extended the liberal principles of juridical equality and consent to the original appropriation, these norms would have been ideological stumbling blocks to the justification of colonial capitalist enterprise in America.

Locke's way out of this bottleneck was to argue that land in America was indeed in the natural common and, more importantly, that this common status itself was a function of Native Americans' consent. This consent, in turn, was a function of the *universal tacit consent of mankind* that Locke ascribed to the origins of money. Conjuring up an agreement that was as mythical as it was paradoxical, Locke reintroduced into his account the element of consent that he had expelled from the act of original appropriation. Without this element, English settlements in America would stand exposed to the charge that they were creatures of conquest, which conferred sovereignty but not property (II. 182, 196), or worse, brute acts of sheer seizure with no legal basis at all. Locke's theoretical fiction of universal consent to money is where land appropriations in America were brought back into the liberal fold.

"Consent" and "agreement" constantly recur in Locke's discussion of money in chapter 5: "the invention of money and the tacit agreement of men to put a value on it, introduced (by consent) larger possessions, and a right to them" (II. 36); "had agreed that a little piece of yellow metal . . . should be worth a great piece of flesh, or a whole heap of corn" (II. 37); "in the consent of the use of their common money" (II. 45); "things that fancy or agreement hath put the value on" (II. 46); "money . . . that by mutual consent men would take in exchange for the truly useful, but perishable supports of life" (II. 47); and "riches . . . have but a fantastical imaginary value" (II. 184). The penultimate section of chapter 5 is where Locke brings the articulation of land, labor, money, and property to a close, and thus worth citing in its entirety:

> But since Gold and Silver, being little useful to the Life of Man in pro-portion to Food, Rayment, and Carriage, has its *value* only from the consent of Men, whereof labour yet makes, in great part, *the measure*; it is plain, that men have agreed to a disproportionate and unequal Possession of the Earth; they having, by tacit and voluntary consent, found out a way how a man may fairly posses more land than he himself could use the product of, by receiving, in exchange for the overplus, gold and silver, which may be hoarded up without injury to any-one . . . This partage of things in an inequality of private possessions, men have made practicable out of the bounds of Societie, and without compact; only by putting a value on gold and silver, and tacitly agreeing in the use of Money. For in Governments, the Laws regulate the right of property, and the possession of land is determined by positive constitu-tions. (II. 50)

The conclusion some interpreters have derived from these passages is that Locke is trying to demonstrate that property based on money is conventional and can-not be justified on the grounds of natural rights.[86] For others, locating the con-sent to money outside the bounds of society amounts to nothing short of the "depoliticization" or "naturalization" of money and the property based on it by excluding their foundations from the domain of political human agency.[87] Put differently, one interpretation focuses on the *presence of consent* and concludes with money-as-convention, whereas the other emphasizes the *absence of com-pact* and arrives at money-as-nature.[88]

I maintain, against this binary, that the indeterminacy of the *consent without compact* that underpins money is the very strength of Locke's theory, in that it allows him to depart from moral injunctions (preserve mankind, labor, and sub-due the earth) and arrive at the necessity of accumulative practices (increasing the common stock of mankind). Yet in the process, the explicitly consensual language around money saves Locke the trouble of holding the difficult posi-tion that God directly commanded men to accumulate capital even if this meant widespread dispossession and inequality of property. In this respect, money remains a peculiar beast, with historical and contingent origins yet theologi-cal and moral impact. It cannot be derived from natural law without commit-ting absurdity; neither can it be reduced to sheer convention without impeding God's intentions.

I submit that the paradoxical and indeterminate status of money is best captured by the oxymoron "natural consent," which finds support from a care-ful reading of some of the passages in the *Second Treatise*. The most striking characteristic of the consent given to the use and value of money is its *univer-sality*. Going back to section 50, *"men"* who "have agreed to a disproportion-ate and unequal possession of the *earth*" are clearly not a particular group of men but all mankind, the protagonist of the *Second Treatise*.[89] A decade later, Locke more clearly reiterates this point in his famous economic tract, *Some Considerations of the Consequences of the Lowering of Interest, and Raising the Value of Money*: "For Mankind, having consented to put an imaginary Value upon Gold and Silver . . . have made them by general consent the common Pledges."[90] Invocation of "mankind" as the subject of consent to money universalizes the normative reach of the implications of monetization and effectively turns it into an *agreement that binds mankind*. This is nowhere more clearly indicated than in perhaps one of the most crucial passages in the *Second Treatise*:

> [Y]et there are *great tracts of Grounds* to be found, which (the Inhabitants thereof not having joined the rest of Mankind, in the consent of the Use of their common money) *lie waste*, and are more than the People, who dwell on it, do, or can make use of, and so still lie in common. Tho' this can scarce happen amongst that part of Mankind, that have consented to the Use of Money. (II. 45)

Note in this passage the curious semantics of *mankind*, which is at once the unanimous consenter to money and a subject riven into, on the one hand, those who use money and abide by the binding power of the original tacit agreement and, on the other, those who do not use money and are therefore the subject of a contractual deficit. This social division spatially maps onto the division of the earth into nonwaste and waste, natural common and property, lands that can be appropriated without the consent of their tenants and lands that are subject to the consent of their proprietors. The penalty (as it were) imposed on Native

Americans for not abiding by the tacit agreement to which they have, or *must have*, consented in the lost recesses of time is the pronouncement of their territories as natural common open to appropriation by the members of a monetized economy like England. In other words, the assumption of universality of the consent to money does not budge in the face of factual contradiction. This presumption can be explained only if one assumes that the universality of money is a *principle of necessity* that binds the entirety of mankind.[91] If Native Americans have not joined the "rest of mankind" in the common consent to money, it is they and not the "rest of mankind" who are at fault. The responsibility for the status of their lands as natural common is placed on the shoulders of Native Americans, and the legitimacy of appropriating their territories can be retraced to an act of mutual consent.

Perhaps even more tellingly for its importance in Locke's theory of property, monetization is the only phenomenon that rests on universal consent in the *Two Treatises*. Other instances of mutual consent in the state of nature, such as marriage, master-servant relations, and exchanges of commodities are particularistic contracts that obligate only the parties involved, whereas the consent to money is singular in its binding force over all mankind.[92] This point can be more emphatically established through a comparison with the only phenomenon whose foundations evince an affinity with those of money. This is the inheritance of property, which Locke treats in the *First Treatise*. Locke asks the question, "how come Children by this right of possessing, before any other, the properties of their Parents upon their Decease" and conjectures:

> 'Twill perhaps be answered, that common consent hath disposed of it, to the Children. Common Practice, we see indeed does so dispose of it but we cannot say, that it is the common consent of Mankind; for that hath never been asked, nor actually given: and if common tacit Consent hath establish'd it, it would make a positive and not Natural right of Children to Inherit the Goods of their Parents: But where the practice is universal, 'tis reasonable to think the Cause is Natural. (I. 88)[93]

Considering the position of money in the light of the logic presented in this passage further underscores its peculiarity. On the one hand, the *tacit consent* underpinning the use of money would clearly position it in the domain of positive law, yet this contradicts Locke's contention that America is natural commons because Native Americans have not joined the common consent to money. On the other hand, the *universality* of this consent and its binding validity for mankind would lead one to conclude that "where the practice is universal, it is reasonable to think the cause it natural"; nevertheless, Locke is incontrovertibly clear about the consensual origins of money. To conclude, if the use of money is natural because it is universal, and hence binds mankind, then it cannot be based on consent; if, in contrast, it is consensual and conventional, then it cannot be natural and hence lacks the power to bind mankind. This leaves money in an ambiguous position located on the border between positive law and natural law.

What the paradoxical consent to money renders visible is the rhetorical gesture by which Locke simultaneously folds all mankind in the universal benefits of his accumulative vision *and* marks off Native Americans as implied deviants from this vision's commercial foundations. Native Americans are excluded from the domain of legitimate proprietorship and consigned to "tenancy" in America until and unless they join the "rest of mankind" in the common consent to money. The indeterminacy of money between natural law and human convention is replicated by the nebulous status of Native Americans, who are simultaneously inside and outside mankind's consent to money, bound by a universal agreement of which they are at once already a part and yet to join. Layers of conceptual ambivalence opened by these theoretical maneuvers enable Locke to arrange inclusionary and exclusionary provisions in ways that authorize the dispossession of Native Americans while capturing them in myths of natural equality, mutual consent, and global prosperity. In other words, Locke's theory of property subtly co-articulates sociospatial displacement and exclusion, on the one hand, and liberal values and the historical promise of progress, on the other. It thereby recasts the foundation of seventeenth-century Atlantic capitalism, the extralegal appropriation of colonial lands, in a distinctly liberal mold. A sustained analysis of Locke's notion of money therefore helps us gain novel insights into the ways in which the socioeconomic and theological-moral aspects of Locke's thought interlock in a bid to sanction the transatlantic process of enclosure through a global vision of material progress underpinned by a universalist ideology of improvement.

These insights have been only partially glimpsed by the existing Locke scholarship due to the perspectival insularity discussed earlier. The foregoing discussion of the morality of accumulation and the liberal myth of universal consent calls for re-evaluating two influential lines of interpretation generated by the colonial turn in Locke scholarship. The first of these, forwarded by James Tully, focuses on Locke's provincial theory of constitutionalism that denies Native Americans sovereignty and reduces them to apolitical tribes dwelling in the state of nature. The second line of commentary, advanced by Uday Mehta, picks up the question of colonial exclusion and disenfranchisement from the perspective of subjectivity and interrogates the implicit presuppositions of rationality and personhood undergirding Locke's abstract universalistic claims.

I suggest that both analyses of colonial exclusion can benefit from a materialist perspective on the colonial interface between Native American and English modes of social reproduction. With the introduction of the money there arise, first, abstract relations of value and the need for civil laws to mediate them, and second, a continuum of subjective maturity keyed to the faculty of abstraction in which Native Americans occupy a primitive stage. Arriving at this interpretive standpoint, however, requires abandoning the habitual treatment of money as a metonym for labor or agriculture, as an invention that "in Locke's scheme, only extended the reach of the plough."[94] The nature of the paradigmatic distinction that money draws between the beginning and the present of the world should be sought in its uniqueness, that is, in its status as the medium of representation and accumulation of abstract exchangeable value.[95] This implies a conception of value that properly belongs to a paradigm of social interdependence mediated by the commodity form or, in other words, to the domain of "the social" as a prepolitical formation.[96] Considering Locke's repeated emphasis on the "value" that labor creates, and bearing in mind that "value," "waste," and "money" appear almost always in the same sections of the *Second Treatise*, I suggest that money emblematizes the difference between the principles of subsistence (use value) and accumulation (exchange value) that structure two contrasting modes of social reproduction. Money does not simply "facilitate" exchange by resolving the inconvenience of barter; it marks in Locke's theory a radical reorientation of production toward commodity exchange, surplus, and profit and thereby a fundamental line of demarcation between properly utilized and underutilized land, between property and common.

This distinction between the paradigms of subsistence and accumulation, semantically mapped onto living hand to mouth and increasing the common stock, can theoretically deepen the constitutionalist ideology of dispossession that James Tully has extrapolated from the *Two Treatises*.[97] Tully argues that Locke viewed aboriginal forms of governance through a "Eurocentric narrative of modern constitutionalism," in which they figured as the primitive ancestors of the European peoples before the latter set up sovereign states through social contracts.[98] The lack of resemblance between Native American and European governmental institutions, especially the conspicuous absence of a bipartite structure of monarchy and parliament among Native Americans, prompted Locke conclude that they led a pre-political existence:

> Thus we see, that the *kings* of the *Indians* in *America*, which is still a pattern of the first ages in *Asia* and *Europe*, . . . are little more than *generals of their armies;* and though they command absolutely in war, yet at home and in time of peace they exercise very little dominion, and have but a very moderate sovereignty, the resolutions of peace and war being ordinarily either in the people, or in a council. (II. 108)

The absence of an institutionalized power to declare war and peace indicated the absence of sovereignty among Native Americans, which, in the tradition of natural jurisprudence, meant that America was still in a state of nature. The basis of the argument, initially developed by Hugo Grotius, was that sovereignty over land, whether that land was cultivated or not, preemptively foreclosed individual claims to appropriation by becoming the very source of property rights.[99] Given that original appropriation was possible exclusively in the state of nature, Tully concludes, Locke's denial of imperium to Native Americans effectively stripped them of the right to exclude Europeans from property claims in America.[100] The contrast that Locke drew between the common in America and the common in England is suggestive:

> [I]n *land* that is *common* in *England*, or any other country, where there
> is plenty of people under government, who have money and commerce,
> no one can inclose or appropriate any part, without the consent of all
> his fellow-commoners; because this is left common by compact, *i. e.* by
> the law of the land, which is not to be violated. And though it be com-
> mon, in respect of some men, it is not so to all mankind. (II. 35)

In contrast, common land in America was common by nature, where "[*a*]*s much land* as a man tills, plants, improves, cultivates, and can use the product of, so much is his *property* (II.32).

It is not coincidental that "government" and "money and commerce" appear together in the passage just quoted. Locke associated the subsistence paradigm of Native Americans with the egalitarian simplicity of a premonetary natural econ-omy, which also characterized the "first ages of Asia and Europe." Regulated by the labor and spoilage provisos, natural economy "did confine every man's *posses-sion* to a very moderate proportion, and such as he might appropriate to himself, without injury to any body, in the first ages of the world" (II. 36). The rudimen-tary and (this is crucial) *concrete* nature of property in game, fruits, or enclosed land made very clear what belonged to whom, by what right, and to what end. The objective immediacy of production and consumption rendered property rights legible and relations of exchange plain. As a result, there existed very little reason for "quarrel and contention," those famous "inconveniences" of the law of nature. Locke encapsulates this logic lucidly in the last paragraph of chapter 5:

> And thus, I think, it is very easy to conceive, without any difficulty,
> *how labour could at first begin a title of property* in the common things
> of nature, and how the spending it upon our uses bounded it. So that
> there could then be no reason of quarrelling about title, nor any doubt

> about the largeness of possession it gave. Right and conveniency went together; for as a man had a right to all he could employ his labour upon, so he had no temptation to labour for more than he could make use of. This left no room for controversy about the title, nor for incroachment on the right of others; what portion a man carved to himself, was easily seen; and it was useless, as well as dishonest, to carve himself too much, or take more than he needed. (II. 51)

The pivotal expression here is "easily seen"—the tree that is felled, the game that is caught, the acorns that are picked, and most importantly, as J. G. A. Pocock reminds us, the land that is tilled by the plough, which visibly inscribes on the surface of the earth the property of those who have labored on it.[101] In sum, the paradigm of subsistence, which rests on the satisfaction of concrete needs through the production and consumption of use-values, leaves little room for ambiguity in property relations. As a result, there is no pressing need for promulgated laws to specify these rights or institutionalized impartial judges to arbitrate property disputes.

What distinguishes the paradigm of accumulation, made possible by the introduction of money, is the increasing mediation of production and exchange by abstract exchangeable values—what is precisely and singularly missing in the subsistence paradigm. Monetization of the economy, production for profit, and commodification of exchange introduce a fundamental element of abstraction into the definition and organization of property. Including money within the concept of property poses a critical problem for Locke's natural jurisprudence, a problem of *legibility* that eclipses in importance the question of labor and improvement.[102] The mediation of progressively complex social relations by intangible and fugitive exchange values multiplies the surfaces of friction between property-owning individuals, sparking contentions and quarrels not because individuals are wicked (natural jurisprudence, unlike civic humanism, is not concerned with social personality) but because the modus operandi of property relations is compounded by monetary abstraction. In the words of Istvan Hont, "[N]atural authority and naïve unconditional trust were feasible only while social and economic life were simple and relatively non-conflictual. As money was invented, wealth accumulated and property rights proliferated, the incidence of social conflict increased dramatically."[103] Against this background of mounting entropy, the intuitively accessible norms of natural law become inadequate to the task of regulating natural liberty and property, and the need arises for "established *standing laws*, promulgated and known to the people," and "*indifferent* and upright *judges*, who are to decide controversies by those laws" in order to secure "the *peace, safety*, and *public good* of the people" (II. 131).[104]

We thus arrive at the logical necessity that monetization be followed by civil government. Because monetization is the necessary condition of economic progress, the inconveniences it occasions in the state of nature cannot be resolved by reverting to a premonetary economy, but instead require the establishment of commonwealths. Abandoning monetization would entail a drastic fall in trade, disappearance of the main motive for improvement beyond providing for the most rudimentary needs, and, consequently, a precipitous decline in the common stock of mankind. Paradoxically, once again, the consent to money emerges in Locke's theory as the only species of consent that cannot be withdrawn. Once locked in place, it necessitates a further act of consent, this time to political society, for securing the conditions of industry, improvement, and accumulation.[105] This necessary connection between monetized economy and constitutional government in Locke's narrative constitutes the matrix that differentiates between the natural common and sovereign territory, between what is open to unilateral appropriation and what requires the consent of its inhabitants, and between America and England.

Social repercussions of monetization speak to a second prominent interpretation of Locke in the colonial context. Adopting a subjectivist lens, Uday Mehta detects the exclusionary tendencies that are "an aspect of [liberalism's] theoretical underpinnings and not an episodic compromise with the practical constraints of implementation."[106] "Liberal strategies of exclusion" operate by qualifying the applicability of liberalism's universal claims by an "implicit and thicker set of social credentials" that underwrite the proper subjectivity requisite for political inclusion.[107] Mehta skillfully unearths the rift between the "universal constituency" of the *Two Treatises*, which rests on an "anthropological minimum" devoid of historical and social specificity, and the "exclusionary conventions" of Locke's *Thoughts Concerning Education*, which prescribe a "pedagogical discipline" for cultivating the sort of reason that "naturally" belongs to the rational, gentlemanly, and civilized subjects.[108] Ruled by the "cosmopolitanism of reason," Locke's liberalism negotiates colonial difference by temporally emplotting it as a story of uneven progress and authorizes "the imperial power [as] simply the instrument required to align a deviant and recalcitrant history with the appropriate future."[109]

I do not contest the colonial implications of rational subjectivity in Locke's thought; however, I find Mehta's epistemological idealism to be analytically limited insofar as it attributes to Locke an undifferentiated refusal to acknowledge colonial difference *as such*, and explains this blanket refusal by the "uniformity of the Euclidian space" and "post-Newtonian algebraic continuity" that governs Locke's liberalism.[110] As I will show, Locke's view of colonial difference was in fact much more variegated and selective than an abstract "teleology of reason" would suggest; it identified certain differences as relevant for justifying colonial disenfranchisement, but it admitted others as legitimate differences or simply passed over them with indifference. Parsing the differences that did matter, however, requires attention to the historically specific social practices that furnished the semantic content of Locke's hierarchy of reason. To this end, I suggest decoding the "teleology of reason" as an index to the teleology of transition from the subsistence to the accumulative paradigm of social reproduction.

In a crucial passage in *Some Thoughts Concerning Education*, Locke states that "he that has no master over his Inclinations, he that knows not how to *resist* the importunity of *present Pleasure or Pain*, for the sake of what reason tells him is fit to be done, wants the true Principle of Virtue and Industry; and is in danger never to be good for anything."[111] The "true Principle of Virtue of Industry" rests with "higher" subjective traits, such as instrumental rationality, moderation, sobriety, and self-discipline, which in turn are rooted in the ability to suspend the urge for immediate gratification in order to achieve an anticipated future goal. These traits, I argue, properly belong to the accumulative paradigm, and find their medium of expression and development in the realm of abstraction opened up by monetization. Money itself is born out of the human faculty of abstraction, and the increasingly complex social relations engendered by monetization in turn require the further honing of this faculty.[112] The field of temporal freedom opened by the use of money is rife with possibilities for exercising future-oriented, calculative, and rational behavior, for comporting oneself in the present on the basis of a projection of one's self in a moment that does not yet exist. The "desire for money" extends into "the expression of the distinctly human characteristic of foresight."[113] Although producing goods for the purpose selling them is certainly driven by the pecuniary pursuit of self-interest, insofar as it involves producing for anonymous and prospective rather than immediate and proximate human needs, it signifies more than this narrow motive.[114] Generalization of commodity production and exchange is at the same time the social process of liberation from the immediacy of quotidian experience and parochial circumstance. In this respect, Locke's theory prefigures Adam Smith's account of commercial society, wherein impersonal market exchange mediates the division of labor and economic interdependence, undermining personal relations of dependence and expanding the domain of individual liberty.

The significance of money and commerce in Locke's overall philosophy falls into even sharper relief if one bears in mind that in the *Essay on Human Understanding* Locke posits the "faculty of *Abstracting*" as the human faculty par excellence, which sets our species apart from lower animals. It is "the faculty to enlarge by any kind of *Abstraction*" that places "a perfect distinction betwixt man and brutes."[115] In the *Essay*, Locke defines human subjectivity as consciousness that persists over time and amid the flux of sense-impressions, consciousness that remains aware of its unity and identity at different temporal and experiential instances.[116] As a number of commentators have noted, "abstracting lifts the mind out of the given flow of sensation and allows it to stand in semisovereign sway over its own contents,"[117] such that the individual "can think of himself, abstractly, as a being that endures from moment to moment."[118] This particular temporal analytic, the future orientation of thought and behavior represents a major philosophical and normative thread that connects Locke's theory of the self to his theory of labor and property. One of the most forceful critics of innate ideas and a towering philosopher of empiricist epistemology, Locke held that selfhood is crafted out of the experience of social practice and convention. Then social practice and convention is where we should look for the conditions of "industrious and rational" human subjectivity. I contend that the emancipation of human beings from production for immediate consumption and their reorientation to accumulative practices constitutes the socioeconomic crucible where futural human subjectivities are forged. As the necessary medium of this transition, monetized exchange functions as the practical grounds for training that mental faculty which distinguishes us as humans, or put more starkly, as a field of potentialities for the consummation of humanity. If my interpretation is plausible, then, from a Lockean perspective, the relative positioning of various individuals, groups, or classes in relation to monetary economy holds normative implications for judging the development and plenitude of their subjectivities.

To be clear, this is not to contend that Locke denied Native Americans the faculty of reason and abstraction. Locke quite clearly parted ways with the Spanish whose justifications of dispossession dehumanized American indigenes as heathens or beasts. He declared in unambiguous terms that all human beings were born with the same faculty of reason that enabled them to discern the moral obligations of natural law. "[T]hey have Light enough to lead them to the knowledge of their maker . . . For the visible Marks of extraordinary Wisdom and Power appear so plainly in all the Works of the Creation, that a rational Creature, who will but seriously reflect on them, cannot miss the discovery of a *Deity*."[119] By the same token, Locke included Native Americans under the protection of religious toleration. "No man whatsoever ought . . . to be deprived of his Terrestrial Enjoyments, upon account of his Religion. Not even Americans, subjected unto a Christian Prince, are to be punished either in Body or Goods, for not imbracing our Faith and Worship."[120] These and other similar remarks have fueled David Armitage's recent objection to Locke's depiction as a "theorist of empire." Squarely rebutting Mehta's argument from cultural difference and hierarchy of reason, Armitage notes Locke's "scepticism about human capacities and his humility about the alleged superiority of Europeans" and concludes, "Locke did not charge Native Americans with irrationality."[121] Particularly indicative of

Locke's humility was his encounter with two Native Americans who had traveled to England, of whom he wrote:

> And this I thinke to be the reason why some Indians I have spoken with, who were otherwise of quick rationall parts could not as we doe count to a 1000. though they could very well count to 20 because their language being scanty & accommodated to the few necessarys of a needy simple life unacquainted either with trade or Mathematiques, had noe words in it to stand for a thousand.[122]

This passage suggests that Locke perceived apparent differences in cognitive capacities as reflections of circumstantial variation rather than innate deficits of rationality, thus cautioning Europeans against superior cultural self-understanding.

I contend, pace Armitage, that if we appraise this passage in the light of the progressive-accumulative paradigm signaled by monetization, we can detect a hierarchical framework, albeit one that is much subtler and more historically grounded than is argued by Mehta. Fully consonant with the link between monetization and abstraction, Locke here explains the limits of numerical reckoning ("Mathematiques") by the simplicity and scarcity of a precommercial subsistence economy ("few necessaries of a needy simple life unacquainted with trade"), which in the *Second Treatise* corresponds to the premonetary stage in the state of nature. That the primitive condition of Native Americans does not issue from an inherent defect of reason does not change their status as primitive and dwelling in the natural common. If anything, possessing an inherent capacity for reason but not fully utilizing it (as attested by the absence of money, lack of trade, and stunted abstraction) places Native Americans in the ambiguous position of "not irrational."[123] Although Native Americans do not lack the faculty of reason with which God has endowed all mankind, they do not partake in the practical conditions that enable the actualization of these capacities. I would go further to suggest that from a Lockean perspective, the absence of monetization among Native Americans instantiates the *nonexercise* of the faculty of abstraction that they surely possess—a non-exercise, the responsibility for which belongs to Native Americans themselves.

Locke's insistence that monetization is the only way to disentangle the transformative powers of labor from the limits of subsistence economy (and thereby pave the way for the full utilization of human faculties) cannot be explained without recourse to the colonial capitalism that mediated the relationship between Native Americans and the English. For Atlantic colonial capitalism consisted of a socioeconomic frontier where the agents of highly commercialized economies confronted nonmonetized communities who were in control of the lands these agents so avidly sought. Accordingly, it was the absence not of monotheism but of monetization that Locke settled on for adjudicating property rights in America. If, therefore, we are to search for Locke's liberal strategies of exclusion in the tacit assumptions that lurk beneath the abstract idiom of natural rights, we should not look to the tired culturalist trope of the universalization of the colonizers' provincial beliefs. For this perspective cannot explain why Locke deemed certain forms of abstraction to be binding on property claims and regarded others as irrelevant, why he claimed that the absence of money rendered American lands open to appropriation and treated Christianity (itself no less abstract than money) as juridically null with respect to proprietorship. As Dipesh Chakrabarty remarks, "The point is not that Enlightenment rationalism is always unreasonable to itself, but rather a matter of documenting how—through what historical process—its "reason," which was not always self-evident to everyone, has been made to look obvious far beyond the ground where it originated."[124] The colonial capitalism of the seventeenth-century Atlantic and its originary position in the global inceptions of capital is a good place to start unraveling this historical process.

Conclusion: Beyond Possessive Individualism

In an exceptionally evocative passage, Patrick Wolfe has observed:

> As John Locke had provided, in texts that would profoundly influence Euroamerican colonial discourse, private property accrued from the admixture of labour and land. To put it very simply, Blacks provided the former and Indians the latter—the application of enslaved Black people's labour to evacuated Indian land produced the White man's property, a primitive accumulation if ever there was one.[125]

The gist of this passage casts into relief several more general issues concerning the imperial turn in political theory and, specifically, the hermeneutic binary of abstract universals and historical difference through which Locke and other members of the pantheon are read into the history of colonial empires. In chapter 1, I sketched some of the shortcomings of this interpretive lens, which magnifies textual enunciation and divides the discursive field into zones of disembodied liberal principles and thick cultural particularisms. I conclude by drawing out the specific implications of my analysis of Locke for this problematic.

First, the foregoing discussion points to the ways in which the putative foundational dichotomies such as abstract/concrete and universal/particular, out of which we fashion our analytic grids for discerning the colonial inflections of political thought, are themselves woven into historically determinate modes of social reproduction. If we are to dissect Locke's universal claims and historical abstractions, perhaps a more accurate scalpel than Euclidian space or post-Newtonian algebra would be "capital," which is universal in its conceptual logic and global in its geographic horizon, and "commodity" in and through which social relations are mediated through abstract exchangeable value.[126] If this sounds like reductive materialism, one need recall that the specific Atlantic context that shaped the orientation of the English toward Native Americans was, by the standards of the time, heavily commercialized. In fact, what constituted the backbone of the English Atlantic, what propelled thousands of men and women from the England to America and hurled many more from Africa to the Caribbean, what spurred settlements and plantations, what regularized trans-oceanic relations of production and exchange, in short, what held the English Atlantic together was a vast network of commodity chains in things and humans, driven by ever-present dreams and plans of profit. One navigated the English Atlantic by the compass of commodity and capital much more reliably than one could England itself.[127]

Viewed through this lens, Locke's universal claims for adjudicating property claims in America appear less to be arbitrary markers of historical difference. Under the "universal constituency" of Locke's theory of property, one can discern the vision of a new socioeconomic order lodged in the capitalist relations crystallizing in the Atlantic basin, a vision with global aspirations to bring mankind within its compass of private property, material productivity, and accumulation of value. To emphasize this point is not so much to reduce as to embed Locke's theory of property in the field of concrete possibilities and relations of the seventeenth-century world-historical conjuncture that delimited political and economic perceptions and priorities. And these perceptions and priorities were the province of not only men of power like Shaftesbury and their intellectual aides like Locke, but also people of middling sorts who invested in colonial trade or joint-stock companies, and the poor who indentured their labor in return for their passage to a new and hopefully more commodious life.

Secondly, applying the analytic of colonial political economy to Locke's theory of property helps to elaborate in more concrete terms the notion of disavowal that I proposed in chapter 1 for interpreting liberal texts. The analysis presented here refers Locke's theory beyond the text itself by treating it as a window on the commodity relations of Atlantic colonial capitalism and the specific problems of ideological justification they engendered. Bracing the liberal self-image of the English exploits against the disturbing implications of lawless conquest in the Atlantic, Locke's theory of property instantiates a crucial moment in the liberal misrecognition of colonial capitalism and the continued authorization of colonial land appropriations. Instead of denying the problem of extralegal appropriation or simply conceding it as a tragic contradiction, Locke acknowledges the problem *eo nomine* and proceeds to contrive narratives and fictions in order to deproblematize it for liberal sensibilities. Locke's interpolation of money in his theory of property caters to a fantastic trove of ideological resources for draping capitalism in liberal garb, including myths of natural consent, oscillating spatial exclusion and temporal inclusion, human communities at once inside and outside mankind, and gray zones of subjectivity inhabited by "not irrational" individuals. Finally, these conceptual maneuvers and fictions around money operate less as cynical strategies Locke employs to hoodwink his audience than "myths" in the anthropological sense of the term. They are stories that Locke tells himself and his English contemporaries to explain their exploits in an expanding, vagarious, and turbulent world.

Finally, the emphasis on Locke's notion of money not only helps us discern subtler boundaries of exclusion than were observed by the colonial interpretations of Locke, but it also suggests hitherto unnoticed connections between England and America that cut across cultural lines. Embedding the problematic of exclusion in the distinct modes of social reproduction implied by money foregrounds economic complexity, social abstraction, and future orientation as criteria of hierarchy. Above all, it brings together Native Americans and the English laboring poor in the common denominator of hand-to-mouth existence. By connecting English enclosures to American land appropriations under the progressive cause of commercial agriculture, it structurally links the dispossessed of England with the soon-to-be dispossessed of America.[128] The "wild Indian" who subsists on the "spontaneous products of the earth" is in this respect akin to the "Labourer" whose "share, being seldom more than a bare subsistence, never allows that Body of Men time or opportunity to raise their Thoughts above that."[129] The subsistence paradigm sets these two groups apart from England's commercial-colonial entrepreneurs, whose privileged position in the monetary economy of the Atlantic renders them the proper historical subjects of Locke's accumulative paradigm. When transposed to the register of Locke's theory of subjectivity, this entrapment in the immediacy of subsistence directly contrasts with the workings of the faculty of abstraction. Differential access to, and status in, a monetized economy conceivably stands indexical to the level of individual and social development on a scale ranging from commanding money for investment to merely subsisting in a monetary economy to being completely outside monetization; from money as capital (M-C-M') to money as medium of exchange (C-M-C) to the total absence of money (C-C); from English capitalists to the English working class to Native Americans.

Insofar as it enables us to perceive this socioeconomic and subjective developmental hierarchy, the focus on money can help us reinterpret a conundrum pointed out by Tully, who countered Macpherson's thesis of possessive individualism with the accurate observation that the dominant mercantilist view of the English population in Locke's time was one of "utilizable" individuals, not quite possessed of their capacities and subject to the state's "authoritative allocation of work" in workhouses or plantations.[130] The class aspect of this distinction and the role of money therein have been identified in a recent essay by Edward Andrew:

> Locke's *Considerations* and *Further Considerations* advocate *laissez-faire* for the propertied and police for the property-less. Locke certainly thought that justice entailed the right of those with money to lend it at market rates and the right of landlords and creditors to be paid with the bullion rate of silver, rather than the clipped but circulating coin of the realm. The right of charity did not extend to debtors, tenant farmers, laborers and consumers who experienced mass starvation from the depletion of coin and the exportation of bullion arising from the government's adoption of Locke's re-coinage scheme.[131]

Pushing this line of analysis beyond England and into the Atlantic can help us identify "possessive individuals" who command money as capital, "utilizable individuals" who are subject to various degrees of unfreedom as they labor under the command of capitalists, and "disposable individuals" who, until and unless they join the global monetary order, are to be swept aside by the tide of capitalist expansion qua primitive accumulation. The gradation of socioeconomic status by quantitatively unequal and qualitatively different access to money, and the subordinate co-articulation of possessive, utilizable, and disposable (possessive-possessed-dispossessed) individuals under the overarching vision of possessive universalism might offer a fresh perspective on one of the longest-standing debates on Locke's political and economic allegiances.

As I indicated at the end of chapter 1, we can discern a specifically modern and capitalist grammar of power and progress in Locke's theory of property that has endured beyond his particular context. The following chapters contend that this grammar was central to eighteenth- and nineteenth-century metropolitan discourses that ordered the social diversity within the British Empire into a legible hierarchy, however fraught and provisional, that reinforced the essentially liberal and capitalist British self-conceptions. Importantly, the socioeconomic parameters of this hierarchical grammar cut across the putative cultural divide between the European self and the non-European Other. As chapter 4 demonstrates, Edward Gibbon Wakefield and many of his contemporaries judged the white settler colonies of Australasia to be "barbarous" and "savage" societies by the social and moral standards of early Victorian Britain. Hailed in Locke's time as the frontrunners of civilization in the wilderness of the New World, British settlers were now recast as civilizational degenerates who needed the direction and intervention of the imperial state for their reclamation.

Before we connect the American moment of settler colonialism to the Australasian moment and examine the changing stakes of imperial expansion from land to labor, we shall tarry with Britain's empire in India. Chapter 3 investigates the eighteenth-century debates over what it meant for Britain to acquire an empire on the subcontinent that was anything but maritime, Protestant, and free. The government of Britain's trade with the territories that were under the rule of the East India Company assumed paramount importance as the test of whether Britain could remain an empire of commerce and liberty. The "commercial barbarism" of the Company policies in India posed the main ideological problem that Edmund Burke had to confront in reclaiming the liberal image of the British Empire.

Not a Partnership in Pepper, Coffee, Calico, or Tobacco

Edmund Burke and the Vicissitudes of Imperial Commerce

> Society is indeed a contract ... but the state ought not to be considered as nothing better than a partnership agreement in a trade of pepper and coffee, callico or tobacco, or some other such low concern, to be taken up for a little temporary interest, and to be dissolved by the fancy of the parties ... it becomes a partnership not only between those who are living, but between those who are living, those who are dead, and those who are to be born. Each contract of each particular state is but a clause in the great primeval contract of eternal society.
>
> —Edmund Burke

If John Locke provided the imperial turn in political theory with its seminal object of inquiry, then Edmund Burke arguably furnished the most controversial one.[1] Interpreters have cut from the cloth of Burke's writings and speeches an entire wardrobe of guises. Some have presented him as a defender of empire that is based on British custom, culture, and imperial responsibility.[2] Others have found in the Irishman an untimely cosmopolitan given to the cause of a less exclusionary, more liberal, and culturally pluralistic empire.[3] In some accounts, he appears an uneasy accomplice in the colonial project and its implicit guilt, striving to absolve the empire of its scandal.[4] In others, he is a true Whig who glorifies empire as the vehicle for commercial grandeur and improvement underwritten by the civilizational categories of the Scottish Enlightenment.[5] In the latest installment of the debate, we see Burke portrayed as an ardently conservative champion of empire and a statesman deeply wary of the spirit of conquest that empire revives.[6]

In chapter 2, I pointed to a disconnect between the colonial and the economic interpretations of Locke's political thought. A closer look at the epigraph that opens this chapter suggests a similar disconnect in Burke scholarship.

Burke's appeal to the "great primeval contract" in this passage has been a staple reference in explicating his anti-Jacobinism, his opposition to radical contractarianism, and his defense of the traditional order against the mercurial forces of commerce embodied in the political ascendancy of "monied men." However, no commentator seems to have detected the exclusively colonial origins of the commodities in the "partnership agreement" that Burke counterposed to his great primeval contract. *Pepper, coffee, calico, and tobacco.* These were colonial commodities traded by European joint-stock companies through complex chains of production and procurement in which methods of extra-economic coercion played a constitutive role. Edmund Burke would devote the latter half of his political career to scrutinizing and criticizing the British East India Company's use of such coercive methods in India, writing searing reports, drafting imperial reform bills, and spearheading the impeachment of Warren Hastings, the former governor-general of Bengal. It was on these efforts to reform and retain the empire in India that Burke celebrated himself "the most; most for the importance; most for the labor; most for the judgment; most for constancy and perseverance in the pursuit" (*W&S*, 9:159).[7] Regardless of whether Burke purposely selected the colonial commodities he mentioned in the passage or invoked them absentmindedly, the selection itself gives a clue about the nature of the problem that so vexed Burke: the venal and temporary contract that represented the mirror opposite and even the dissolution of constitutive bonds of society was of a *colonial capitalist* nature.

This chapter argues that Burke's acidic criticism of the Company's economic policies and his exertions to reform its administration aimed at upholding the free and commercial image of Britain while maintaining its necessarily extractive empire in India. I contend that Burke traced the root cause of plunder, famine, and depopulation in Bengal to the "imperious commerce" carried out by the Company. He accused company agents of abusing their newfound political power to maximize private profits as their political accomplices in Britain shielded their conduct from effective parliamentary scrutiny. Burke admitted that conquest and expropriation lay at the origins of all government and property, the British Empire in India not excepted. However, instead of *institutionalizing* political power as the basis of private property, contract enforcement, and market exchange (the necessary institutional conditions of a commercial society), the Company *instrumentalized* political power to extract and remit back home as much surplus from India as possible.

The consequent "drain of wealth" did not only decimate Britain's Indian subjects. More importantly, it defamed Britain's image as a modern empire of liberty and commerce that ought to have been an exception and an example to other European empires of plunder and extortion. Burke was unambiguously invested in this Whig self-image of Britain and knew well that his reform efforts could only have a fighting chance if he persuaded his audience that the British Empire was ceasing to be characteristically British. As he clung to the empire in India as a potential source of British power and prosperity, he addressed the problem of its illiberality by attributing it to the congenitally misshapen merchant sovereignty of the Company. The British Empire could be liberal and commercial without losing its imperial nature if the economic and political functions of the Company were separated, the former liberalized and the latter entrusted to Britain's imperial Parliament. Britain's Indian subjects could enjoy security of property, freedom of contract, and market equality regardless of their race and religion.[8] Put differently, the ideological challenge to which Burke rose was to imagine an "imperial commerce" as the antidote to "imperious commerce," which could restore the empire to liberality.

I begin with situating Burke's writings and speeches in the political, economic, and ideological context of eighteenth-century colonial capitalism in British India. I construct a brief yet pointed account of the political economy of the early British rule in the subcontinent that Burke targeted with his criticisms and reform attempts. I hold that far from being an agent of sheer mercantilist plunder or the "stillbirth of capital" in South Asia,[9] the Company policies forcibly reorganized and reoriented economic activity in the Indian Ocean in line with the priorities of capital accumulation even if this meant an overall decline in the productivity of Indian agriculture and manufactures. To Burke's liberal economic sensibilities, the coercive methods of merchant capitalism appeared to be a peculiar scheme for looting Indian wealth. Although Burke resorted to the classical idiom of "corruption" to indict this system, I contend that he was giving expression to a historically novel contradiction between the liberal values of a commercial ideal (which he shared with Adam Smith) and the systematic violation of these values by commercial capitalism in India.

Against this political economic backdrop, I provide a close analysis of Burke's commercial ideal, the primary ideological prism through which Burke viewed, imagined, and judged Britain's liberal self-image. I reconstruct from Burke's writings a decisively liberal economic (though not political) vision that endorsed the pursuit of material interest, an ethos of productivity, and self-regulating markets. Most importantly, Burke prescribed a wall of separation between political power and economic transactions, which sustained legal equality and contractual freedom as the pillars of public utility and equity. Enshrined in the constitutional arrangements and laws of Britain, properly constituted political power made the accumulation of capital through voluntary, mutually beneficial, and fair commercial relations possible.

In British India, the runaway merchant-sovereignty of the company subverted this separation and turned political power into an instrument of expropriation and exploitation. I build up a detailed account of these colonial subversions of the commercial ideal. Burke often described Company policies in India as "barbarous," but he also intimated that it was an unprecedented, *commercial* form of barbarism. His attempt to salvage the essential liberality of commerce depended on disavowing its violent and rapacious eruptions in India, because the latter revealed the same principle of self-interested exchange that animated capital accumulation in Europe to be the main motive force behind plunder in the colonies. Burke's fervent denunciation of Company rule can be understood as an attempt to shore up the increasingly blurred distinctions between civilized commerce and unabashed pillage, enlightened self-interest and unbridled rapacity, and mercantile principle and political power.

I finally turn the lens of imperial political economy back on questions of cultural alterity and civilizational hierarchy, and re-evaluate the recent arguments on Burke's cosmopolitan critique, ambivalent embrace, or conservative defense of empire. I contend that Burke's defense of Indians rested on his view of India as a "commercial society." As a category of political economy and stadial history, commercial society was distinguished by a sublime socioeconomic complexity that had led Adam Smith to the providential metaphor of the invisible hand. Burke's designation of India as a commercial society on par with Britain and France led him to defend that country from the rude, visible hands of the Company's political despotism. Conversely, the primitive socioeconomic simplicity of "savage" Native Americans and "barbarous" Africans sanctioned Burke's derogatory attitude toward them, rendering their subjection to the British Empire's austere civilizing dominion morally justifiable. Recovering the place of political economic analysis in Burke's appraisal of the nature, management, and problems of the British Empire, I conclude, can more clearly illuminate the consistency of his differential judgments of non-Europeans than can the existing culturalist interpretations.

Empire and Commercial Capitalism in India

At the time Burke entered the House of Commons in 1765, the spoils of the Seven Years' War with France (1756–1763) and the East India Company's military victories against the Mughal Empire had brought vast territorial possessions in North America and India under the British dominion, and along with them, large populations of French Catholics, Hindus, and Muslims. Britain's increasingly territorial, extractive, and heterogeneous empire made it more difficult to speak of it as commercial, maritime, Protestant, and free. Burke's political career therefore overlapped with not only imperial dismemberment in America and retrenchment in India, but also a concomitant search for a new imperial ideology that could square the established British self-understandings with the changing imperial realities on the ground.

The East India Company, like its Dutch and French counterparts, had started out as a joint-stock trading company in 1600, chartered to carry out England's trade with regions to the east of the Cape of Good Hope. For a century and a half, the Company operated from fortified coastal factories in Bombay, Calcutta, Surat, and Madras, under the grant and jurisdiction of the Mughal Empire. The conventional narrative that the Company was a trader-turned-sovereign has been challenged by revisionist histories that stress the quasi-sovereign powers (such as making wars and treaties, territorial acquisition, and administration of justice) enshrined its founding charter.[10] Yet the Company's exercise of these powers in India remained spatially circumscribed and politically subordinate to Mughal authority.[11] In economic terms, this meant that in addition to paying customs duties on their exports, the Company was bound by the regulations laid down by Nawabs (local governors) and barred from engaging in inland trade, and it had to rely on networks of local intermediaries to procure from local producers the commodities it exported.[12]

The picture changed rather rapidly in the second half of the eighteenth century, when the increased militarization of the Indian Ocean because of the Anglo-French rivalry coincided with the centrifugal political forces that undermined Mughal authority in the subcontinent. The Company emerged as a formidable military and political contender in the region, exploiting rivalries between local rulers in order to secure a territorial foothold. The victory against the Nawab of Bengal at the Battle of Plassey (1757) established a decisive bridgehead and introduced the British as a regional power. More fateful was the victory against the Mughal emperor himself at the Battle of Buxar (1764). The ensuing Treaty of Allahabad (1765) granted the Company the *diwani* right to collect the revenues of Bengal, Bihar, and Orissa on behalf of the emperor. Thereafter, the Company transformed into an unexampled hybrid of a joint-stock company and a fiscal-military state.[13] On the one hand, it continued its trading operations, distributed dividends to its shareholders, and invested in British public debt. On the other, it raised revenue, principally from land taxes and opium and salt monopolies, to finance its military campaigns and territorial expansion against the Maratha and Mysore kingdoms on the subcontinent.

The institutional hybridity soon inflected economic policy and practice on the ground. The Company began financing its exports from India through the "investment of surplus revenue in commodities," abandoning "trade for trade's sake . . . in order to facilitate the transfer of tribute to London."[14] Paralleling the use of public resources for commercial purposes was the use of public authority for penetrating and dominating the local markets that supplied the Company exports, especially in textiles, tea, and opium. "Political power," P. J. Marshall remarks, "notoriously enabled private trade to move from the sea inland and for large profits to be extracted from fixing prices and eliminating competition."[15] Removing local intermediaries, imposing monopoly pricing at the point of production, prohibiting weavers from selling their cloth on the open market, foisting loans and advances on farmers and artisans, creating debt peonage and indenture, forcing the cultivation of cash crops, and mortgaging prospective harvests—all supported in the last instance by the threat of physical coercion—figured among the Company's strategies for minimizing costs and maximizing profits.

The conventional view of the economic effects of British imperialism in India, popular among mainstream and critical historians alike, has been one of "drain of wealth"—though there is disagreement over whether this drain contributed to the Industrial Revolution and metropolitan economic development in any meaningful way.[16] The major shortcoming of this metro-centric accounting viewpoint (which mainly tallies imperial credits and debits) is its inability to grasp the social transformation in late eighteenth-century India as a *capitalist* transformation, part and parcel of the history of global capitalism outlined chapter 1. A much more productive approach is offered by Jairus Banaji's conception of "company capitalism," a form of capitalist organization regnant between the sixteenth and eighteenth centuries, which networked local markets into a world market, indirectly dominated local labor regimes, and "brought about the kind of capitalist world economy that large-scale industry took for granted when it began its own expansion in the nineteenth century."[17] Taking his cue from Marx's underserved reflections on merchant capitalism, Banaji draws attention to the competitive pressures that push commercial capitalists beyond the simplistic formula of buying cheap and selling dear and compel them to "*seek some measure of control over production.*"[18] This point is echoed in Giovanni Arrighi and Jason Moore's discussion of hegemonic cycles of capitalist accumulation, in which the British cycle is distinguished from the previous (Genoese and Dutch) cycles by capitalist merchants' direct intrusion into agro-industrial production processes in both Europe and the colonies.[19]

Commercial capitalism therefore shares with industrial capitalism the *reorganization of production* for the extraction of surplus value, even though the reorganization of labor proceeds through different methods and the extraction of surplus is mediated by different sociohistorical forms in each case. Commercial capitalism relies on strategies of "formal subsumption" that leave existing social forms of production (such as peasant households or artisanal manufacturers) formally intact, yet destroy their economic independence by rendering their viability as economic units conditional on their ability to yield a surplus that can be realized as profit.[20] The power of commercial capital in this case, as Marx observed in *Grundrisse*, consists in gradually restricting direct producers "to one kind of work in which they become dependent on selling, on the *buyer*, the *merchant*, and ultimately produce only *for* and *through* him."[21] Obstacles and resistance to the subordination of productive activity to the demand for remittable surplus are overcome or circumvented with the help of extra-economic coercion and market rigging. These strategies, though incompatible with a *liberal* definition of capitalism that excludes force and fraud, do not change the capitalist priorities of surplus extraction and accumulation that guide formal subsumption.

In colonial India, British company capitalism proceeded primarily through the monopolization and command of the textile market, followed by deindustrialization, peasantization, and the commercialization of agriculture, especially after the Permanent Settlement of Bengal in 1793.[22] Use of military force and creation of monopolies constituted the primary strategies of company capitalism for confiscating and conscripting Indian land and labor into global circuits of capital. Armed trading, which was a signature anomaly in the Indian Ocean, enabled Europeans to "maintain and extend their Asian bridgeheads, and dominate local trade through the use of terror and force."[23] This dynamic played out rather dramatically in textile manufacturing, the principal export sector of precolonial India. At the same time, Britain protected its domestic manufactures with the Calico Act of 1721, the Company used its "new combination of economic and political power" in India to "gain greater control over textile manufacturing, especially by increasing control over weavers. . . . Monopolizing the market became the way to drive down weavers' incomes and drive up the selling prices of particular goods."[24] Similarly, Indian peasants and agricultural laborers, working predominantly in the cultivation of cash crops like indigo, were bonded by forms of debt peonage and forced to generate a surplus for the Company, landlords, financiers, and agricultural middlemen in the form of tax, rent, and interest.

Although the threat of physical coercion and corporal punishment was never too distant, the "advances system" formed the main vector of formal subsumption and merchant control over Indian manufactures and agriculture. The elimination of competition in the credit and commodity markets left producers dependent for operating funds on Company merchants and their agents, who now dictated both the terms of credit and the terms of sale. Regarding the merchant domination of the textile industry, Sven Beckert writes, "[T]hrough its Indian agents, the company now made direct advances to weavers . . . [who] were now compelled to take advances from particular merchants. . . . Extensive new regulations attached weavers legally to the company, making them unable to sell their cloth on the open market."[25] Andrew Sartori summarizes the imbrication of coercion and capital in the commercialization of Indian agriculture:

> The cultivators were thus already positioned de facto as wage laborers producing surplus out of the capital of the planters. Advances

functioned as wages foisted upon the cultivator through either the force of necessity (want of cash) or direct coercion (the threat of dispossession through rent enhancement or naked violence), and forcibly depressed to such a level as to ensure so that the product thus secured would return surplus value.[26]

Despite its appearance as a usurious expropriation of direct producers by non-market coercion, the advances system constituted a strategy of "vertical concentration" by which commercial capital articulated the dispersed labor power of a myriad of households to global networks of accumulation.[27] The subsequent economic regression of the region in terms of manufacturing output and the share of global trade was not so much the preemption of India's transition to capitalist modernity, or what Siraj Ahmed has called the "stillbirth of capital,"[28] as its moment of simultaneous "global integration and regional peripheralization."[29]

In short, the systemic exploitation of the peasantry primarily through non-market means, the investment of agricultural tax revenues in the financing of exports to Europe and China, and the Company's manipulation of regional rivalries to expropriate local princes coalesced into a process of colonial primitive accumulation of subordinating local economic activity, extraction of surplus, and absorption of the region into the global movement of capital, wherein Britain increasingly occupied the epicenter.

To Burke and his eighteenth-century contemporaries, however, who obviously did not have access to the Marxian concepts used here, the process of primitive accumulation and formal subsumption in India appeared to be a gigantic and elaborate system for carrying away the region's wealth (this much was conceded by Marx himself, who wrote, "commercial capital, when it holds a dominant position, is thus in all cases a system of plunder").[30] As I will argue in detail, the prime imperial pathology that Burke diagnosed in India was the corruption of his idealized image of "commerce" by its adulteration with *imperium*, giving birth to the bastard of "imperious commerce." As Richard Bourke puts it crisply, "[T]erritorial sovereignty had politicized the commercial enterprise of the East India Company."[31] This "politicization of commerce" qua economic instrumentalization of political power, was for Burke the taproot of a whole range of disorders that immiserated Indians and brought shame upon the British name. "Imperious commerce" (strictly speaking, a contradiction in terms) condensed the tension between the liberal ideal and the illiberal origins of commercial capitalism in India. Burke, more than anybody else, knew that the latter had to be covered by a "secret veil" if the former were to survive.

The Company's startling ascendancy amid the political and economic upheavals in India generated a number of ideological challenges for Britain's political classes that are relevant for the analysis that follows. The first of these was the problem of imperial rule over socially and culturally alien populations on the subcontinent, who were thought to be unaccustomed to the institutions of free government. The problem, however, was neither unprecedented nor unsurmountable; Britain's Atlantic empire featured a long history of despotic rule over racialized others, above all, enslaved Africans and the conquered Irish.[32] In fact, Marshall notes the surprising alacrity with which Burke incorporated India into the British Empire at a time when a fear of corruption and decline inspired by classical interpretations of Roman history had instilled doubt and anxiety in his contemporaries.[33] Partly accounting for this readiness was Burke's belief that God, for inscrutable reasons, had providentially led the British down the path of dominion and conquest in India.[34] In contrast to the American colonies, the Indian empire lacked historical, cultural, and customary ties to the metropole that could serve to legitimize imperial sovereignty. In the face of alien rule, invoking divine design lent support to the British rule—by providence if not by consent, in trust derived from God if not from the Indians.[35]

A second, more controversial matter concerned the form of merchant sovereignty that the British rule assumed in India and the constitutional entanglements it engendered between the British state, the East India Company, and the Mughal Empire. That a joint-stock trading company chartered by the British Crown to carry out commerce should exercise sovereign authority in Bengal proved difficult to settle and would remain so until the establishment of the British Raj.[36] Initially cautious about impinging on the corporate rights of the Company, Burke eventually came to agree with Adam Smith's vituperation of merchant sovereignty and pressed for transferring the Company's political function to the Parliament.[37] For Burke, Britain's imperial constitution dictated protecting the well-being of Britain's provincial subjects rather than sacrificing them to metropolitan interests. The Company policy of maximizing short-term profits without regard for the long-term prosperity of Indians had proven that merchants made the worst sovereigns. The trust of government therefore had to be placed in Britain's Parliament, which had, for better or for worse, been "imperialized" in the 1760 by the abandonment of the "salutary neglect" toward the colonies. Parliamentary control of Indian administration would offer a bulwark against corruption in the East and at the same time place Indian patronage beyond the reach of the Crown.[38]

The final and most pressing problem was the political economy of governing India, a critical yet often underemphasized dimension of Burke's imperial thought.[39] It is at the level of political economic argument that one can most lucidly delineate Burke's secular reasons for maintaining the empire as an instrument of wealth and power *and* his criticism of imperial practice in India for being economically destructive and morally repugnant to the British liberal character.

As has been noted by Robert Travers, eighteenth-century theories of political economy supplied empire builders and their critics with an alternative language with which to formulate questions of authority, law, liberty, and justice unencumbered by the notions of ancient constitution and republican virtue.[40] Marshall observes that the "writings of the Company's servants in the this period often reveal a taste for theorizing about such matters as social development or political economy."[41] Especially after the Seven Years' War, political economy increasingly became the idiom of choice among statesmen for framing the problems of modern statecraft.[42] A key tenet of this discourse was what is now labeled the "commercial reason of state": a rationality of rule that recognized the dependency of modern states on international trade for wealth and revenue, and the consequent necessity for states to act as armed business concerns and compete against their rivals for a share of global commerce.[43] The commercial reason of state found its principal and, in Istvan Hont's words, "murderously intense" area of application in imperialism beyond Europe precisely because, as I argued in the chapter 1, the colonies lay "beyond the line" of *jus publicum Europeaum*.[44] In the Asian theater, this was manifested in the "idea of force"—that is, the belief in the inescapability of militarized trading in the absence of shared laws, customs, and conventions that reined the use of violence and coercion in economic dealings.

Burke fully owned this premise, and as we shall see, though he advocated the free operation of commerce *within* sovereign borders, he was no cosmopolitan free trader from principle. In this spirit, he openly admitted in 1757 that the slave trade, though morally dubious, served the "necessity we are under of peopling our colonies."[45] In his plea to conciliate the American colonies in 1775, he reminded his audience of the meteoric rise of the Atlantic commerce that had become "interwoven" into the fabric of British prosperity (*W&S*, 3:11–16). Addressing the House of Commons on the corruption in India, he emphasized the "interest which this nation [Britain] has in the commerce and revenues of that country" (*W&S*, 5:381) and warned his peers, "The greatest body of your revenue, your most numerous armies, your most important commerce, the richest source of your public credit . . . are on the point of being converted into a mystery of the state" (*W&S*, 5:491).[46] To preserve "the British Empire in the east," Burke invited the British political elite to "stretch and expand" their political vision in proportion to their imperial project and to formulate "a general, comprehensive, well-connected, and well-proportioned view of the whole of our dominions, and a just sense of their true bearings and relations" (*W&S*, 5:492).[47] With these exhortations, he was trying to align imperial politics with a new comprehension of empire as an economic totality of interdependent peripheries that ought to be deliberately integrated and governed by policy.[48] The Indian empire in particular "would be, if managed properly, a wondrous possession of potentially enormous commercial value."[49] In an unadorned expression of this position in 1769,

Burke praised Robert Clive's acquisition of "such a world of commerce; . . . such manufactures and revenues, as I believe never was laid before any committee in so short words. . . . Europe will envy, the East will envy:I hope we shall remain an envied people. (*W&S*, 2:220).

Unfortunately, Burke's hopes did not bear out. A steady stream of "reports of wars, famines, the overthrow of Nawabs and the indiscipline of company servants" in the 1770s gradually eroded Burke's resolve to defend the chartered rights of the Company against the encroachments of the British state, a position he held onto as late as 1781.[50] His service on the Parliamentary Select Committee between 1781 and 1783, which gave him a very detailed picture of the Indian affairs, represented a decisive turning point in his view of the administration of the Indian empire.[51] By 1783, he had lost faith not in the empire itself but in the Company's capacity to discharge the duties that the empire entailed. Accordingly, he began to call for abridging the Company charter and asserting the "universal laws of morality" over and against corporate rights. Indictments of corruption, embezzlement, extortion, and oppression leveled at the Indian government, Burke now believed, neither were partisan pretexts to capture the Company nor could be explained away as the isolated misdemeanors of a few wayward agents. The consistent financial problems the Company had experienced for over a decade despite having taxed its once-opulent provinces to the point of repeated famines could only be explained by systemic corruption.

Burke found the intellectual resources necessary for pressing this point in the modern discourse of political economy, more precisely, in the premises that governments existed to secure the conditions of general material welfare and that the "political conditions of economic success were everywhere similar."[52] He thereby joined those who questioned "the assumption that the normal state of India was one of prosperity" and held that "it might also be necessary for the Company to adopt positive policies which would change and develop their provinces in order to create wealth."[53] On these assumptions, both the ends and the means of British sovereignty in India gained transparency and simplicity, notwithstanding the vast geographical distance and cultural difference between Britain and India. By the same token, the abject failure of the Company to perform its governmental obligations appeared plain and incontrovertible. A complete overhaul of the Indian administration was imperative to purge the rot and restore the Indian economy to its former prosperity.

At stake in the governance of Britain's empire was not only her power and prosperity but also her national character, image, and reputation. As Jennifer Pitts explains, "Burke took his speeches on empire and international justice as occasions for imagining the British nation."[54] In an idiomatic expression of the "empire of liberty," Burke wrote, "Without subordination, it would not be one empire; without freedom, it would not be the British Empire" (*W&S*, 2:50). As one commentator has recently noted, "Throughout his career Burke adhered to the idea that among European and Asian powers, the British polity was the best constituted to protect individual rights and the general welfare."[55] This deep commitment to an idealized image of the British polity persistently colored Burke's judgments on imperial policy. He imagined the British imperial conduct to be the showcase of its political integrity and imagined other European nations, all of humanity, and even God himself to be watching and judging it.

A major leitmotif of Burke's writings on empire was the hazards it posed to the liberal values and institutions that defined the English nation, hazards that nonetheless could be avoided or contained by principled and prudent statesmanship. For instance, in his much acclaimed "Speech on Conciliation," he hailed England as a "great, commercial nation," "a nation, in whose veins the blood of freedom circulates" (*W&S*, 3: 114, 130). He objected to the imperious handling of the American crisis on the grounds that it threatened to "subvert the maxims" that kept alive the English "spirit of liberty" (*W&S*, 3: 127). During the war with the colonies, Burke begrudgingly watched his premonition come true. "Liberty is being made unpopular to Englishmen," he declaimed, "contending for an imaginary power, we are acquiring the spirit of domination, and to lose the relish of honest equality" (*W&S*, 3:328–29). If the free and commercial image of the British Empire proved hard to uphold on the American front, it was even more slippery, awkward, and difficult to apply to the Indian dominions. Fortified in territorial possessions acquired by conquest and wielding administrative, judicial, and revenue powers over culturally alien populations accustomed to "Asiatic despotism," the "empire acquired in India was, disturbingly, a great deal more Roman than that lost in America."[56] The Greek model of colonization had always been cherished in the English political imaginary as natural, voluntary, and based on historical ties; whereas the Roman model was associated with the "spirit of domination" that Burke dreaded.[57] Against this background, it is not surprising that he sounded more alarmed when remarking on the British self-image as refracted through *imperium* in India.

H. V. Bowen notes the proliferation of "charges of misrule against the Company" that "carried especially great weight before 1790 as a steady stream of Company servants returned to Britain to be accused of corruption, greed, tyranny, and a host of other crimes thought to besmirch the good name of Britain."[58] Burke joined the fray in 1781 in a speech that targeted the Company's clandestine involvement in wars between Indian rulers.[59] Disturbed by the possibility that this strategy was alienating the local rulers and could drive them to court other European powers, Burke resented that Indians considered "the most despotic empires as more liberal than Britain" (*W&S*, 5:136–37). The proper solution would be to completely publicize the inquiry into the Company's Indian dealings, and if the House showed the political integrity of chastising its own citizens for their misconduct in distant provinces, "Europe would stand astonished and awed by your conduct" (*W&S*, 5:138). In defense of Fox's India Bill, he warned that administrative reform in India would "turn out a matter of great disgrace or great glory to the whole British nation. We are on a conspicuous stage, and the world marks our demeanor" (*W&S*, 5:381). The Company's shady dealings, breaches of contract, and mercenary wars for pecuniary aggrandizement constituted a "most atrocious violation of public faith" and "damned our reputation in India" (*W&S*, 5:395, 397). The collusion between the delinquent company servants and the Court of Directors in London perpetuated the abuses in India and brought repugnance upon "*the honour and policy of this nation, . . . great calamities on India, and enormous expences on the East India Company*" (*W&S*, 5: 438).[60] Principles of justice and prudence called for a vote to strike down "a tyranny that exists to the disgrace of this nation, and the destruction of so large a part of the human species" (*W&S*, 5:451).

One year later, Burke's "Speech on Almas Ali Khan" again rang with alarm over the "disgraceful brand," "indelible stain," "ignominy and abhorrence" that stuck to the British honor and character (*W&S*, 5:474–75). Burke was convinced that the infamy of the Indian plunder and oppression had drawn the "scorn and derision of the world, . . . interested the curiosity and roused the indignation of all Europe, and . . . could descend to posterity unbroken" (*W&S*, 5:462). The same concern was repeated in "Speech on Nabob of Arcot's Debts," in 1785, which asserted the futility of trying to "separate it [India] from our public interest and national reputation," and summoned the "audience formed by the other States of Europe . . . the discerning and critical company before which [the British government] acts" (*W&S*, 5:550, 552). Burke's obsession with the idea that Britain was tested by its imperial conduct in India rose to a crescendo in his inaugural speech at the opening of Hastings Impeachment in 1788:

> My Lords, it is not only the interest of a great Empire which is concerned, which is now a most considerable part of the British Empire; but, my Lords, the credit and honour of the British nation will itself be decided by this decision. My Lords, they will stand or fall thereby. We are to decide by the case of this gentleman whether the crimes of individuals are to be turned into public guilt and national ignominy, or whether this nation will convert these offences, which have thrown a transient shade on its glory, into a judgment that will reflect on the permanent lustre, honour, justice and humanity of this Kingdom . . . Situated as this Kingdom is—and, thank God, an object of envy to the rest of the world for its greatness and its power—its conduct, in that very elevated situation to which it has arisen, will undoubtedly be scrutinized. (*W&S*, 6:271, 277)

Britain's economic and political power, precisely because it derived in great part from its overseas empire, raised doubts about the manner in which the empire was acquired and governed. These passages indicate Burke's concern to ascertain before the British, the European, and the Indian public that imperial and commercial grandeur could and ought to be made compatible with moral conduct and good government.

There is a broad consensus among commentators that the main danger that Burke perceived in imperial expansion was "political corruption," a classical trope based on the lessons of a once-virtuous Roman Empire dragged to dissolution by the plundered "Eastern riches."[61] The specter of Rome incarnate was "Indianism," by which Burke denoted a political "cabal" formed by Company servants in India, the Court of Proprietors and the Court of Directors in London, and a growing number of members of Parliament who owed their seats and political allegiance to the money, influence, and interests of the Company.[62] In his speech on the Sixth Article of Impeachment, Burke conjured up a dreadful image of Indianism as a disease infecting the British body politic:"These people pour in upon us everyday. They not only bring with them the wealth they have, but they bring with them into our country the vices by which they were acquired," with many more awaiting to "let loose all the corrupt wealth of India acquired by the oppression of that country to the corruption of all liberties." (*W&S*, 7:62–63).[63] These and other expressions of the classical fear of corruption, coupled with his providential rhetoric, have lent credence to the conclusion that Burke's was a "premodern political conception of empire"[64] and that he proposed imperial reform in order to salvage the "precapitalist morality of governance of England."[65]

While this interpretation of Burke's anxieties is at first glance plausible, I think it remains superficial and incomplete. A closer examination of Indianism reveals that the classical language of corruption was the medium in which Burke expressed a uniquely modern problem. To return Burke to the main theme of this study, this was the contradiction between, on the one hand, the liberal conception that commercial capitalism was based on contractual transactions between juridical equals in a free market devoid of political power, and on the other, the historical role of political power and extra-economic coercion in engendering the institutional background conditions commercial capitalism. The wealth extracted from India as tribute or "forced trade in booty"[66] was capitalized through Company stocks, dividends, and landed investments, thereby underwriting what Anthony Hopkins and Peter Cain have famously labeled the "gentlemanly capitalism" of the metropole.[67] However, the methods of extracting and transferring that surplus appeared reprehensible according to the gentlemanly, civilized categories by which the British metropole imagined itself. Burke was a perceptive observer of this uneasy symbiosis and tried to navigate it by

drawing on a syncretic ideological arsenal of political economy, ancient constitutionalism, Whig history, and Scottish stadial history.

Burke conceived of Britain as a "commercial society" that incorporated an
agrarian capitalist economy based on private property in land, agricultural
improvement, and wage labor; specialization, the technical division of labor,
and efficiency in manufactures; a large and highly monetarized national market
in consumer and capital goods; a complex system of credit and national debt;
and a legal structure of civil liberties that reproduced these conditions by securing private property and enforcing contracts between legally free and equal persons. He not only affirmed this economic reality but, in somewhat un-Burkean
fashion, elevated its principles to a normative model of political economy.[68]
An examination of Burke's ideas on property, labor, capital, and markets shows
that he unhesitantly drew upon the central tenets of the discourse of political
economy and hewed to a set of liberal principles of economic fairness.[69] The
primal liberal norms of juridical equality and contractual freedom were woven
into what I call Burke's "commercial ideal," which comprised the utility of self-
interest in creating wealth and accumulating capital, universal benefits of economic growth, equity of the market in distributing wealth, and laissez-faire in
agricultural and labor markets.

Burke's Commercial Ideal

The conviction that the free pursuit of material interest, combined with a productive ethic of labor,[70] would simultaneously improve personal fortunes and
contribute to the overall wealth of the society was a staple of eighteenth-century
political economy.[71] This premise appeared in Burke's economic remarks as early
as 1765 and persisted until 1797. Lambasting the restrictive economic policies
of anti-Popery Laws in Ireland, Burke extolled the "desire of acquisition" as
"always a passion of long views." "Confine a man to a momentary possession and
you at once cut off that laudable avarice which every wise state cherished as one
of its first principles" (W&S, 9:477). Curtailing that laudable avarice with profit
ceilings and short tenure terms in landed property resulted in "famishing the
present hour and squandering all upon prospect and futurity" (W&S, 9:477).[72]
Three decades later, Burke revisited the "desire of accumulation," this time to
defend the monied property that floated the national debt during the Anglo-
French War. The desire of accumulation was

> a principle without which the means of their service to the state could
> not exist. The love of lucre, though sometimes carried to a ridiculous,
> sometimes to a vicious excess, is the grand cause of prosperity to all

states. In this natural, this reasonable, this powerful, this prolifick principle ... it is for the statesmen to employ it as it finds it ... he is to make
use of the general energies of nature, to take them as he finds them.
(*W&S*, 9:347–48)

Burke was not endorsing self-interest here simply as a "useful" principle. The
analogy between the "energies of nature" and the "natural, reasonable, powerful, and prolific" principle indicates that the desire of accumulation was akin to
an elemental force in society. Self-interest was less a moral than an epistemological issue, as the question now became how to use the knowledge of men's
self-interest and establish the conditions under which it would augment general prosperity. This question was addressed in Burke's "Speech on Economical
Reform," which betrayed a Lockean commitment to useful knowledge in the
service of material and moral improvement:[73]

> Those things which are not practicable, are not desirable. There is noth-
> ing in the world really beneficial, that does not lie within the reach of an
> informed understanding, and a well directed pursuit. There is nothing
> that God has judged good for us, that he has not given us the means to
> accomplish, both in the natural and moral world. (*W&S*, 3:546)

Burke boasted that his economic proposals were rooted not in "airy speculation" but "in real life, and in real human nature ... in the business and bosoms
of men" (*W&S*, 3:534). Properly managed, the desire to accumulate lodged in
men's bosoms could be a universally beneficent force and it was incumbent on
the prudent politician to channel it toward "universal opulence."[74]

It is important to stress that the self-interest that Burke accepted and praised
here was not the destructive urge derided by the Classical-Christian tradition.
It was instead akin to Smith's "desire of bettering our condition, a desire which,
though generally calm and dispassionate, comes with us from the womb, and
never leaves us till we go into the grave."[75] That is to say, Burke's notion was
already inflected by the transformation of destructive passions into the constant and predictable motive of accumulation, insightfully theorized by Albert
Hirschman.[76] For Burke (unlike for Smith and other Scottish Enlightenment
thinkers), this transformation was indebted less to *doux commerce* than to the
civilized manners fostered by Christianity and social prescription, which had
over time attenuated the conquering spirit of arrogant nobility that had characterized the ancient Britons.[77] Thus rendered calm and dispassionate, self-
interest implied two conditions that we have already encountered in the analysis
of Locke's political economy. First, that the self-interested subject behave in a
rational, settled, and, most importantly, accumulative and a future-oriented

manner. This subjective disposition translated into saving, foresight, and investment by the propertied classes (farmers, merchants, and the like), and "patience, labor, sobriety, frugality, and religion" for the laboring classes (*W&S*, 9:121, 130–32). Both classes "augment the common stock . . . by their industry or their self-denial" (*W&S*, 9:349). The second condition, following from the first, stipulated that labor and consumption be concentrated in productive activities. The first of these conditions had its antithesis in the "thoughtless, loitering, and dissipated life" in Ireland (*W&S*, 9:477), while the second condition was contravened by the unproductive consumption that sustained the "unprofitable titles" of the royal household targeted by Burke's economic reform proposals (*W&S*, 3:483).[78] The harness that tied self-interest to public prosperity was woven from the strips of a Whig ethos of rational industry and Smithian policy of fostering productive consumption.

If the security of property formed the backbone of the Whig worldview in general, Burke's particular views on private property and labor suggest a capitalistic socioeconomic vision. First, Burke not only favored the private possession of land as a factor of production, but he also argued for the concentration of capital as much as possible. In his economic reform proposals, Burke justified his advocacy of the sale of crown and forest lands on the grounds that such dispersed possessions "are of a nature more proper for private management, than public administration"; with the sales, "property is transferred from hands that are not fit for that property to those who are. The buyer and seller must mutually profit by such a bargain" (*W&S*, 3:506). This call for the privatization of public lands becomes more intelligible if one bears in mind that Burke's political career coincided with the onset of the Parliamentary Enclosures that stretched between the mid-eighteenth and mid-nineteenth centuries.[79] One can conjecture that Burke had a positive attitude to the whole enclosure process, given that he perceived in the enclosure of crown lands the same principles "upon which you have acted in private inclosures. I shall never quit precedents where I find them applicable" (*W&S*, 3:506).[80] Public lands were not only to be sold, they were to be cheap enough so as to leave the purchasers with adequate "capital" for cultivating the land. The principal revenue to be obtained from "these uncultivated wastes" was not from the sales but from the "improvement and population of the kingdom," which required that the "unprofitable landed estates of the crown" be disposed of and "thrown into the mass of private property" (*W&S*, 3:507). Burke expressed the same preference for the concentration of capital (landed or otherwise) more powerfully in *Thoughts and Details on Scarcity*, in which he stated that the "monopoly of authority . . . is an evil; but the monopoly of capital is the contrary. It is a great benefit, and a benefit particularly to the poor" (*W&S*, 9:132–33). The reasoning behind this endorsement was the familiar Smithian concatenation of the accumulation of stock, division of labor, increased productivity, expedited accumulation, universal opulence, and the improved condition of the laboring population.

Private property does not function as capital unless it is used to employ and exploit a structurally dependent labor force. One finds strong assumptions and normative prescriptions of wage labor in Burke's later writings that are congruent with a capitalist outlook. The laboring classes of Britain were those who had nothing but their labor power to sell:"As to the common people, their stock is in their persons and in their earnings" and they were to be paid "according to the operation of general capital" (*W&S*, 9:352).[81] The labor power of the common people is "a commodity, like every other," "an article of trade . . . subject to all the laws and principles of trade" (*W&S*, 9:122, 126). As Corey Robin has recently pointed out, even as Burke wrote about labor, he "paid almost exclusive attention to the needs of capital."[82] Similarly, although his political reflections in this period were suffused by a revulsion at the abstract ideal of natural equality, his economic writings exhibited a clear "endorsement of the capitalist abstraction of labor."[83] Burke had no scruples about treating the laboring classes as an undifferentiated mass and their labor as an abstract factor of production, the value of which was determined by supply and demand on the labor market. Wages were set not by the "necessity of the vender, but [by] the necessity of the purchaser" and whether one could fetch subsistence wages on the market was "totally beside the question in this way of viewing it" (*W&S*, 9:126). Intervening in the wage contract was a direct and, in a government's hands, an "arbitrary tax" that encroached upon property (*W&S*, 9:123, 126).[84] Minimum wage or outdoor relief amounted to "trifling with the condition of mankind" for it pushed "those who must labour or the world cannot exist" to "seek resources . . . in something else other than their own industry, frugality, and sobriety" (*W&S*, 9:355).[85] That capital accumulation accrued from the surplus value generated by the laborer was similarly unequivocal:"the labour, so far as that labour is concerned, shall be sufficient to pay the employer a profit on his capital" (*W&S*, 9:123).[86] This relation of surplus transfer was couched in the language of a "natural and just" chain of subordination with enterprising capitalist farmers at the top, descending to agricultural laborers, beasts of burden, and inanimate instruments (*W&S*, 9:125).[87] Regardless of his religious-providential language, it is not difficult to detect the capitalist parameters of Burke's prescription of concentrated private property in factors of production and the employment of wage labor for profit.

If capital accumulation was one major pillar of Burke's commercial ideal, the other was the equity of the market. Left to its own operations, the market not only contributed to "general and publick utility" (*W&S*, 9:456), but it also ensured that the transactions were equitable. Burke emphatically asserted in *Thoughts and Details on Scarcity* that the "market alone can settle the price" and does so with an astonishing "truth, correctness, celerity, and general equity"

(*W&S*, 9:134). Thus, amid the rising grain prices, food riots, and the government plans to intervene in grain markets in the early 1790s, Burke held fast to the notion that only the market could offer a "fair test of scarcity and plenty" (*W&S*, 9:134).[88] Finally, his belief in the natural tendency of the markets to convert self-interested behavior into societal prosperity went beyond Smith's metaphorical invisible hand and bordered on the providential belief that "the benign and wise disposer of all things . . . obliges men, whether they will or not, in pursuing their own selfish interests, to connect the general good with their own individual success" (*W&S*, 9:125).

The equity of the market manifested itself above all in contractual freedom and the "great rule of equality" in commercial transactions (*W&S*, 9:456). This principle, which underwrote the moral superiority of the free market over all other forms of productive organization, was nowhere more unequivocally asserted than in the *Scarcity* essay. There, Burke expressed his preference "to leave all dealing, in which there is no force or fraud, collusion or combination, entirely to the persons mutually concerned in the matter contracted for" (*W&S*, 9:123). Defending this preference with Smith's reasoning that the contracting parties knew their interests and their particular circumstances better than any third party, Burke predicated the *equity* and thereby the *validity* of the contract exclusively on the volition of the contractors. If the parties were not "completely [masters of the intercourse], they are not free, and therefore their contracts are void" (*W&S*, 9:124). With each party looking to "all possible profit, which, without force or fraud, he can make," the contract implied compromise and identity of interest (*W&S*, 9:130). Most crucially, in labor contracts "it is absolutely impossible that their free contracts can be onerous to either party" (*W&S*, 9:124–25). While Burke had his misgivings about the theories of *social contract*, these passages unmistakably point to Burke's conviction that legal freedom and equality, and the categorical exclusion of deception and coercion, rendered *economic contract* the most fair and morally elevated form of organizing material production and distribution.[89] The difficulty of interpolating Burke's philosophical principles notwithstanding, the foregoing exposition strongly suggests that his economic principles were predominantly *liberal*.

The providential aura with which Burke consecrated the market became even more salient when he later defended the "laws of commerce, which are the laws of nature, and consequently the laws of God" against the improvident hands of government (*W&S*, 9:137). Laissez-faire constituted the final pillar of Burke's vision of Britain as a commercial society. He reprimanded government intervention in the market not only as inefficient in that it distorted the "truth and correctness" of prices and wages, but also as detrimental to "general equity" insofar as it violated contractual freedom. "The moment that government appears at market, all principles of market will be subverted," and a "monopoly of authority" will emerge under the "appearance of a monopoly of capital" (*W&S*, 9:135). The idea that "to provide us in our necessities . . . is in the power of government" was merely a "vain presumption" of statesmen (*W&S*, 9:120).[90] The economic role that Burke reserved for government conformed to a modern-day textbook description of laissez-faire. While government could "prevent much evil, it can to very little positive good" (*W&S*, 9:120); "the office of the judge cannot dictate the contract. It is his business to see that it be enforced" (*W&S*, 9:124). There could be "no authority on earth" to "judge what profit and advantage ought to be" (*W&S*, 9:125). The "truly and properly public" function of the state was to maintain public peace, order, and safety: "Let government protect and encourage industry, repress violence and discountenance fraud, it is all they have to do. In other respects, the less they meddle in these affairs, the better; the rest is in the hands of our Master and theirs" (*W&S*, 9:355).

The final and foundational principle of Burke's political economy, one that laid down the groundwork for the public utility of self-interest and the equity of the market, was a simple yet strict configuration between political power and commercial relations. The ultimate reference point of Burke's political economy, both analytical and normative, was the Scottish Enlightenment understanding of "commercial society."[91] As the most developed and sophisticated stage of human development, commercial society represented the terminus of "a history which explained the hidden causes of civilization's progress from its barbarous to it polished states in terms of changes in the means of subsistence and the distribution of property."[92] Sovereign power had an indispensable role to play in making commercial society possible. A complex web of market-mediated interdependence between specialized producers formed the very tissue of commercial society, which depended on a public authority with the institutional capacity to protect property, enforce contracts, and prevent force and fraud.

When properly *institutionalized*, political power safeguarded civil liberties, chiefly the security of person and property and protection from arbitrary government, which in turn rendered economic transactions with strangers on the market tolerably secure and predictable. Political power made markets; markets promoted the division of labor, productivity, and universal opulence. On this score, Burke followed the increasingly popular conception of civil liberties and their commercial function as independent from political liberties as well as from cultural particularities.[93] Commercial civilization was no longer the exclusive province of republics and could develop under a range of different constitutional regimes, such as monarchies or mixed governments. As a forerunner of this argument, Hume had designated France a "civilized monarchy" because of its protection of civil liberties and (when compared to Britain, admittedly inferior) commercial progress.[94] Taking a step further, Burke added India to the family of commercial societies, arguing against the prejudice of Asiatic despotism that

India was an economically developed society governed by a system of laws.[95] As I will elaborate, his ideal of "imperial commerce" envisioned the commercial societies of England and India conjoined into a single economic space encircled by Britain's imperial constitution, enjoying the same civil liberties under the auspices of the British imperial Parliament.

On the other hand, when political power was *instrumentalized* to attain economic ends, it degenerated into force and fraud, the very pathogens of commercial society that it ought to eradicate. Once considerations of private profit goaded the actions of those vested with public authority, sovereign powers of legislation and executive prerogative turned into forces of insecurity and instability by subjecting commercial dealings to the contingent interests and arbitrary measures of the powerful. Coercion and fraud upended markets and sapped the incentive for industry, investment, division of labor, and economic growth. Put formulaically, political power was a noncommercial precondition of commerce, an institutional framework that enclosed and enabled an economic space that was itself devoid of political power.[96] For that precise reason, the exercise of political power had to remain noncommercial in its guiding principles. Otherwise the inevitable outcome was, in Bourke's words, the "politicisation of commerce," as was fast happening in India.[97] Finally, just as the political conditions of economic success were relatively uniform across cultural and political divides, the politicization of commerce yielded recognizably similar outcomes wherever it occurred. If the expropriations in India were the overture in the unraveling of the commercial civilization as Burke knew it, the confiscations of the French Revolution were the main act. If the dangers of Indianism and Jacobinism were not destroyed root and branch, Burke feared, the coda would be performed in Britain.

In India, each and every one of the principles of the commercial ideal was breached by the Company rule (*W&S*, 5:306). Burke found the situation scandalous for three reasons. First, the British who were trampling on commercial principles were themselves members of a liberal, commercial society; they had "come from a learned and enlightened part of Europe, in the most enlightened period of its time . . . from the bosom of a free Country" (*W&S*, 6:315). Secondly, their atrocities threatened to destroy a society that was as complex and commercialized as their own, and arguably more ancient and opulent. Thirdly, their mode of plundering India rested on the most offensive fusion of political power and commercial interest. Together, these considerations suggested that India's desolation followed not so much from a precommercial spirit of conquest befitting the Goths and Tartars as from one of the actuating principles of commerce itself. The natural desire to accumulate that animated commercial society and powered the "great wheel of circulation" was the main force behind the havoc in India. "Beyond the line," commerce descended into piracy, self-interest into rapacity, and civilization into barbarity.

Imperious Commerce

The commercial ideal in India remained just that: an ideal. Wherever the Company managed to extend its sovereign prerogative (institutionally through the Council of Bengal and individually through its servants), its "imperious Commerce" had breached "every just principle of commerce" in the subcontinent. (*W&S*, 5:244, 306). The immediate effect was the abrogation of juridical equality in commercial transactions between the Company agents and the local traders and producers. The Company's strategy to uphold nominal Mughal authority as a cover for its effective control over Bengal did not deceive Burke: "[T]he English are now a people who appear in India as a conquering nation" and any commercial dealing with them was a "dealing with *power*" (*W&S*, 5:271). "The constitution of the company began in commerce and ended in Empire" (*W&S*, 6:283). One of the first things the Company did with its newfound power was to eliminate all native intermediaries between the manufacturers and itself, thereby rendering its agents "magistrates in the Markets in which they dealt as traders" (*W&S*, 5:245, 259, 427). The stones of legal asymmetry had paved the road to "forced and exorbitant gains of a trade carried on by power" and invariably entailed the dispossession and oppression of the natives (*W&S*, 5:246).

The necessary corollary of the juridical inequality was the evaporation of contractual freedom in the sale and purchase of labor power and commodities, whereby unilateral coercion and extortion replaced volition, compromise, and mutual benefit overseen by an impartial judge.[98] Under Company rule, forms of bonded labor proliferated, driven in equal parts by the advances system and the corrupt scheme of tax farming introduced by Hastings, which pushed cultivators and artisans ever deeper into debt. Burke scornfully remarked that the elimination of local middlemen, coupled with the advances system, reduced the Indian weavers to "virtual vassalage" and instituted "debt peonage" under a "most violent and arbitrary power" (*W&S*, 5:259–60). A public and competitive market in credit and auctions, which could have freed the Indian producers from "debt bondage," was deliberately thwarted by Company policies (*W&S*, 5:268–69). Adding insult to the injury, laborers who had been "defrauded" into debt bondage would be "delivered over like Cattle in Succession to different Masters, who, under Pretence of buying up the Balances due to their preceding employers, find Means of keeping them in perpetual *Slavery*" (*W&S*, 5:290). Those who managed to evade debt bondage and hold on to some stock discovered that they had no control over how they invested it. The monopoly powers of the Company in cash crops, especially opium, were used to force farmers to cultivate these crops instead of grain, even after the dearth and high costs of food led to the 1769–1770 famine that decimated the Bengali population (*W&S*, 5:270–71, 274).

Subversion of contractual freedom was compounded by the loss of security of property, which manifested itself in confiscation at all levels of social hierarchy. Expropriation of the Indian nobility by the British found its most emphatic account in Burke's "Speech on Almas Ali Khan," when he accused the Company of having invented "the crime of having money . . . like the sin against the Holy Ghost in Christianity" (*W&S*, 5:464–67). In this scheme, wealthy Indian nobles would be first accused of treason on fabricated and expedient grounds, and then punished by confiscation and even death.[99] If the state's confiscation of property was an anathema to Burke's Whig sensibilities, its conduct under the pretext of a legal trial was a macabre travesty of justice, more execrable than the open use of sheer force. Burke pithily captured this perversion in the speech opening the impeachment, when he referred to Hastings as "the great criminal" who "has the law in his hand" (*W&S*, 6:290). Instrumentalizing the law in the service of expropriation brought an indelible disgrace upon the British nation, which Burke thought to "have better institutions for the preservations of the rights of men than any other Country in the World" (*W&S*, 6:352). Predation on property also struck Indian farmers and manufacturers, who were first indebted by the arbitrary pricing of the Company, and then visited by Company agents who acted in the power of lenders of usurious loans, assessors of the accruing debts, and finally bailiffs to seize the debtors' property (*W&S*, 5:259–60). Finally, the lowest strata of Indian society, the *ryots* who worked the land of *zamindars*, were "ruined and made desperate" under the British monopoly by extortionate taxes, not only on land (twice the rate in England), but also on such necessaries of life as salt (*W&S*, 5:463). Burke described the situation starkly in the "Speech on the Nabob of Arcot's Debts":

> Every man of rank and landed fortune being long since extinguished, the remaining miserable last cultivator, who grows to the soil, after having his back scored by the farmer, has it again flayed by the whip of the assignee, and is thus by a ravenous, because a short-lived succession of claimants, lashed from oppressor to oppressor, whilst a single drop of blood is left as the means of extorting a single grain of corn. (*W&S*, 5:532–33)

The fusion of political power and commerce reached its apex in the "revenue investment" system of the Company, which Burke examined in painstaking detail in the *Ninth Report*.[100] After the Company obtained revenue rights of Bengal in 1765, it began to finance its Indian exports with the taxes it levied in that province. This constituted a "new system of trade, carried on through the medium of power and public revenue," which, Burke asserted clearly, was "not commerce" but "annual plunder," or "tribute" disguised as "investment" (*W&S*,

5:221, 223–26, 231). Insofar as it was driven by narrow and immediate monetary concerns, the revenue investment system trumped the common sense that the welfare of the natives was essential for the investment of capital, sustained profits, and steady revenue (*W&S*, 5:221).[101] The "vast extraction of wealth" from India was maintained not, as it ought to have been, by the "improvement" of the country but by raising the land rents and by annulling the payments due to local powers, backed up in the last instance by the military force of the Company (*W&S*, 5:231–32). Commerce, conducted under the rule of a power that was itself a party in economic transactions, became a zero-sum game, whereby the enrichment of the British meant the impoverishment of Indians. In contrast to the Muslim conquerors before them, the British did not take responsibility for the dominions they conquered; instead, driven by an "insatiable lust for plunder," they carried away whatever they found available.[102] Under the pretext of patronage and alliance, the Company impoverished local rulers and their dominions (*W&S*, 5:396, 401–7).[103] Indian riches thus obtained were siphoned out of the realm, making "the transport of its plunder . . . the only traffic of the country" (*W&S*, 5:427). After providing a detailed account of the "deep, silent flow of wealth from the Carnatic," which he estimated at 20 million pounds between 1760 and 1780, Burke would ask rhetorically, "What are the articles of commerce or the branches of manufacture which these gentlemen have carried thence to enrich India?" (*W&S*, 5:492, 494).[104]

Even more outrageously, despite its intensive pillage of the Indian wealth, the East India Company constantly teetered on the verge of bankruptcy, and had to be bailed out by the British government on more than one occasion.[105] Having usurped sovereign power, the Company had abandoned commercial principles. It was indifferent to the prices paid on the open market; it engaged in the systematic breach of contracts; it had poor and fraudulent accounting, bringing upon itself insolvency, improvident borrowing, and ruined credit (*W&S*, 5:242–43). In short, "no trace of equitable government is to be found in their politics; not one trace of commercial principle in their mercantile dealings" (*W&S*, 5:432–33). Mismanagement and private embezzlement of funds drained the coffers. The system of revenue investment had become a vehicle for remitting private fortunes to England at the expense of *both* the British and Indian publics, vindicating Burke's conviction that there could not be public utility where there was no equity (*W&S*, 5:235, 242, 448). "It is there the public is robbed," Burke exclaimed, "in its army, in its civil administration, in its credit, in its investment which forms the commercial connection between that country and Europe. There is the robbery" (*W&S*, 5:531).

Finally, Burke repeatedly underscored that violations of the free market, legal equality, free labor, and free contract were not occasional; the subversion was "regular, permanent, and systematical" (*W&S*, 5:433). Such violations could not be attributed to the corruption of a few servants. Instead, they sprung from the degeneracy of the public authority itself: "[T]he hand of government, which ought never to appear but to protect, is felt as the instrument in every act of oppression" (*W&S*, 5:272). The Indian administration represented a complete inversion of the functions that Burke ascribed to government in commercial society: instead of protecting property, it confiscated; instead of enforcing contracts, it dictated; instead of promoting the welfare of the population, it impoverished and depopulated.

Put more starkly, although the Company had become de facto (and arguably de jure) sovereign with the acquisition of the *diwani*, it continued to treat its new dominions as if they were foreign lands and alien peoples, located beyond the line where the "idea of force" still set the rules of engagement. Imperious commerce was the perverse continuation of armed trading within a state's own borders. Its ultimate effect was to demolish the very institutional foundations of commercial (and therefore civil) society.[106]

Burke's ideas for remedying these perversions betrayed a remarkably Smithian streak. The broad premise was to regenerate the economic morass created by the Company through the prudent introduction of competitive markets under the watchful eye of Parliamentary supervision. The Anglo-Indian trade had to be restored to "a Bottom truly Commercial," which would necessitate confining the economic operations of the Company to the "main Spring of the Commercial Machine, the *Principles of Profit and Loss*" (*W&S*, 5:241). As regards the Company's abuse of its trading privileges in Bengal's internal commerce, Burke applauded the Nawab's decision to abolish all duties on trade (and thereby equalize the terms of competition) as a "forcible, simple and equitable" retaliation against the "oppressions of the monopoly" (*W&S*, 5:244–45).[107] In the same spirit, he extolled the virtues of "rivalship" to redeem and reinvigorate the Indian manufactures, a notion that would later reappear as "market of competition" in the *Scarcity* essay (*W&S*, 5:268; *W&S*, 9:135). Finally, inveighing against opium and salt monopolies, he advocated the "unerring standard of the public market" to regulate the inland trade in necessities (*W&S*, 5:278). Political economy of the commercial ideal illuminated the path to administrative reform.

The eighteenth-century discourse of political economy informed Burke's criticisms of the Indian empire in another major way. Political economy, especially as articulated by the Scottish philosophers, was as much a discourse of progress from savagery to civilization as it was a theory of the division of labor, trade, growth, rents, wages, and profits. The Company contravened Burke's commercial ideal not only in its economic policy but also in its moral categories of civilization. "Barbarism" was Burke's label of choice when he judged the moral character of the Company's enormities. In his "Speech on Almas Ali Khan," Burke referred to Indians as "millions of our fellow-creatures . . . whom our barbarous policy had ruined" (*W&S*, 5:463), and poured his scorn on the Company agents' actions as "barbarities" of an "inhuman system" (*W&S*, 5:471). Two years later, he once again designated Hastings's policies as "crimes of barbarity" (*W&S*, 5:65). His derogation of the British in India reached hateful proportions in the Opening Speech, when he damned "the Company's service" as "the very filth and dregs of mankind, the most degenerate public body that has ever existed in the world" (*W&S*, 6:290).

It might at first glance appear strange to see Burke referring to the British exploits in India as "barbarous," given his high esteem for the standing of Britain as a liberal, enlightened, civilized society. The invective loses some of its curiosity, however, if one considers that the idea of civilized Europeans relapsing into savagery at colonial frontiers was a popular trope among the eighteenth-century European literati.[108] Expressed in the idiom of stadial history, British character in India suffered from a civilizational regress, sliding from the civility of commercial societies to the barbarism of nomadic societies. This trope had already appeared in Burke's remarks on the English colonies in America a decade earlier. Opposing the proposed restrictions on settler expansion beyond the Appalachians, he warned that House that the colonists would not only defy such proscription, but in the process "they would change the manners with the habits of their life; would soon forget a government by which they were disowned; would become *Hordes of English Tartars*; and, pouring down upon your unfortified frontiers a fierce and irresistible cavalry, become masters of your Governors and Counsellors" (*W&S*, 3:129; emphasis added). The British lost their polished manners in proportion to their social and geographical distance from the institutional order and the civilizing influence of the metropole.[109] In America this civilizational distance issued from the settlement of the outback, where imperatives of survival in an alien and hostile natural environment eroded the fine appurtenances of civilized life as the settlers broke in the wilderness. In India, the distance from the metropole was compounded by the estrangement, fear, and revulsion induced by an alien cultural environment, driving the British to isolate themselves, develop sterner attitudes, and lose all possibility of sympathy with their subjects.[110] Young Company servants in India, who received Burke's undisguised contempt, exemplified this combination of transience and indifference. They had neither the chance to grow roots in Britain nor intention to do so in India, rendering them, in one of Burke's most harrowing metaphors, "birds of passage and prey" that descended in endless waves upon the hapless country (*W&S*, 6:286–90; *W&S*, 5:402). Equally distressing for Burke was the return of the Company servants to Britain as wealthy nabobs, whom he portrayed with evocations of barbarian hordes pressing into the heart of civilization:"These people pour in upon us everyday. They not only bring with them the wealth they have, but they bring with them into our country the vices by which [that wealth was] acquired" (*W&S*, 7:62–63). Taken together, these remarks on the American and Indian dominions indicate that for Burke the imperial frontier was a dangerous space, where civility degenerated into barbarism and polished manners dissipated in the violent grab for land and riches.

Notwithstanding the classical imagery of barbarians raiding civilized settlements, the key terms in which Burke condemned the Company rule crucially suggest that the plunder of India represented a novel species of *commercial barbarism*, one that had its conditions of possibility and motivating force in modern commercial capitalism. The British depredations in India had little in common with the pre-feudal barbarism of the Goths, the ancient Britons, or the warlike Greco-Roman citizens of antiquity.[111] The cruelties of empire in the East, pace Bourke, did not simply revive the atavistic "spirit of conquest" typical of martial nobilities, which had been tamed into polished manners by religion and prescription.[112] As Partha Chatterjee puts it succinctly, "[I]t was conquest by a commercial nation that had now brought disaster to the country."[113] The new commercial barbarism sprung up from the alliance of the state and capital that found its distinctly modern organizational form in Asia in the militarized joint-stock trading company, just as it had given rise to the modern slave plantation in the Atlantic. Burke's contemporaries had already noticed the unsettling connection between the commercialization of European economies and the increased severity of economic extraction in their overseas empires.[114] Alexander Dow, the notable eighteenth-century Orientalist, had noted India's particular misfortune of being "subdued by a society whose business was commerce," citing "monopolies," "an exclusive trade," and "additional taxations" as the principal methods of ruination.[115] On Burke's account, the politicization of commerce in India had turned the "reasonable, powerful, and prolifick principle" of self-interest from a "grand cause of prosperity" into a supremely destructive force. The natural "desire of acquisition" fueled "extortion, usury, and peculation" (*W&S*, 5:496), the "laudable avarice" became violent "rapacity" (*W&S*, 6:275), and the prosperity they ought to have caused turned into "ruination" and "depopulation." Burke captured the paradox of commercial barbarism most lucidly when he wrote that "commerce, which enriches every other country in the world, was bringing Bengal to total ruin" (*W&S*, 6:278, 428).[116]

If the barbarizing tendencies of the imperial frontier in the West made Tartars out of Englishmen, in the East it turned them into "banyans." Members of the merchant caste, banyans were native intermediaries who acted as commercial agents on behalf of Company servants in the procurement of commodities. Burke's opinion on banyans bordered on loathing; he described them in one instance as creatures "*whose fathers they* [the Indian nobility] *would not have set with the dogs of their flock*" (*W&S*, 5:426). For Burke, the banyan personified the sacrifice of morality at the altar of self-interest, the reduction of all social relations to the venal, and temporary collusion for material gain. On the one hand, ban-yans manipulated their masters' dependency on their local knowledge and con-nections; on the other, they leveraged their masters' political power and privilege to aggrandize themselves in the commercial deals they concluded, freely extort-ing, robbing, and oppressing local producers (*W&S*, 6:292–93). For Burke, the "system of banyans" in Bengal represented the dissolution of human sociability in the ether of vulgar material gain, just as the collusion of Paul Benfield and the Nawab of Arcot in their "magnificent plan of universal plunder" had rendered them "the determined enemies of human intercourse itself" (*W&S*, 5:516–18). In this system, money was the only interracial glue that bound depraved Company servants and devious banyans, perverted partners in plunder and peculation, who otherwise would not have an iota of human sociability between them. The collusion between banyans and Company agents crystallized the unprincipled economy of extortion in India and laid bare the dark underside of Burke's commercial ideal. When self-interest and market exchange fused with political power, they became the very solvent of society. If Parliament allowed Indianism to go unchecked, Burke warned the House, it would be Britain's turn to "become a Chain of Twisters, prevaricators, dissemblers Liars, a nation of *Banyans*" (*W&S*, 7:62). To bring the discussion full circle, it was not capitalism but colonial capitalism that Burke found threatening to his image of civilization and society, the great primeval contract between generations.

To summarize, we can see that the political economic moorings of Burke's cri-tique were tied to his image of Britain as a commercial society, whose commer-cial civility had degenerated into commercial barbarism at the imperial frontier. Burke's castigation of the Company rule for engaging in extortion and plunder performed an ideological excision that separated the extra-economic coercion of commercial capitalism in India, painted this illiberality as a resurgence of pre-commercial barbarism, and posited it as the very antithesis of commerce. Burke thereby salvaged the essential liberality of the British Empire, an empire of com-merce and liberty, by redefining the formative violence of capitalism as a colo-nial aberration, rather than the very means by which Indian land and labor were brought within the fold of capital. Framed as a colonial anomaly, the violence of "imperious commerce" appeared to be an incidental problem remediable by administrative reform. A reformed "imperial commerce" could reconcile the principle of empire and the principle of commerce—that is, accommodate legal equality and market freedoms under political subordination and cultural differ-ence. The "vision of a reformed, national empire," in Ahmed's words, "looked forward to the nineteenth-century liberal apology for empire, which claimed that when Parliament eliminated the East India Company's monopoly in 1813, empire transcended the merchant's private interest and joined the nation-state's progressive history."[117]

Burke's "Peculiar Universalism" Revisited

Although my interpretation has deliberately concentrated on questions of metropolitan self-perception and imperial ideology, the perspective of political economy adopted here also sheds light on Burke's perception of the non-Europeans whom the British encountered in the course of imperial expansion. Earlier studies on Burke and empire place much stock in his vindication of the Indians against British depredations, which they construe as expressing a marked, if atypical, universalism. Frederick Whelan has attributed Burke's criticisms to his deep conviction in the existence of a natural moral law that furnished governmental conduct with basic maxims irrespective of social and cultural variation.[118] Burke derided Hastings's extraordinary methods in India as taking refuge in "geographical morality," suggesting that the Indians were equally entitled to a government that secured civil rights, dispensed justice, and promoted welfare.[119] For Uday Mehta, Burke's universalism resided in his "cosmopolitanism of sentiment," which took exception with eighteenth-century liberalism that infantilized Indians and prescribed imperial tutelage. Burke recognized that the human condition was defined by constitutive links between social belonging, intersubjective ties, and political identity. On that basis, he validated the cultural particularity of India as deserving recognition and respect, rather than folding it into a linear narrative of progress and civilization.[120] Jennifer Pitts, though she disagrees with Mehta's unfavorable verdict on eighteenth-century liberalism, has similarly observed a cosmopolitan disposition or "peculiar universalism" in Burke's protest against the parochial morality of the British public opinion.[121] Burke strove to expand the moral horizon of the British political classes and kindle sympathy with the Indians by representing the latter's society as one not unlike that of the British. In his speech on Fox's India Bill, he remarked that the British remained aloof to the oppression and suffering in India mostly because they were "so little acquainted with Indian details . . . that it is very difficult for our sympathy to fix upon these objects" (*W&S*, 5:403–4). His strategy of choice was to construct social and geographic analogies between India and Europe, which aimed to familiarize his audience with what appeared to them inscrutably alien and thus susceptible to indifference.

More recent accounts have questioned Burke's cosmopolitan commitments by enlarging the scope of inquiry to include his statements on Native Americans and Africans. This broader focus reveals, in Duncan Bell's words, that "India was the exception, not the rule in Burke's sympathies."[122] Bell's verdict takes its cue from Daniel O'Neill's reconstruction of Burke's "conservative logic of empire." O'Neill contends that Burke asserted the sovereign authority of the British state over its overseas subjects through a combination of "orientalist" strategies of othering and "ornamentalist" strategies of familiarizing.[123] Social class, race, and level of civilization furnished the classificatory grid with which Burke ordered the heterogeneity of the empire in a hierarchical fashion, prescribing different governmental measures for different stations in this hierarchy. On O'Neill's account, Burke viewed Indian society through ornamentalist lenses that highlighted its similarity to Britain, and reserved orientalist arguments for Native Americans and enslaved Africans. His veneration of the former could thus exist quite consistently alongside his haughty paternalism, if not contempt or animosity, for the latter.[124]

Indeed, a brief overview Burke's remarks on the non-Europeans in Britain's Atlantic empire suggests that his misgivings about the government of India had little to do with the presence of an imperious and violent government per se. There is little reason to doubt that he saw in empire an instrument for civilizing the savage and the barbarian, by means of conquest and despotism if necessary.[125] For instance, in *An Account of the European Settlements*, in which he defended the slave trade on economic grounds, Burke proposed the use of an "iron rod" for "ruling" (though not for "crushing") African slaves in the British Caribbean.[126] The "Sketch of a Negro Code," drafted two decades later, betrayed the same tutelary civilizing mission. Africans occupied a barbarous stage in the scale of civilization, whereby they lacked the social manners requisite for an orderly form of freedom that was compatible with civilized society. If, following Scottish stadial theory, the manners needed to support civil liberties were a function of customs and conventions (rather than innate virtues), then the direction and discipline of the British Empire could very well create the conditions for the emancipation of African slaves. In this vein, Burke proposed a regime of paternal despotism, in which to forge barbarous Africans into industrious, God-fearing, conjugal, and responsible subjects. The pivotal premise of the "Sketch" was that "the habits of industry and sobriety and the means of acquiring and preserving property, are the proper and reasonable preparatives of freedom" (*W&S*, 3:578–79). Braided around this premise were practical provisions that included educating slaves in schools and churches, training in crafts, promoting monogamous families, and offering the possibility of manumission if they proved their excellence in a mechanical art or liberal knowledge (*W&S*, 3:574–80). However, just as the barbarous could be brought into civilization, the civilized could regress into barbarism, as the experiences on the colonial frontiers had attested. For the former slaves, the punishment for civilizational relapse would be re-enslavement. The "Sketch" tasked England's Lord Protector of Negroes and justices of peace with deciding on the civilizational progress of each African and redrawing the legal line between personhood and property accordingly. If a "free Negro" was proven to be "incorrigibly idle, dissolute, and vicious, it shall be lawful . . . to sell the said free Negro into Slavery" (*W&S*, 3:581).

If Burke granted the black "crew of fierce, foreign barbarians and slaves" of the Atlantic half a chance at civilization, he placed Native Americans entirely beyond the pale (*W&S*, 3:359). He described them as "fierce tribes of Savages and Cannibals, in whom the traces of human nature are effaced by ignorance and barbarity" (*W&S*, 3:281), and admonished their recruitment in the conflict with the colonists:

> To call from that Wilderness, which is not yet reclaimed [by] the spir-
> ited Enterprise of your American brethren and which they looked to as
> the [present] [object] for the growing industry of future generations,
> every Class of savages and Cannibals the most cruel and ferocious ever
> [known] to lay waste with fire hatchet with Murders, and Sanguinary
> Tortures of the Inhabitants, the most beautiful work of Skill and Labour
> by which the creation and the name of God was ever glorified by his
> creatures. (*W&S*, 3:180; brackets in the original)

Save for a rhetorical wish for "bringing those unhappy part of mankind into civility, order, piety, and virtuous discipline," Burke projected the political era-sure and total removal of the American indigenes (*W&S*, 3:282). Betraying a Lockean streak, he categorically denied them any rights to property or sov-ereignty on the continent, reducing them to floating vagrants in the British Empire. "There is but one single nation in America—and that is the English," he proclaimed, "The Indians are no longer a people in any proper acceptation of the Word—but several gangs of Banditti scattered along a wild of a great civilized empire—A Banditti of the most cruel and atrocious kind such as infest many such empires" (*W&S*, 3:365). In another Lockean moment, he praised English settlers for turning "a savage wilderness into a glorious empire" and for making "the most extensive and the only honourable conquests, not by destroying but by promoting the wealth, the number, and the happiness of the human race" (*W&S*, 3:166). Clearly, Burke's "cosmopolitanism of sentiment" or his "peculiar universalism" did not extend to the Native Americans who had been losing their lands and people to European incursions and diseases.[127]

That Burke lavished the sympathy on the Indians that he dramatically with-held from other nonwhite peoples being expropriated, oppressed, and enslaved under the British Empire poses a conundrum. One response has been to take Burke's writings on India (and, to some extent, Ireland) as representative of his true cosmopolitan sympathies, explain his remarks on African slaves as a reluc-tant compromise with the commercial reason of state, and ignore or historicize his position on Native Americans.[128] This line of interpretation, however, avoids a sustained discussion of the a priori grounds for elevating India to the para-digmatic case, and it leaves a whole legion of questions unanswered. Why, for instance, Burke did not opt for compromise on the Company rule as he did on the slave trade? Conversely, why did he not condemn slavery for corrupting the moral character of the British nation by habituating Englishmen to despotic manners, or why did the West Indian absentee planters in Parliament not perturb him the way returned nabobs did?[129] Why did conquest of and the revolutions against the natives of America received his wholehearted approbation, whereas the same in India drew his white-hot indignation? In short, what distinguished the "fellow-creatures," (*W&S*, 5:463) "fellow subjects of the people of England" (*W&S*, 5:62), and "our distressed fellow citizens" (*W&S*, 5:553) in India from the "crew of fierce, foreign barbarians and slaves" and "Banditti of the most cruel and atrocious kind"?

Parting ways with recent explanations of Burke's political conservatism, my solution to this conundrum points to Burke's economic liberalism and, more specifically, the discourse of political economy in which it was embedded.[130] In addition to offering a new language for reformulating the problems of imperial rule, political economy in the last third of the eighteenth century was, above all, a specialized language for grasping and expressing the workings of the "commercial society" as a unique social formation based on a complex structure of economic interdependence.[131] In this sense, political economy was deeply consonant with Burke's "Whig social theory" that held "commercial progress to be a part of the science of human nature."[132] Commercial societies had developed out of the simplicity of the savage, barbarous, and agrarian modes of life through the increased division of labor and the market-mediated cooperation among specialized producers, which in the process generated material prosperity and polished social manners. This new state of affairs, when the unsocial sociability of market transactions constituted the fabric of everyday life (or, as Smith famously described it, "Every man thus lives by exchanging . . . and the society grows to be what is properly called a commercial society"), tested the conceptual resources of Burke's contemporaries.[133] At the edge of this historical horizon stood Britain, with an entrenched capitalist agrarian and manufacturing economy, a vast colonial and commercial network, and an intricate system of private and public credit. As the "first self-conscious commercial society" in Europe, Britain supplied eighteenth-century European intellectuals with a signature object of fascination, delight, envy, anxiety, grief, and fear.[134] It also gave Scottish social theory, which Burke imbibed, its exemplary object of inquiry and analysis.

The most important feature of commercial society, one that is central to Burke's economic liberalism and to his differential treatment of non-Europeans, was its unprecedented socioeconomic complexity. The sheer number, diversity, and dispersal of interests in a commercial society made it utterly impossible to comprehend and coordinate these interests from a political center. At an incandescent moment in his lectures on classical political economy, and apropos of Adam Smith's metaphor of the invisible hand, Michel Foucault explains:

> Invisibility is absolutely indispensable . . . the world of the economy must be and can only be obscure to the sovereign . . . it is impossible for the sovereign to have a point of view on the economic mechanism which totalizes every element and enables them to be combined artificially or voluntarily. . . . In the middle of the eighteenth century, political economy denounces the paralogism of political totalization of the economic process.[135]

In Burkean terms, commercial society's complexity rendered it a sublime, awe-inspiring social totality that refused a panoptic perspective from which it could be grasped. A number of Burke scholars have taken note of this problem, albeit somewhat obliquely. For instance, Hampsher-Monk has argued that for Burke, "political society" was a "miraculous assemblage of institutions, rules, moral beliefs, customs, habits, and dispositions."[136] Macpherson has likewise observed the centrality of "harmony in the natural and political world" to Burke's social thought.[137] Systemic harmony in a social formation of such magnitude and intricacy could not possibly be the result of deliberate design, save by God, which has led David Bromwich to conclude that for Burke "society" was a "work of art without a maker."[138]

These observations are correct but partial insofar as they mistake "political society" or "society" as such for a historically specific social formation of "commercial society." It was only the presence of a complex multitude of contending or, in Burke's words, "discordant powers" that "the harmony of the universe" could spontaneously arise and thwart the "arbitrary power" that characterized simpler societies (*W&S*, 8:86). The fortuitous interplay of social manners and the economic division of labor that had produced wealth, leisure, arts, letters, and civilization in Europe belonged exclusively to commercial societies. This was the fundamental premise behind Burke's laissez-faire pronouncements, such as when he equated "the laws of commerce" with "the laws of nature, and consequently the laws of God," designating the economy as a domain inscrutable and mysterious to men and transparent only to God (*W&S*, 9:137). In the same spirit, commercial affairs constituted a "department of things [that] manners alone can regulate. To these, great politicians may give a leaning, but they cannot give a law" (*W&S*, 9:144). In a commercial society, "interest, habit, and the tacit convention that arise from a thousand nameless circumstances, produce a tact that regulates without difficulty," though one that often fell victim to "zeal of regulation," "coercive guidance," and "magistrates exercising stiff, and often inapplicable rules" (*W&S*, 9:126–28).

Central to this explanation is Burke's judgment on the capacity of human reason, which in *Reflections* he famously claimed to be rather "small" when it was held in "private stock" (*W&S*, 8:138).[139] Statesmen, Burke continued, had to resort to the "bank and capital of ages" in confronting the economic and political problems of their times. In view of the foregoing discussion, I contend that these remarks were intended to humble not human reason per se but human reason that made the hubristic claim to know, comprehend, regulate, and revolutionize a commercial society. It was in the face of the sublime complexity and opacity of commercial society that the capacity of human reason proved to be puny and powerless. This point can be inferred from the similar terms in which Burke criticized government intervention in the economy in Britain and condemned the radical attempts to radically remake French society after the Revolution. British politicians' "zeal of regulation" and "coercive guidance" found their counterpart in French legislators' "categorical tables" and "metaphysical taxonomies" that confused and violated the "diversity of interest, that must exist, and must contend in all complex society" (*W&S*, 8:231–32).

Viewed through this theoretical perspective, Burke's veneration and defense of India appears in a light that dispels the semblance of an unconditional veneration for cultural difference or a cosmopolitan sentiment and reveals his universal morality to be laden with civilizational asymmetries. Burke made it plain that in his view what aligned India's miseries with those of postrevolutionary France was India's status as a commercial society. India

> does not consist of an abject and barbarous populace; much less of gangs of savages, like the Guaranies and Chiquitos, who wander on the waste borders of the river of Amazons, or the Plate; but a people for ages civilized and cultivated; cultivated by all the arts of polished life, whilst we were yet in the woods. There, have been princes once of great dignity, authority, and opulence. There, are to be found the chiefs of tribes and nations. There, is to be found an antient and venerable priesthood, the depository of their laws, learning, and history, the guides of the people whilst living, and their consolation in death; a nobility of great antiquity and renown; a multitude of cities, not exceeded in population and trade by those of the first class in Europe; merchants and bankers, individual houses of whom have once vied in capital with the Bank of England; whose credit had often supported a tottering state, and preserved their governments in the midst of war and desolation; millions of ingenious manufacturers and mechanicks; millions of the most diligent, and not the least intelligent, tillers of the earth. Here are to be found almost all the religions professed by men, the Bramincal, the Mussulmen, the Eastern and the Western Christians. (*W&S*, 5:389–90)

India not only boasted agriculture, manufacture, and credit on par with European polities. It also had a grand nobility and institutionalized religion, which were indispensable to Burke's social vision of a civilized society.[140] At the beginning of the impeachment proceedings, Burke complemented the socioeconomic analysis of India with a discourse on the Indian government in which he documented, in assiduous detail, its legal tradition and conformity to rule of law (*W&S*, 6:352–67). Contrary to British preconceptions, India was not an example of "Asiatic despotism" but possessed a constitutional government and civil liberties very much like those of Britain. The Indian sovereign

> cannot dispose of the life, of the property, or, of the liberty, of any of his subjects, but by what is called the Fetfa, or sentence of the law. He cannot declare peace or war without the same sentence of the law; so much is he more than European sovereigns a subject of strict law, that he cannot declare war or peace without it. Then if he can neither touch life nor property, if he cannot lay a tax upon his subjects, or declare peace or War, I leave it to your Lordships to say whether he can be called, according to the principles of that constitution, an arbitrary power. (*W&S*, 6:354)

In short, if Burke was trying to induce sympathy with the Indians by familiarizing it in a language accessible to his audience, then he was trying to induce sympathy for another commercial society. As Indian society exhibited the same level of social complexity and inscrutability as the English and French societies, it ought to have been accorded the same protection against the undiscerning, ignorant, and zealous policies of the magistrates.

Yet, as Burke's contrast of the Indians with the Amazonian "gangs of savages" indicates, not all non-Europeans were equally entitled to liberal modes of government. The same factor of socioeconomic complexity that reined in the prerogative of reason in civilized commercial societies could authorize its self-assured dominion over primitive societies of savages and barbarians. Especially at the interface between unequal civilizations, human reason cultivated in a commercial society could assume without arrogance a pedagogical-civilizational mission over less civilized societies typified by primitive modes of subsistence, elementary conceptions of property, crude relations of exchange, unrefined passions, and consequently barbarous social manners. Over such pre-commercial societies, the political rule of a civilized empire had to be despotic in some measure because, as Pocock writes, there "the exchange of goods and services is so underdeveloped that the normal human relationship is between master and slave, lord and serf. Only as commerce develops do social relations become capable of generating civil authority."[141] This theoretical assumption goes some way to explain why the "contrivance of our reason" that Burke deemed to be "fallible and feeble" in the case of French society broke out triumphant when he drafted his despotic regimen for civilizing Africans or called for the extirpation of American natives. The simplicity of savage or barbarous societies denied them the safeguards against the haughtiness of reason.

Finally, the link between properly institutionalized political power and progress of commercial society can be further illustrated by the thematic continuity between Burke's remarks on the devastation of India and his description of the destruction of France by the revolutionaries.[142] Commerce, trade, manufacture had for ages grown in the shade of the Indian nobility, religion, and constitution that protected life, liberty, and property. Under the British power, however, "that country suffers, almost every year, the miseries of a revolution" and witnessed "the most ancient and most revered institutions, of ages and nations" being trampled by the juvenile arrogance and rapacity of the Company agents (*W&S*, 5:427). The same rude hands that would later destroy the French nobility and religion, which formed the "protecting principles" of "commerce, trade, and manufacture," had already begun their work in India (*W&S*, 8:130). Through massive confiscation of landed property, they had reduced men of rank and status to a "state of indigence, depression and contempt" (*W&S*, 8:155). Animated, if not by the "barbarous philosophy" of the revolutionaries, then certainly by an urge for material gain no less barbarous, they had torn apart the "system of manners" such that their dominion in India, like the laws of French revolutionary government, was now "supported only by their own terrors" (*W&S*, 8:128–29). Having drowned equity and public utility, justice and prosperity, they remained a pack of "gross, stupid, ferocious, and at the same time, poor and sordid barbarians, destitute of religion, honour or manly pride" (*W&S*, 8:131). The rapacity with which Company continued of a sort of armed trading within its Indian dominions resembled the ruthlessness of the revolutionaries who "treat France exactly like a country of conquest" (*W&S*, 8:230). The simplicity of self-interest that ripped through the complex texture of institutions, customs and values in one commercial society foreshadowed the destruction wrought by the simplicity of radical reason in the next.

To conclude, the level of socioeconomic complexity not only indexed the stages of social progress from savagery and civilization; it also designated the specific forms of political authority commensurate with each stage. The proper correspondence between the level of social development and the form of political power constituted a standard for ascertaining the justice of political rule. The rules of engagement and modes of government suitable in dealing with barbarian subjects were different than those admissible when interacting with civilized subjects. Burke believed that India was a civilized, commercial society like Britain and France, and ought to have been governed accordingly. The failure to do so amounted to injustice by the standards of Burke's universal moral law. Yet the same moral law was informed by civilizational categories that rendered such primitive, noncommercial peoples as Native Americans and Africans legitimately liable to the same practices that Burke deemed unjust in India. The inflection of Burke's universal moral law by civilizational categories, themselves keyed to categories of political economy, might explain Burke's self-righteous advocacy of the Indian cause alongside his unhesitant derogation of Africans and Native Americans. While the universal law of morality and justice provided for gradually bringing savages and barbarians into the ways of civility, trying to assume a similar tutelary role vis-à-vis another commercial society was profoundly haughty, unjust, and scandalous. And it was *this* scandal, the arrogance of revolutionary reason and its pretensions to remake commercial societies, that Burke denounced in India, cursed in France, and dreaded in Britain.

Conclusion: Imperial Frontiersmen, Gentlemanly Capitalists

Burke's efforts at impeaching Warren Hastings and reforming the Indian government were tokens of his faith in the possibility of a British Empire cleansed of imperial arrogance, one that remained an empire but conducted equitable trade with its conquered subjects in India, or to use Jeanne Morefield's recent coinage, an "empire without imperialism."[143] Burke's criticism of commercial capitalism in India formed the crucible in which he separated commerce from empire, refined commerce as a liberal economic ideal, and salvaged the morality of empire by displacing its violence onto the Company.[144] Burke was not the only political economist to engage in such theoretical purification. As I have argued elsewhere, Hume and Smith also grappled with the coercive methods of commercial capitalism as manifested in colonial slavery and settler colonialism. They both also acknowledged and disavowed the constitutive role of imperial violence in the history of global commerce, Hume by confining his discussion of slavery almost entirely to the ancient Greco-Roman practice, and Smith by representing modern settler colonialism in the pacific image of Ancient Greek colonization.[145] The crucial difference between Burke and the two Scotsmen, however, was that Hume and Smith expunged the imperial baggage of global commerce in order to posit the commercial principle as the antithesis of empire tout court. By contrast, Burke, as a believer in the trust of empire and its material benefits, isolated the liberal essence of commerce in order to re-amalgamate it with reformed imperial rule. Burke's vision of regenerating the imperious commerce of the Company into an imperial commerce under the British rule of law not only matched Hume and Smith's innovations in building a commercial ideal but also far outstripped them in contributing to the imagination of the British Empire as the empire of liberty.

To the extent that Burke succeeded in laying at the Company's door the responsibility for the coercive transformation of the Indian economy, he exonerated from illiberality not only the British Empire but also its aggressive species of commercial capitalism that forcibly inserted Indian land and labor into global circuits of capital accumulation. Primitive accumulation had been going on in the Atlantic and nourishing British capitalism for some time, but it became a problem for Burke for the first time when it cut against the grain of his civilizational categories by despoiling another commercial society. Per Burke's suggestion, Britain could have re-established a "truly commercial" relation to India but only at the cost of a massive negative balance of trade, as had been the case until the East India Company reversed it by instrumentalizing its sovereign powers and violating the "just principles of commerce." Insofar as the imperial relation was the historically specific political shell in which primitive accumulation in India was carried out, and insofar as Burke could not relinquish the British Empire, the only recourse available to him was to publicly castigate the agents of primitive accumulation in order to expel the "odium of primitive despoliation" from his idealized image of the British Empire.

Dissecting Burke's imperial thought along the axes of commercial capitalism and idiom of political economy yields a different picture than submitted by the culturalist interpretations that either recruit Burke to a cosmopolitan respect for cultural pluralism or reinstate him as a traditionalist exponent of aristocracy and religion. Locked in a debate that revolves around the parameters of difference/similarity and particularism/universalism, these approaches have given remarkably short shrift to economic analysis in the writings of a statesman who proudly announced that he had "made political oeconomy an object of my humble studies, from my very early youth to near the end of my service in parliament" (*W&S*, 9:159–60), and whom Adam Smith described as "the only man I ever knew who, without communication, thought on economic subjects exactly as I."[146] Instead of offering a liberal critique or conservative defense of empire, I have highlighted Burke's economic liberalism as grounds for simultaneously criticizing existing imperial practices *and* vindicating a reformed empire as the necessary and sufficient framework for equitable commercial relations between Britain's imperial subjects.[147]

Burke certainly did not conceive all of Britain's non-European subjects to be equally entitled to civil liberties required to participate in commercial transactions on free and equal terms. Here, too, the discourse of political economy and especially the element of social complexity can offer a nuanced account of his differentiation between the empire's civilized and uncivilized subjects and his prescription of free and despotic modes of government. It also brings into focus unexpected uses of the discourse of civilization and savagery, as when Burke described the Company behavior as "barbarous," suggesting an (at least partial) Orientalist denigration of the British together with an Ornamentalist sympathy for the Indians. Foregrounding the idiom of political economy therefore does not so much refute the cosmopolitan or conservative valences of Burke's thought as clarify why liberal-inclusionary dispositions obtained in certain cases (India), and illiberal-exclusionary attitudes in others (Africa, America). It offers a finer-grained picture of which cultural differences are selectively recoded into civilizational deficits for purposes of imperial rule, which also reveals Burke's assessment of the political authority of reason to be relative to the civilizational status of the society in question. Finally, it can attune us to the those elements in British imperial ideology that cut across the so-called "turn to empire" at the turn of the nineteenth century.[148] If, as O'Neill maintains, Burke's arguments for the empire's civilizing mission "look a good deal more like the arguments of James and J. S. Mill," the implied ideological continuity is to be sought less in a conservative reverence for aristocracy and religion (which the Mills, as Philosophic Radicals, held in low esteem) than in shared premises of political economy.[149]

As the next chapter demonstrates, the core premises of liberal political economy lent themselves to a rather different project of imperial expansion in the first half of the nineteenth century. The Colonial Reform Movement led by Edward Gibbon Wakefield urged British political and public opinion to grant renewed attention to settler colonialism as a solution, on the one hand, to the explosive "social question" in Britain and, on the other, to labor shortages in Britain's colonies that spawned a new species of frontier barbarism. Lockean theory of property by then had been firmly locked in place as far as "vacant lands" were concerned, and the free trade sentiments had the ideological wind in their sails. This time, the stakes of the debate was neither private property nor free exchange but free labor.

Letters from Sydney

Edward Gibbon Wakefield and the Problem of Colonial Labor

The whole world is before you. Open new channels for the most productive employment of English capital. Let the English buy bread from
every people that has bread to sell cheap. Make England, for all that is
produced by steam, the work-shop of the world. If, after this, there be
capital and people to spare, imitate the ancient Greeks; take a lesson
from the Americans, who, as their capital and population increase, find
room for both by means of colonization.
—Edward G. Wakefield

Edward Gibbon Wakefield rarely figures in the recent scholarship on liberalism
empire, and then as a marginal figure whose significance is limited to his influence on John Stuart Mill's views on colonization.[1] Such neglect, if unfortunate, is
unsurprising. After all, Wakefield's writings principally addressed matters of settler colonialism, and as Duncan Bell has recently argued, this mode of imperial
expansion has been eclipsed in the literature by the overwhelming attention to
imperial dependencies such as India and the British West Indies.[2] Additionally,
Wakefield developed and expressed his ideas in the medium of classical political
economy, which, as I discussed in chapter 1, is hardly a prime object of interest
for most scholars of political theory.[3] Yet, I would argue that it is precisely this
intersection of settler colonialism and political economy that renders Wakefield
worthy of attention in the history of liberalism and empire. In the last quarter of
the eighteenth century, liberal critics of imperial expansion such as Adam Smith,
James Mill, and Jeremy Bentham enlisted the new science of political economy
to their objection to acquiring and maintaining colonies. In the second quarter of
the nineteenth century, proponents of British settler colonialism similarly mobilized political economy in advancing their expansionist agenda, this time in a
distinctly liberal, postmercantilist key.[4] Adopting the normative premises of the
earlier critics, early Victorian liberal imperialists rechristened the empire as the
historical avatar of capitalist civilization, a peaceful and progressive formation

that thrived on investment and production and expanded through trade and colonial settlement. As a self-proclaimed political economist, colonial entrepreneur, and publicist, Wakefield stood in the vanguard of this ideological renewal of the British Empire as the empire of liberty.

This chapter investigates the status of "labor" in Britain's imperial economy as the chief ideological problem Wakefield had to contend with in imagining capitalism in liberal terms. I contend that Wakefield's political economic analysis and his theory of colonization turned on reconciling the idea of "free labor" with the capitalist domination of laborers both in the metropole and in the colonies. More specifically, his proposals for the imperial state creating a landless colonial proletariat amounted to a premeditated strategy of primitive accumulation that ran afoul of the liberal principles that he professed. Wakefield explicitly intended his colonial reform agenda to save capitalism in the metropole and to secure it in the colonies by resolving a dual "labor problem." Saving capitalism in England depended on addressing the political problem of heightened worker militancy that was being fueled by unemployment, poverty, and revolutionary currents. Breaking with Ricardian orthodoxy, Wakefield ascribed the source of the problem to a systemic glut of capital and labor that was driving down profits and accelerating proletarianization. It was therefore imperative to find fresh sites of profitable investment for excess English capital and labor. By contrast, securing capitalism in the colonies required alleviating the problem of labor shortage in the colonies. The root of this problem lay in the expedient of relieving population pressure at home by "shoveling out paupers" to Britain's settler dominions. Given the availability of cheap colonial land, emigrants quickly abandoned wage labor to become independent landed proprietors. Such schemes of "spontaneous colonization" led to the dispersal of capital and labor in the colonies and prevented their economies from advancing beyond primitive agrarian self-provisioning.

In both its metropolitan and colonial manifestations, the labor problem represented a threat to capitalist social relations that Victorians like Wakefield equated with civilization per se. The prospect of workers' political empowerment in Britain portended the confiscation and redistribution of property, which would reverse Britain's social and economic progress and throw the country into poverty and barbarism. In the colonies, the absence of a reliable workforce inhibited socioeconomic progress, and the resultant primitive agrarianism effected a sort of civilizational regress in the morals and manners of colonial emigrants. Once members of a civilized commercial society, British emigrants gradually lapsed into a "rude" mode of life that was thought to characterize barbarous peoples in the precommercial stages of social development. They exhibited the settler variant of the frontier barbarism discussed in chapter 3, which gave the colonies and colonial emigration ill repute.[5]

Wakefield addressed these problems within a political economic frame that conceived Britain and its colonies as a unified system of capital and labor flows. His proposed theory of "systematic colonization," he argued, would resolve both labor problems in one stroke. Imposing an arbitrarily inflated price on colonial lands would compel emigrants to work for wages for a while before they could purchase land. The proceeds from the sale of such lands, in turn, would fund the emigration of future colonists, thereby keeping the colonial labor market well stocked while reducing metropolitan unemployment. Wakefield assigned a critical role to the juridico-political agency of the British imperial state in implementing systematic colonization, primarily through establishing preemptive crown rights in land, chartering colonization companies, and administering the sufficient price policy. Operating like hydraulic circuit, systematic colonization would channel excess capital and labor from the metropole to the colonies and at the same time ensure that colonial labor remained subordinate to the direction of colonial capitalists. Karl Marx would later devote a full chapter in *Capital* to the analysis of Wakefield's theory, which he described as a scheme of "primitive accumulation" that sought to preemptively divorce emigrants from land, the chief means of production in the colonies. Systematic colonization crystallized the interlocking cascades of capitalist dispossession that gave birth to global networks of capital. The dispossessed of the British Isles became the agents of indigenous dispossession in North America and the Antipodes (a process that Marx himself ignored), only to be dispossessed again by the colonial capitalists of the empire.

Wakefield's plan did not only promise to save Britain's capitalist civilization. It also promised to do so in a broadly liberal manner. Colonial entrepreneurs had previously mitigated the colonial labor shortage by resorting to manifold and frequently racialized forms of bonded labor, such as indenture, convict transportation, and chattel slavery. Wakefield's intellectual career, by contrast, began in the wake of the British Parliament's abolition of the slave trade and coincided with the abolition of the slavery itself, during which the ideal of "free labor" was white hot in the crucible of abolitionist fervor. The solution to the colonial labor problem therefore necessitated the creation of a class of dependent laborers without abridging their basic civil liberties. White male colonial emigrants posed a particularly thorny case insofar as they, unlike Britain's "uncivilized" brown and black wards, were considered to be mature and civilized enough to direct their own persons, labor, and property.[6] Wakefield's theory skillfully navigated this conundrum by deploying the juridico-political power of the state at the level of institutional design, leaving laborers free to respond to the structurally engineered background conditions of domination. Unlike slaves or indentured laborers, colonial emigrants would fully enjoy contractual freedom and juridical equality in dealing with their prospective employers, on whom they would nonetheless depend for employment and livelihood.

As Wakefield's critics were quick to note, the coercion implicit in this orchestrated dependency and the juridico-political power of the state that underwrote it posed an ideological problem for Wakefield who, like other classical political economists, claimed to be a principled exponent of laissez-faire. I argue that Wakefield ultimately could not find a way out of this contradiction. The priority he accorded to salvaging capitalist civilization overrode his commitment to the principles of juridical equality and contractual freedom. The more he struggled to justify colonial dispossession, the more glaringly he betrayed an illiberal and paternalistic stance on the government of putatively free laborers. Unable to exorcise paternalism from his theory, he ultimately disavowed it by draping it in fictions of contractual dispossession. His notion of a "settler compact," which supposedly re-enacted the primordial agreement of mankind to divide itself into capitalists and laborers, represented a sterling example of the of mythical origin story that, for Marx, signaled classical political economy's inability to account for the violent historical beginnings of the capitalist mode of production.

My argument begins with analyzing Wakefield's explication of the labor problem in its metropolitan and colonial moments, which roughly map onto the problems of the overaccumulation of capital and the inadequacies of spontaneous colonization. I contextualize the first moment in the debates about economic stagnation and the "social question" that preoccupied British political economy in the first half of the nineteenth century. I situate the second moment in the broader controversy on the legal and moral status of labor that flared in the context of British abolitionism. Both debates were animated, I maintain, as much by political and economic concerns for the stable reproduction of capitalist relations as by deeper anxieties about moral and civilizational values that implicated British self-conceptions. I then go on to examine Wakefield's theory of systematic colonization as an imperial program for establishing colonial land and labor markets and instituting the conditions of "settler capitalism." I reconstruct the ideological challenge that colonial primitive accumulation (qua state-led proletarianization) presented to the ideal of free labor, and dissect Wakefield's myths of contractual dispossession as an attempt to confront this challenge.

In focusing on the labor problem, it is not my intention to ignore the disaster that nineteenth-century British settler colonialism spelled for the indigenous peoples of North America and Australasia.[7] But I do not dwell on indigenous dispossession here because the ideological quandaries that it once posed for liberal metropolitan thought had more or less been settled by the 1830s. The Lockean grammar of agricultural and commercial improvement, compounded by eighteenth-century stadial categories of civilization and savagery, had sedimented into a discernible ideology of dispossession that early Victorians found readily at hand. The real test of the liberality of the empire and its capitalist economy at this conjuncture was not its treatment of indigenous peoples (though some imperial philanthropists and missionaries did think otherwise) but its position on human bondage.

Political Labor Problem: The Metropole

Since the middle of the eighteenth century, a major source of befuddlement for British intellectuals had been the simultaneous appearance of unprecedented wealth and poverty in their country, a counterintuitive unity that proved to be permanent and fueled debate over its economic causes as well as its political and moral consequences.[8] By the first decades of the nineteenth century, the disquietude had reached a new pitch as the age of English industrial supremacy entailed the dramatic pauperization of the English laboring classes. In his magisterial study of the social and economic crisis in Britain, Boyd Hilton describes the second quarter of the nineteenth century as the point at which "inequality and absolute poverty peak[ed]," giving rise to what Thomas Carlyle called the "Condition-of-England question."[9] To contemporary observers, the problem appeared as one of runaway population pressure. The absolute increase in Britain's population was exacerbated by the Parliamentary Enclosures that intensified between 1795 and 1815, and again by the collapse of agricultural prices with the end of the Napoleonic Wars.[10] As large landowners concentrated their holdings and raised rents in the countryside, landless laborers flooded Britain's rising industrial towns, forming the abundant and cheap labor force that fueled mushrooming factories. Although English manufacturing output expanded rapidly, it did so in violent spurts and contractions, and the urban poor whose livelihood depended on nonagricultural employment felt the violent fluctuations of the business cycle. Not only the laboring poor but the professional classes and businessmen also bore the brunt of the "huge commercial and financial crises in 1811, 1825, 1837, and 1847" that increased risk, indebtedness, and bankruptcy, leading to a "surge in suicides."[11]

In the field of political economy, these socioeconomic convulsions effected a general shift of mood from the earlier optimism of Adam Smith to the skepticism of Thomas Malthus and David Ricardo. By the 1820s, the belief in the equilibrating tendencies of the market had become the orthodox position, condensed into Say's Law, which denied the possibility of a terminal economic crisis due to systemic overproduction, though it allowed for short-term sectoral gluts. The challenge to the orthodoxy was spearheaded by Malthus's view of industrial capitalism as an inherently disharmonious totality ridden with systemic imbalances.[12] The ensuing controversy revolved around the problem of falling profits, which posed "a problem of primary importance in British political economy" insofar as it threw into sharp relief the question of stability and sustainability of industrial capitalism.[13]

The orthodox school, with Ricardo at the helm and the Utilitarian philosophers in tow, admitted falling profits but did not perceive the danger to be fatal. They held that profits tended to decline because the expansion of cultivation to less fertile marginal lands inflated the price of food and subsequently the wage bill. However, countervailing tendencies, such as productivity gains from the division of labor and free trade in foodstuffs, could stave off a systemic crisis for the foreseeable future. As long as profits were reinvested (as it was assumed that they would be, no matter how low the profit margin), it would create demand for labor and sustain wages above the subsistence level. The heterodox opinion, espoused by Malthus, Thomas Chalmers, and Robert Torrens, was less sanguine. Its adherents ascribed falling profits to the paucity of profitable investment opportunities in Britain, with the implication that a general glut was a real possibility. Systemic low returns on capital would encourage hoarding over investing. The growing differential between economic and demographic expansion would lead to an overstocked labor market, pushing up unemployment and depressing wages. The source of economic stagnation and social distress, pace Ricardians, was not the insufficient accumulation of capital but its "superabundance," or overaccumulation. Excess capital that could not be profitably invested in employing labor was left idle, thus ceasing to be productive capital. It was driven into speculation, devaluation, and bankruptcy. The paradoxical outcome was a wealthy yet distressed economy, saturated with capital and labor but suffering from stagnation, unemployment, low wages, and low profits.[14]

Wakefield's view of the social conditions in England broadly followed heterodox lights. This should not come as a surprise, for Wakefield's own biography reflected the socioeconomic predicaments surveyed by Hilton.[15] He was born to a Quaker middle-class family, received some schooling, and held some minor diplomatic posts. Driven by frustrated ambitions for social status and a political career, he abducted the fifteen-year-old daughter of a wealthy and influential manufacturer and beguiled her into marrying him. He was caught by his new wife's family, who denounced the marriage and had it annulled by a special act of Parliament. This escapade earned Wakefield a three-year sentence in the Newgate Gaol and lifetime of public notoriety. His time in jail proved formative of his assessment of Britain's social condition and possible ways of improving it. During his sentence, he observed the porous line that separated poverty and criminality in London and realized that he was hardly alone in being forced into desperate actions by economic circumstances.[16] His interaction with other inmates, especially those sentenced to transportation to Australia incited an interest in matters of colonization. In his own words, "Whilst in Newgate, I had the occasion to read with care every book concerning New South Wales and Van Diemen's Land, as well as a long series of newspapers published in these colonies. Becoming thus pretty well acquainted with the true prospect of a convict about to be transported, and being in the habit of conversing on the subject with such prisoners gave me a perfect opportunity of ascertaining the state of their feelings."[17] As Tony Ballantyne notes, in Newgate, Wakefield came to conceive "population, emigration, poverty and crime as interlocking problems that not only plagued the development of British society 'at home,' but were also distorting the growth of new society in New South Wales."[18]

Wakefield published the results of his "research" in Newgate in a series of short epistolary pieces that appeared anonymously in the *Morning Chronicle* and later reappeared as a book entitled *A Letter from Sydney* (1829).[19] This book contained in embryonic form all the major themes that Wakefield developed in his subsequent writings, including the colonial labor problem, ills of spontaneous emigration, and the remedy of systematic colonization. The *Plan of Company to Be Established for the Purpose of Founding a Colony in Southern Australia* (1830), in addition to systematizing the message of *A Letter from Sydney*, offered policy blueprints for prospective colonization societies and land companies, including those founded by Wakefield and his associates.[20] *England and America*, published anonymously in 1833, represented Wakefield's real debut in political economy and colonial policy. The book's theoretical force derived from explaining the social question in England and economic underdevelopment in the colonies within a single, coherent, and elegant analytic framework that exhibited an ardent utilitarianism. Policy circles found strong appeal in its promise of alleviating the social question at home through a self-financing system of colonial emigration, which would additionally transform settler colonies into a source of imperial wealth and revenue. Wakefield publicized these ideas in a tireless stream of pamphlets and articles that appeared in the radical journal *The Spectator*, as well as in a promotional book, suggestively entitled *The British Colonization of New Zealand* (1837). His last major work, *A View of the Art of Colonization* (1849), was a sprawling book that found lukewarm reception mainly because, excepting some important expansions on the role of government in colonization, its theses overlapped to a great extent with those in *England and America*.

His prospects of a political career foreclosed by his damaged reputation, Wakefield set out to promote his colonization plans indirectly by recruiting political economists, members of Parliament, and public officials to his cause.[21] He was a very active and familiar figure in Philosophical Radical circles that agitated for sociopolitical reform.[22] His fusion of utilitarianism with a revitalized colonial program represented his signature contribution to the radical reform agenda. This fusion gave birth to the Colonial Reform Movement, which boasted among its adherents a coterie of parliamentarians, most notably Charles Buller, Robert

Torrens, William Hutt, William Molesworth, and Charles Tennant.[23] Above all, the Colonial Reform Movement distinguished itself from earlier mercantilist rationales that had been thoroughly discredited by liberals and political economists. The "novelty and inner unity" of Wakefield's doctrine, Bernard Semmel remarks, was rooted in formulating "positive programmes of empire based on the new economic science."[24] Once a formidable weapon of anti-imperial critique, in Wakefield's hands, political economy turned into a resource for reimagining and rejuvenating the empire. On this score, Wakefield celebrated himself for persuading an elderly Jeremy Bentham to embrace systematic colonization, and John Stuart Mill's writings on the colonies borrowed from Wakefield's theory lock, stock, and barrel.[25]

A number of contemporary Antipodean historians have dismissed Wakefield's colonization efforts as a racket hatched by a mercurial adventurer who hoped to thereby secure a fortune and social status for himself and his family.[26] Such ad hominem dismissals overlook the sophistication and coherence of Wakefield's account of England's social problems and his imperial solutions to it. His combination of heterodox political economy with a global scope of analysis, I contend, placed Wakefield at the front lines of the ideological renewal of the British Empire as a globe-spanning liberal polity and the vanguard of capitalist civilization.

In the first half of *England and America* (1833), Wakefield examined the economic causes, social effects, and the potential political consequences of the overaccumulation of capital in England. The book opened with a paean to English wealth. English economic activity thrived on the application of scientific knowledge to production, strong property rights, long tenures, economies of scale, and large time horizons. The productivity of English agriculture set "more than two-thirds [of the population] free to follow other pursuits" in the cities (EA, 332). The "congregation in one place vast numbers," "steam power," and "large factories" honed the competitive edge of the English manufactures in foreign markets, and rendered "improvement" and "rapid material progress" the signature feature of "the greatest commercial nation in the world" (EA, 332–36). The strongest indicator of economic performance was above all the "abundance of CAPITAL," evidenced by the "facility with which in any part of England, funds are raised for any undertaking that offers the least chance of profit" (EA, 324).

Such wealth was paradoxically accompanied by the "misery of the bulk of the people" and the "uneasiness of the middle class" that Wakefield treated in the following three chapters. The end of the Napoleonic Wars, he held, had sealed a major outlet into which the English agriculture and industry had been pouring the output of their expanding capacity. "War ceasing," he wrote, "great masses of capital were no longer wasted every year but were accumulated in England" (EA, 376). The ensuing glut in the commodity markets and diminishing returns on capital investment discouraged the investment of savings. "Capital creates capital," declared Wakefield, and in England, "by reason of the vast masses of capital already invested, there seems but little room for the profitable investment of more, millions accumulate so rapidly, that funds are never wanted for even the most hazardous undertakings" (EA, 324). Wakefield was effectively assailing Say's Law by contending that postwar England had been suffering from systemic overproduction. Since 1815, low profits had struck farming, manufacture, commerce, and retail simultaneously. "Each distress has lasted fifteen years, and all the distresses together make a permanent general distress . . . [a] steady national distress" (EA, 355). Excess capital that could find no space for investment in England regularly flowed out to unproductive speculative ventures, "glutting distant markets," inflating short-lived bubbles (such as in South American mines or foreign securities), and facing "occasional destruction on the grandest scale" (EA, 357–58).[27]

If the problem remained confined to the cyclical destruction of excess capital, there would be no cause for alarm. However, in England rural dispossession and urbanization had rendered the bulk of the population dependent on the labor market. Furthermore, the end of the war recalled to England not only capital but also the labor that had gone to fight the revolutionary armies. The lack of new investment meant growing unemployment and the approximation of wages to the "minimum" level. As greater competition for jobs in an "overstocked labor market" drove down wages, the influx into England of "barbarous and easily satisfied Irishmen" and the factory system that rendered "the work performed by man's labor more simple and easy" combined to depress wages below what used to be acceptable pay for the English workman (EA, 343–44). The "pauperization" of English workers was compounded by chronic proletarianization of the middle classes because of capitalist competition at narrow profit margins (EA, 339). Large enterprises could weather the low profit rate by virtue of their scale, whereas small capitalists, whether in agriculture, manufactures, or commerce, frequently sunk into bankruptcy, leaving behind "hundreds and thousands of people who lost their capital" and joined the ranks of the laboring class (EA, 356). Pauperization and proletarianization paved the way to the ruthless exploitation of the poor masses, especially women and children, who were particularly vulnerable. Wakefield's middle-class philanthropy blossomed in his sympathetic account of children recruited through the parish apprenticeship system who perished toiling in millineries or sweeping chimneys, women whom necessity forced into "prostitution for bread," many who disappeared into the pit of crime and ended up in "fine jails," and those who sought consolation in the gin-shops that dotted poor neighborhoods (EA, 347–51). In radical fashion, Wakefield rebuked the haughty moralism of his time, instead explaining metropolitan social pathologies with reference to socioeconomic conditions. "Not vice and misery, Mr. Malthus," he declaimed, but "misery and vice is the order of checks to population . . . In England, those who compose the bulk of the people are too cheap to be happy" (EA, 353).[28]

At the heart of the problem lay the division of the population into a capitalist and a laboring class, which was paradoxically the very fount of England's economic power. England represented the first society in which "a complete separation has taken place between capitalists and workmen, [and] the labouring class compose the vast majority of the people" (EA, 338). In all of his writings, Wakefield designated the existence of "a class of laborers for hire" as the precondition of social progress, insofar as this fundamental class division enabled the division of labor under the rational direction of capital that boosted labor productivity (EA, 325–26).[29] All "modern states, which deserve to be called civilized" boasted "a class whose only property is their labor, and who live by the sale of that property to the other classes" (EA, 337).[30] However, the employment of wage labor depended on the investment of capital, which in turn required a reasonable expectation of profit. Low or declining profitability vitiated the incentive to invest, generating a simultaneous glut in capital markets (low interest rates and speculation) and labor markets (unemployment and underemployment). In Wakefield's view, capital-centric orthodox political economy could not crack the enigma of economic stagnation despite low interest rates and low wages. The "worship of capital" had led "Bentham, Ricardo, Mill, M'Culloch, and others" to erroneously conflate "capital" and "production" (EA, 371). Wakefield retorted, "It does not follow that, because labour is employed by capital, capital always finds a field in which to employ labour" (EA, 517). The causes of unemployment and poverty had to be sought elsewhere than a dearth of capital.

Wakefield dissected this problem by introducing a third variable into the capital-labor binary, namely, the "field of employment." Weaving together Smith's theory of capitalist competition and Ricardo's theory of diminishing returns, this notion sought to explain falling profits by the shrinking opportunities for the profitable investment of capital. Although Wakefield most frequently identified the field of employment with fertile land (EA, 375), he employed the term more capaciously to refer to productivity, specialization, and comparative advantage in the use of land and the expanse of the markets in which surplus could be realized (AC, 804).[31] The key variable was the proportion between the amount of capital and the field of employment in any given country. This ratio decided the level of profits and wages, which in turn set the trend of economic expansion or stagnation.[32] Readily available fertile land comprised an abundant source of foodstuffs and raw material that reduced the costs of labor and of industrial inputs. The resulting high profits and high real wages created further incentives for investment and employment. The best illustration of a large field-to-capital ratio was America, where capital, no matter how fast it accumulated, found profits from improvement and agriculture in the fresh lands opened up by the westward expansion.[33] By contrast, in England, "[b]oth the capital and the people increased faster than the field of production was enlarged" (EA, 376). The dearth of uncultivated fertile land, combined with the Corn Laws that reduced access to the produce of fertile lands elsewhere, constricted the field in which English capital could circulate.[34]

Wakefield utilized hydraulic imagery to express the dynamic between capital and the field. The trope of "want of room"—that is, too narrow a field of employment—studded his writings. The "competition of capital with capital" for limited opportunities was "the immediate cause of all other competitions" (AC, 798). Inadequate investment left "less room for the subordinate classes," ratcheting up competition among laborers, as well as among "professional classes," who were virtually "snatching the bread out of each other's mouths" (EA, 360–62). Cyclical economic crises, or "alternations of hoarding, wasting, and panic," escalated toward a general crisis of social reproduction at all levels of society (AC, 798). Laboring classes drifted into pauperization and moral degradation. Sons of the lesser gentry found themselves excluded from respectable career opportunities, which in turn undercut the prospects of marriage for the daughters of the same class (EA, 363–65). Small capitalists joined the ranks of workers, and wealthy manufacturing and commercial classes slowly abandoned the "old-fashioned" habits of industry for financial speculation and cultivated the "spirit of the gambler" (AC, 799).[35]

Of particular concern was the distress of the laboring classes in the second half of the nineteenth century, as indicated by the stagnant or even declining real wages, rising age of marriage, increasing mortality rates, undernourishment, and the return of infectious diseases.[36] Such social misery, contemporaries dreaded, would almost certainly translate into a radical working-class movement that even the anti-establishmentarian reformists found terrifying. British political opinion in the first half of the nineteenth century, Hilton writes, was suffused by a "constant sensation of fear—fear of revolution, of the masses, of crime, famine, and poverty, of disorder and instability."[37] Moral panic over working-class degeneration blurred into the "demonization of the poor as potential revolutionaries" in a kaleidoscope of "crime, delinquency, sexual depravity, and Jacobinism," which merged into a "one great phantasmagoria of the mad, bad, and dangerous people."[38] Wakefield echoed the common sentiment when he warned that "if their condition be such that it must be worse before it can be better, the crisis is coming" (EA, 353). Such apprehensions were not entirely unfounded. Socialism and Chartism were riding the wave of popular radicalization that had sprouted in the early nineteenth century, and despite such repressive reactions as the Peterloo Massacre and Six Acts, the laboring classes continued agitating for universal suffrage.[39] Adding to these sources of political duress, and most immediate for Wakefield's context, Swing Riots erupted in 1830 in the south and east of the

English countryside. The rural poor destroyed agricultural machinery, set fire to ricks, demolished tithe barns, and gave Wakefield the occasion to air his views on the social question in a pamphlet, entitled *Swing Unmasked*.[40]

Malthus had advised relegating the problem of social distress to natural solutions and waiting until the edifying effects of poverty, such as watching one's children starve to death, instilled moral habits of abstention in the poor.[41] For Wakefield, the social and political mobilization of the working class rendered such passive fatalism unviable, if not disastrous. The political agitation of the middle classes against the corrupt aristocratic order had taught the working classes "to be thoroughly discontented with their lot" and instilled in them the belief that "their misery was owing to bad government" (EA, 391). Furthermore, the July Revolution of 1830 revealed to urban laborers the power of the "barricades," which in turn convinced the British political elite that "the nation had outgrown its laws" (EA, 394–95). Haunted by the specter of urban revolt and pounded by public pressure, Parliament finally passed the Reform Act of 1832. Although subsequent electoral reforms appeased the middle classes, persistent property qualifications frustrated the laboring masses and gave new vigor to Chartism. "The new constitution of England was obtained by physical force.... Those who compose the physical force know this, are proud of it, and will never forget it. Universal suffrage was, is, and will be the object of the working classes" (EA, 399–400).

Wakefield argued that Britain's political classes could neither risk an open confrontation with the working class nor concede adult male suffrage under the existing circumstances. On the one hand, England's preponderantly urban proletariat and complex market economy ruled out violent conflict and outright repression (AC, 793–94). In a commercial society, where the majority depended on the market for income and subsistence, social upheaval spelled economic collapse and further political turmoil. "The regular course of industry depends so much on confidence and credit," Wakefield conjectured, that "any social convulsion, if it should last but a week, must produce a series of convulsions, one more violent than the other" (EA, 400; also see AC, 795). On the other hand, the laboring poor could not be readily granted the vote, for their degraded state deprived them of the reason and foresight necessary for exercising political power. Laws promulgated by the representatives of a "poor, discontent and ignorant" multitude would invariably aim at a "revolution in property" (EA, 404). "A ruined man is a dangerous citizen," he cautioned, "and I suspect that there are at all times in this country more people who have been ruined than in any other country" (AC, 799). Even though Wakefield admitted that the pre-1832 economic legislation had impoverished the lower orders through public debt and high interest rates, a counterexpropriation through inflationary measures would amount to rectifying "one great robbery [by] another great robbery"

(EA, 404). Under "a legislature moved by the wretched . . . there would be no end to confiscation" (EA, 405). Insecurity of property would decimate investor confidence, freeze credit markets, ignite capital flight, and terminate in an economic meltdown that would shatter the welfare of all classes (AC, 794–95). As Edmund Burke did before him, Wakefield looked to "the political economy of the French Revolution" for an estimation of the economic costs of confiscation in England, which he judged to be "synonymous with destruction" (EA, 405; AC, 795). If, as Thomas Holt remarks, the British "defined civilization in their own terms . . . as [they] shaped and were shaped by a capitalist political economy," then at stake in the social question was the survival of capitalist civilization.[42] In Wakefield's words, the very "existence [of the English] as a wealthy and civilized nation" depended on the success of the "great experiment" of reconciling democracy and capitalism (EA, 410).[43]

Wakefield's proposed solution to the problem of democracy, like his inquiry into the social question, followed the compass of political economy. If the "misery and ignorance" of the English laboring population disposed it to abuse political power, then the policy response had to tackle the economic roots of popular misery and ignorance. "Nature herself forbids that you should make a wise and virtuous people out of a starving one," Wakefield wrote, and only by providing the working class with "high wages, leisure, peace of mind, and instruction" that one could cultivate "prudence and wisdom" necessary for self-rule (EA, 410). Wakefield's policy recommendations evinced a humble realism in that they did not arrogate to put the population problem to rest once and for all. Instead, they contrived to provide some breathing room for British policymakers to socialize and educate the working classes into the responsible exercise of political power. He reckoned that maintaining high wages "for twenty years or so" and bestowing "comfort and knowledge upon *one generation* of the poorer class might be a step to the permanent cure of misery and vice." (EA, 407).[44]

Wakefield maintained that the general level of wages could be raised only by expanding the field in which surplus English capital could employ surplus English labor. One measure to achieve a more balanced capital-field ratio would be to repeal the Corn Laws, which would give English capital access to a larger field of production beyond Britain through international trade. As long as Britain could buy cheap grain cultivated in America, she would effectively expand the field of production, reduce the costs of reproducing British labor, and raise real wages and profits simultaneously.[45] More importantly, Wakefield contended that the repeal itself would not suffice to resolve England's problems. Relying on free trade alone would not only expose England to the vagaries of the world market in food (a point also emphasized by Malthus and Torrens) but also complicate the financing of imports. By the 1830s, English manufactures were beginning to feel the sting of the American and European tariffs,[46] which led

Wakefield to consider the establishment of a free-trade emporium off the coast of China, where English manufactures and Indian opium could be exchanged for silver, which in turn could finance food imports from America and Europe (EA, 431–60).[47] Yet he found this scheme to be too convoluted and encumbered with high transaction costs and vulnerabilities. A more politically and economically secure path forward, he conjectured, would be to turn Britain's imperial possessions into agricultural hinterlands and export markets. These satellite economies would absorb surplus British labor and capital, produce cheap food and raw materials, and import British manufactures.[48] Crucially, the economic nexus between the metropole and the colonies would rest on shared cultural values, manners, and tastes rather than enforced trade monopolies. This liberal provision distinguished Wakefield's vision of an "empire of free trade" from both the mercantilism of the "old colonial system" and alternative plans of a British "imperial *Zollverein*."[49] Wakefield's consequent proclamation of a "new colonial system" was grandiose and visionary:

> The whole world is before you. Open new channels for the most productive employment of English capital. Let the English buy bread from every people that has bread to sell cheap. Make England, for all that is produced by steam, the work-shop of the world. If, after this, there be capital and people to spare, imitate the ancient Greeks; take a lesson from the Americans, who, as their capital and population increase, find room for both by means of colonization. You have abundance, super-abundance of capital; provide profitable employment for it, and you will improve the condition of all classes at once. . . . Invest it in colonization; so that, as it flies off, it may take with it, and employ a corresponding amount of labor, if there be any . . . . May the explanation assist to point out a way, by which the English shall escape from that corrupting and irritating state of political economy, which seems fit to precede the dissolution of empires! (EA, 411)

Dissociating class politics from the social question was critical to Wakefield's agenda. By identifying insufficient field of employment as the taproot of the crisis and by suggesting free trade and colonization as its solution, he excluded capitalist class division from the parameters of the problem. Although he openly admitted, in Semmel's words, of an "industrial and commercial system operating most inharmoniously and requiring a constant expansion of the fields of production and employment," he asserted a deeper harmony of class interests beneath the turbulent surface.[50] "The agricultural laborer is a miserable wretch, no doubt," Wakefield wrote, "because he obtains but a very small share of the produce of his labor; but this is a question, not of distribution, but of production" (EA,

329). Depressed wages signaled not the avarice of employers but extremely low profit margins at which they had to conduct business. "Masters and servants have one and the same interest," Wakefield claimed, and "both classes, capitalists and laborers are fighting for room" (EA, 372–74). Ascribing the misery of the laboring class to the distribution of wealth did not just confuse the principal cause of the problem; it dangerously introduced "bad blood" between the two classes.

Although a solid theoretical case for repealing the Corn Laws was in place, entrenched landed interests obstructed its practical realization. In direct contrast, colonial emigration had been practically underway, but it lacked the blessing of a scientific theory that would help order, accelerate, and regulate it. Wakefield set for himself the task of enlisting political economy to the cause of his "new colonial system," which would undercut the orthodox indictments that the colonies were nothing more than outdoor relief for the aristocracy. This would involve demonstrating that *all classes* in England would gain by colonization, if properly conceived and executed. Wakefield rose to the challenge.

Economic Labor Problem: The Colony

Wakefield was hardly the first to view Britain's colonies as a potential solution to the mother country's social pathologies.[51] Some of his contemporaries had already surmised that "emigration would help resolve the menacing specter of overpopulation and act as a safety valve for popular discontent that was beginning to sweep the country in the aftermath of a severe economic depression and chronic post-war employment."[52] As Karen O'Brien puts it poignantly, the archetypal white settler in the early nineteenth century featured "not so much as a standard-bearer of Britain's civilizing mission, but a casualty of industrialization, war, and poverty, and as an economic migrant."[53] The main figure behind emigration schemes in the 1820s was Sir Robert Wilmot-Horton, the Tory undersecretary of state for War and the Colonies. Wilmot-Horton's emigration policies turned on the assumption that financing the passage and settlement of the indigent would costs less in the long term than sustaining them at home.[54] Beyond this economic rationale, colonial emigration appealed to the ascendant Tory romanticism that despised the moral ravages of urbanization and industrialization and idolized "return to the land" in the colonies as a path to regeneration.[55] Classical political economists, on the other hand, were divided on the issue. Ricardo, James Mill, Bentham, McCulloch, and Malthus expressed skepticism about the feasibility of colonization as an economic remedy.[56] Torrens and Nassau Senior, by contrast, vociferously advocated state-assisted emigration, though they disagreed with Wilmot-Horton's system of financing it by mortgaging the poor rates.

Wakefield criticized Wilmot-Horton's colonial emigration policies as economically inefficient, socially stigmatized, and politically vulnerable. The proposals lacked an overarching logic or "system" in the utilitarian sense of a totalizing calculation of ends and means. Instead, in the words of the Colonial Reformer Charles Buller, they desperately aimed at "shovelling out paupers to where they may die without shocking their betters with the sight or sound of their last agony."[57] The flaw was evident first and foremost in Wilmot-Horton's plans for financing colonial emigration, which proposed mortgaging poor rates to meet the costs of relocating paupers and setting them up as small landowners. After a year, new settlers were expected to start repaying their mortgages by selling their agricultural produce. For Wakefield, this plan was a pipe dream. Most emigrants had no experience in the cultivation of the soil, and smallholder agriculture generally resulted in subsistence rather than market economies. Consequently, the financial burden of assisted emigration would remain perpetually on the shoulders of the English taxpayer. Second, the tone and provisions of Wilmot-Horton's plans appealed only to "the scum of the mother country," the most wretched and desperate of the English paupers (PC, 282). The odium of destitution, vice, and social degradation that attached to the name "colony" discouraged self-respecting English workers, professionals, and capitalists, thereby inhibiting the flow of private capital and labor to the colonies. Finally, the mode of land disposal laid out by Wilmot-Horton consisted of huge grants by the crown, opening the door to patronage, speculation, and corruption. It carried grist to the mill of the political economists who decried colonies as the larder of the old, unproductive, parasitic aristocracy.[58]

Equally importantly, spontaneous colonization in the colonies also failed because it inadvertently promoted economically backward and socially degenerate frontier settlements. The loose, unregulated, and sporadic manner in which vast colonial lands were settled led to the dispersal of emigrants and their stock. Wakefield identified such dispersal as the root cause of all the economic and social pathologies that plagued all known colonies, pathologies that coalesced into the civilizational relapse of the settlers into a state of barbarism. This perception of "frontier pathology" was conditioned by a developmental grid of civilization and savagery that recoded social difference into a normative civilizational hierarchy.[59] The Scottish Enlightenment's stadial history had laid down the theoretical groundwork of this developmentalist framework, and Adam Smith was the main conduit between the Scottish tradition and Wakefield's political economy and moral philosophy.[60] By the early nineteenth century, these civilizational categories had become, albeit in simplified and even vulgar forms, the basic furniture of social and political thought in Britain and the "anthropological, legal, and moral framework with which early Victorians categorized non-European peoples."[61] Imputations of savagery and barbarism, as we have seen, often served to justify the dispossession, enslavement, and exploitation of non-European peoples. But the same discourse also shaped the Britons' image of themselves as it was reflected in the mirror of colonial encounters.[62] In "settler mythscapes," colonialists like Wakefield looked past the indigenous people and fixated on land, which they imagined to be vacant, timeless, and brimming with promises of affirming the civilized self by building virtuous and prosperous polities.[63]

On Wakefield's account, spontaneous colonization not only stalled the advance of civilization in vacant lands, but it also eroded whatever civilization emigrants carried with them to the colonies. The threat lurking at the frontier was one of "reverse conversion," an unnatural regression from commercial society to semi-nomadic barbarism.[64] Wakefield encapsulated the stakes of the colonial pathology in a forceful passage about American colonists:

> [T]he people of America may, in this respect be likened to the Tartar conquerors of China, who, being themselves barbarous, consider all but themselves barbarians . . . This narrowness of mind, arising from ignorance, seems proper to the barbarous conquerors of China; but in colonies planted by the most civilized nations, it is a degenerate sentiment, a step backwards from civilization to barbarism, and out of the course of nature, which seems favorable, stoppages reckoned, to the improvement of mankind. (EA, 466–67)

Although the problem was most acute in America, it was by no means peculiar to it. Wakefield adduced "the rudeness, the semi-barbarism of what are called back-settlements in Canada and New Brunswick" (AC, 871) and the "semi-barbarous, Tartarian, ill-cultivated, poverty-stricken wilderness" of the Australian bush (EA, 112) to support his thesis that every colonist "gradually learns to like the baser order of things, takes a pleasure in the coarse licence and physical excitement of less civilized life" (AC, 873). Amid massive differentiation in natural environment and national background, what remained strikingly constant was the social deterioration of colonists into a rude, parochial, narrow-minded, and superstitious people beset by relative material and absolute cultural poverty (LS, 119). This constancy led Wakefield to turn to social and economic causes of civilizational regress that he deemed to be the "natural and inevitable [outcome] of a faulty mode of colonization" (EA, 464).

Wakefield singled out the system of royal land grants as the germ of the colonial labor problem that was spawning the entire range of colonial pathologies. The abundance of fertile land that could be obtained for a trifle placed landownership within easy reach of laborers.[65] As soon as a laborer saved enough to buy land, he ceased working for wages and became a proprietor himself. In doing so, he reduced the colonial labor supply and pushed up wage rates, making it easier for other laborers to become landowners (LS, 110–12). The expensive and unreliable labor supply precluded any possibility of large-scale economic undertakings that required large labor and capital outlays, discouraging investment and reinforcing the tendency toward smallholder subsistence economies. Importing more laborers, for instance, "five thousand starving peasants" from England or even "twenty thousand industrious and skillful Chinese," would be to no avail. They, too, would disperse and become landowners as soon as they could (LS, 108–9).[66]

The disposition of colonial laborers to become smallholders upended the separation between labor and capital on which Wakefield predicated the entire edifice of capitalist civilization. A precarious class division stunted the social and technical division of labor and restricted the scale of production to a very modest level. Furthermore, inadequate transportation, meager urbanization, and poorly integrated commodity markets in the colonies would make it nigh impossible to monetize agricultural surplus (LS, 103–4). This further reinforced subsistence farming geared toward producing "a sufficiency of mere necessaries of life" (PC, 295). For example, echoing John Locke's ruminations on enclosure in the absence of monetization, he wrote, "[M]any a New South Wales farmer grows no more corn than will supply his family, because he could be unable to remove a surplus quantity from his own barn" (LS, 132). Consequently, "there is little division of labor, and you might roll in plenty, without possessing anything of exchangeable value. You must do everything yourself; and flocks in the wilderness are not worth much more than the wilderness itself" (LS, 107). An economy characterized by production for immediate needs resulted in

> a barbarous condition, like that of every people scattered over a territory immense in proportion to their numbers; every man is obliged to occupy himself with questions of daily bread; there is neither leisure nor reward for the investigation of abstract truth; money-getting is the universal object; taste, science, morals, manners, abstract politics are subjects of little interest. (LS, 119)

Wakefield's association of subsistence agriculture with barbarism might appear odd, as this civilizational category was conventionally reserved for pastoralist nomads like the "Tartars." The key to this puzzle is Wakefield's view that settlers were "earth-scratchers" (EA, 493)—that is, horticulturalists who did not "improve" the land with the plow and manure, but "mov[ed] from one piece of land to another as the natural fertility of each piece is exhausted" (EA, 488n). Most Enlightenment thinkers, as J. G. A. Pocock reminds us, did not see the horticultural practices of indigenous peoples as constituting cultivation proper, and Wakefield was simply extending this categorization to colonists. "The Americans have only scratched [the earth] instead of cultivating," he wrote (LS, 157). Accordingly, "they had not escaped from the vagrant condition, and were no further from savagery."[67] Under such conditions of quasi-vagrancy, prerequisites of civilization such as intensive agriculture, monetary economy, and literacy (at once the signs and the conditions of durable, continuous social intercourse) led only the most incipient and rudimentary existence in the colonies.[68]

Wakefield's examination of the colonial labor problem once again resorted to hydraulic imagery, with "dispersal" and "spreading" inverting the "want of room" in the metropole:

> But rudeness and civilization are effects as well as causes. By going further back, by substituting dispersed for rude, and concentrated for civilized, we get nearer, at least, to the truth. In the history of the world, there is no example of a society at once dispersed and highly civilized; while there are instances without end, in the history of colonization, of societies which, being civilized, became barbarous as soon as they were dispersed over an extensive territory. (EA, 468)

The division of labor and socioeconomic complexity that characterized commercial societies depended on a certain level of social density and mutual interdependence that disintegrated under the centrifugal pull of cheap land in the colonies.[69] "[S]uperabundance of good land belong[s] to many savage nations," Wakefield declared, and "men's minds [are] as narrow as their territory is extensive, preventing the native growth of liberal feeling and polished manners" (EA, 483; LS, 122). The inverse proportion between abundant land and civilizational integrity manifested itself universally. For example, in South Australia, "the power to spread at will" stretched the social texture ever thinner, culminating in the "present Tartar state" of the colonists (LS, 152). In North America, Elizabethan land grants, Jefferson's Louisiana Purchase, and Jackson's land policies had paved the way for an "uncouth, ignorant, and violent . . . mass of North Americans," and spawned the "white savages of Kentucky" (LS, 114, 124). To the South, the same logic manifested itself in post-independence Argentina, whose inhabitants eventually spread over the Pampas and became nomadic gauchos who "subsist . . . on the flesh of wild cattle, . . . and have lost most of the arts of civilized life" (EA, 483). "The savage descendants of Spaniards" were mirrored by the farmers of South Africa, the "most ignorant and brutal race of men" as well as by the "hordes of savages" of French Louisiana (EA, 528, 532). Wakefield called such settler societies a "new people" whom he defined as a people who "though they continually increase in number, make no progress in the art of living; who, in respect to wealth, knowledge, skill, taste, and whatever belongs to civilization, have degenerated from their ancestors; . . . we mean, in two words, a people who become rotten before they are ripe" (LS, 151–52). "New people" signified a civilizational rather than temporal status: not young, but degenerate.

In addition to material penury and cultural vulgarity, social degeneracy also instantiated in the subversion of the social order in the colonies. In *A Letter from Sydney*, Wakefield's fictional Australian colonist expressed his revulsion for his former servant, who, having become "an Australian aristocrat," "has grown enormously fat, feeds upon greasy dainties, drinks oceans of bottled porter and port wine" (LS, 105). As a result of labor scarcity, the colonist continued, "I became a slave of my slaves. Can you think of a more hateful existence?" (LS, 106). The same subversion extended to women in the colonial society. "Fancy [a vulgar body in England] converted, by sudden elevation to the first place anywhere into a vulgar fine lady" (LS, 120).[70] Cheap, abundant land acted as a solvent of not only capitalist property relations but also the structures of dependency and power that they subtended.

To summarize, in the colonies, civilization decomposed because there was *too much room*. Sparse population and inadequate communication vitiated the material conditions of civilization (social complexity, productivity, surplus), undermined its cultural corollaries (leisure, arts, sciences, manners), and subverted social hierarchies (status, deference, order). In the metropole, civilization threatened to *implode* under the ever-increasing pressure of capital and labor pressing against the claustrophobic confines of the field of employment. In the colonies, labor and capital dissipated in the immensities of the same field of employment. As the socioeconomic conditions of commercial society crumbled, its civilization slowly languished in a state of fatal torpor.

In tackling the labor problem in the colonies, Wakefield introduced "the degree of social concentration," a "category of political economy" that denoted the social pressure necessary to secure "the combination of labor necessary to obtain the greatest quantity of produce from a given number of hours' work and a given quantity of capital" (PC, 304). The task was to devise a way to compel laborers to work for capitalists, thereby making possible the social and technical division of labor, without squeezing them to the point of discontent and revolt. Wakefield's colonial framework of analysis had rewarded him with a vital political economic discovery: people worked for a wage only to the extent that they had to. This was in fact an old mercantilist insight that had been lost to classical political economy.[71] Wakefield had to retrieve it from the colonies, where he repeatedly observed a "passion to own land" that was coupled with a pervasive pattern of subsistence farming. "The desire of becoming a land proprietor, for the gratification of which [the laborer] is willing to make great sacrifices" constituted the most trenchant obstacle to social cooperation and division of labor, because "by a *small quantity* of labor on new soil, he produces a sufficiency of the mere necessaries of life . . . and contents himself with producing little more" (PC, 297–98).

The sterling case was once again American settlements, "where a passion for owning land prevents the existence of a class of laborers for hire; and where, consequently, half of the crop is sometimes left to rot upon the ground" (EA, 326). Wakefield would later elevate these initial observations to the status of universal principle, and proclaim that "the passion for owning land . . . belongs to human nature," and "property in land is the object of one of the strongest and most general of human desires" (AC, 929, 937). It was this desire for direct access to land and land's abundance in the colonies that gave rise to the colonial labor problem.[72] In England, the "passion to own land" remained effectively under check, because primitive accumulation qua enclosures had advanced to a degree where the laboring classes had no choice but to work on somebody else's land on the condition of producing a profit for the farmer and rent for the landlord. The "social pressure" necessary to keep laborers at work was sustained by strong private-property rights in factors of production and by the compulsion of market mechanisms. Capitalist relations that obtained between factors of production in the metropole evaporated in the colony. As the laborers brought from England abandoned their would-be employers to set up their own freeholds, the initial stock fell prey to "unproductive consumption" (PC, 289).[73]

Capital, which self-evidently referred to "stock" and "money" in the metropolitan political economy, was revealed to be a *social relationship* the moment it dissolved into its constituent elements in the colony. Wakefield's fictional Australian colonist lamented, "I could fill pages with an account of the number of things, which would be of great value in England, which would be considered capital in any densely peopled country, but which we throw away as rubbish" (LS, 112). Land and instruments of production ceased to be "capital" because, Wakefield observed, "capital which cannot be employed, which lies idle for want of employment, is as if it did not exist" (EA, 373). Marx was perhaps the first to discern the significance of this observation for a study of the capitalist mode of production. In the section on the "so-called primitive accumulation," he wrote, "It is the great merit of E. G. Wakefield to have discovered, not something new *about* the colonies, but, *in* the colonies, the truth about capitalist relations in the mother country"—namely, "that capital is not a thing, but a social relation between persons which is mediated through things."[74]

For Wakefield, the relational nature of capital manifested itself most unmistakably in colonial labor relations. In a critical passage, he wrote, "What the capitalist brings to the colony in the shape of labor, *ceases to be labor* the moment it reaches the colony" (EA, 553; emphasis mine). The colonial context threw into sharp relief the specific social preconditions of "labor" as a category of political economy—that is, as "capital-positing labor," as labor that contributes to the self-valorization of capital.[75] At a more general level, "the passion to own land" expressed the disposition of laborers to seek relatively direct access to the means of subsistence without the compulsion to generate a surplus for capitalist employers—a disposition that found (literally) fertile soil for its development in the colonies. Similarly, colonial experience revealed large-scale cooperation and division of labor, which "seems in old countries like a natural property of labour" itself" (AC, 846), to be historical and fragile achievements. Marx would hone this point further in *Capital*, arguing that classical political economists conceived of cooperative production only in the image of the division of labor in manufactures, which led them to confuse the enterprise of the capitalist for the productive powers of social labor.[76] Wakefield's verdict on his fellow political economists was that "in treating of colonies, [they] have worked with no other tools than those which they were accustomed to use in explaining the phenomena of an old country, to facts that never existed in the colony" (EA, 525).

The intensity of Wakefield's abhorrence of the colonial life merged with his portentous outlook on England's troubles. In a perverse way, economic regress and civilizational erosion at the colonial frontier offered a vague indication of the possible consequences of an economic crisis and civilizational bust in England. A postrevolutionary England would not be a postcapitalist society (as Marx sanguinely presaged) but would revert to a precapitalist state akin to the condition of the colonies. Confiscation and redistribution of property by social revolution or political democracy would destroy the division between capitalists and laborers that undergirded capitalist civilization. The forcible redistribution of property would mean *peasantization,* a return to the rude lifestyle that characterized "less civilized" countries such as Ireland, Portugal, and America. This augured the end of civilization as the early Victorians knew it. Wakefield warned that class conflict in England "must end in England's ruin; which might make England a *hunting field, or a place fit to receive convicts from America*" (EA, 405–6; emphasis added). The allusion to the wilderness of the colonial frontier and the penal colonies of South Australia is incontrovertible. Social development was precarious and reversible. Just as the commercial barbarism of the East India Company agents had scandalized Burke, the civilizational decline of English settlers offended Wakefield. The problem did not end with exporting surplus English labor and capital to the colonies. As Pat Moloney reminds us, "Victorians had more than their capital invested in such schemes. Civilization and savagery defined who *they* were."[77] Wakefield's colonization plans would remain defective if salvaging civilization in England could only be obtained at the cost of barbarizing Englishmen abroad.

Wakefield admitted that not all colonies in modern history had fallen prey to the barbarizing tendencies of an open frontier. The coastal towns of North America and the West Indies had long been engines of prosperity and could hardly be called barbarous in the sense Wakefield described. In these colonial settlements, the colonial labor problem was resolved through the employment of bonded labor, of which chattel slavery represented the most brutal and con-troversial type. Wakefield wrote *A Letter from Sydney* and *England and America* in the heat of the public and official debates over the emancipation of slaves in the British West Indies, and his analysis bore the marks of, and intervened in, these debates. During and after the emancipation, the planters set their sights on the East Indian labor reserves and mobilized their connections in the Colonial Office to arrange the migration of indentured laborers to the West Indies. Madhavi Kale's excellent analysis of the indenture controversy reveals the acuity of the colonial labor problem that animated these schemes, as well as the British and policymakers' dilemmas in reconciling the ideology of "free labor" that increas-ingly defined the British self-image with the pressing need for a viable solution to colonial labor shortages.[78] Initially denounced by the abolitionists as yet another form of slavery, Indian indentured servitude ultimately offered a middle ground for a "liberal compromise" between colonial entrepreneurs and the exponents of free labor.[79] Given Wakefield's efforts to popularize his theory, it should not come as a surprise that he was explicitly invoked as an authority by at least one West Indian planter, William Burnley, who adduced his theory lock, stock, and barrel in advocating the importation of labor to the British Caribbean.[80]

Wakefield's view of slavery evinced the same political economic perspective he applied to pauperism in England. Parting ways Adam Smith, who had attrib-uted slavery to the "love of domination and tyrannizing" in all men, Wakefield tied the practice to "not moral but economic circumstances: they relate not to vice and virtue, but to production" (AC, 928).[81] "I can conceive that slavery was revived for something else than the gratification of man's worst propensities" (LS, 113). He traced the "original cause of slavery" to "the discovery of waste countries" with "*super*abundance of land in proportion to people," and explained continuation of the practice by the "disproportion which has ever since existed in those countries between the demand and the supply of labor" (EA, 479; LS, 113). Enslavement of American Indians, African chattel slavery, and a host of other types of "virtual slavery," including redemptioning, indenture, convict labor, and apprenticeship, had served as historical remedies to the colonial labor problem, enabling the concentration of labor in large-scale agriculture, especially in export staples such as sugar, tobacco, and cotton (EA, 470–80; AC 849–53).[82] Wakefield's account was broadly accurate. Prior to the onset of the slave trade, convict transportation and indenture were the principal means for populating the West Indian plantations with white (and during Cromwell's reign, predominantly Irish) bonded laborers.[83] Similarly, commercial agriculture and pastoralism began to progress in Australia, and a discernible form of set-tler capitalism emerged only when the flows of convict transports increased in the second decade of the nineteenth century.[84] Wakefield noted that the unreli-ability of the transportation system would make many an Australian capitalist long for "African slaves," which they would no doubt obtain "if public opinion in England did not forbid it" (LS, 135–36; EA, 485). Accordingly, "if Australasia should become independent tomorrow, these people would find some means of establishing slavery in spite of all the saints" (LS, 114).

Wakefield was effectively qualifying the conventional argument that free labor was economically superior to slave labor because of the high cost of maintaining slaves and the low productivity of their labor. This argument, which had been adumbrated by political economists and public moralists at least since Adam Smith, constituted, in Andrew Porter's words, the principal "capitalist" argument in the liberal "humanitarian armoury."[85] Wakefield contended that economic productivity was, first and foremost, a function of social cooperation and the division of labor, and only secondarily a creature of individual skill or willingness to work. If social cooperation and a division of labor were in place, then free laborers were preferable to bondsmen, since they did not carry the motivational blight that afflicted slaves. Wakefield admitted that "slave labour is on the whole much more costly than the labour of hired freemen," but added, "when slavery is adopted, there is no choice: it is adopted because at the time and under the circumstances there is no other way of getting the labourers to work with constancy and in combination" (AC, 927–28). In the colonies, free labor was the very solvent of the conditions of productivity because of its tendency to disperse. Consequently, slavery represented the only viable instrument for securing a labor force large, pliable, and regular enough to undertake specialized production and economies of scale.[86] This had dawned on Wakefield's fictional Australian capitalist, who "had not bound [his workers] by indentures, for [he] was weak enough to think that free agents would prove better servants than bondsmen" (LS, 106). Indeed, as Henry Taylor, one of the architects of emancipation in the West Indies remarked, "free agents" proved more advantageous than slaves on all counts except "in the continuity and the certainty of [the] supply of labor."[87] As Holt stresses, however, considerations of "continuity and certainty" were precisely what guided colonial capitalists' policies of labor recruitment.[88]

Slavery, execrated in Britain as a most barbaric form of domination, formed the central pillar of civilization in the colonies. "Had slavery never existed," Wakefield contended, a Jamaican planter "would, in the natural course of things, have been a little West Indian farmer, perhaps scarcely be able to read—certainly not fit to be a member of civilized society" (LS, 113). Thanks to the "riches, leisure, and instruction" afforded by the surplus generated by slaves and realized in the European and American markets, planter societies could cultivate the civilized features characteristic of commercial peoples. The link between colonial slave economies and capitalist civilization was a theme that more broadly pervaded the abolition debates and stamped not only planters' but also policymakers' anxieties surrounding the emancipation and apprenticeship. "The worst fears of the men who had fashioned British policy," writes Holt, was the perceived tendency of the freed people "to establish independent freeholds," as expressed in a planter's warning that "our present apprentices will answer to our necessities only in proportion to the facilities of their becoming petty settlers being withheld from them."[89] The danger of peasantization registered itself in a civilizational, as well as an economic, key, wherein subsistence farming, market gardening, and petty commodity production outside the wage relation conjured up visions of "savage indolence" and "cultural regression."[90] The "Malthusian and Wakefieldian dicta" that "ex-slaves be prevented from obtaining land" became the official policy of the day in an effort to counter, in the words of Lord Glenelg (secretary of state for War and the Colonies), "the natural tendency of the population to spread over the surface of the country, each man settling where he may, or roving from place to place in pursuit of virgin soil."[91]

The absence of colonial slavery meant the stall of civilization, while its abolition meant civilizational decay. However, its "economic remedy" notwithstanding, Wakefield deemed slavery to be "full of moral and political evils from which the method of hired labor is exempt" (AC, 928). The "political and social malady" of slavery above all offended the liberal sensibilities associated with the English character (AC, 853). The origins of these sensibilities were rooted in the transvaluation of social values during the consolidation of capitalism in eighteenth-century England, where the polished individual of commercial society was increasingly and favorably juxtaposed to the slave-owning, rude, and barbarous figure of the ancient Greco-Roman citizen.[92] As Pocock puts it lucidly, the modern liberal ideology rested on the premise that "[i]n the pre-commercial society the exchange of goods and services is so underdeveloped that the normal human relationship is that between master and slave, lord and serf. Only as commerce develops do social relations become capable of generating civil authority."[93] Colonial slavery, insofar as it planted one foot of the slave-owner firmly in the soil of brute force, represented a condition as "artificially distanced from civil society as that of savagery was naturally remote."[94] Although slavery resolved the colonial labor problem, it did so through naked coercion that openly contravened the principles of consent and contract, which, increasingly, demarcated the British political and moral self-conceptions. At once constitutive of and pitted against the idea of "free labor," slavery became, in David Brion Davis's words, a "unique moral aberration," no longer compatible with the liberal "attitudes toward labor, property, and individual responsibility" and the "needs and values of the emerging capitalist order."[95] The forcible expropriation and exploitation inherent in enslavement glared too disturbingly in the face of the relatively subtle, flexible, and institutionally relayed forms of labor control and social discipline that were being developed and disseminated in England in this period.[96] Seen in this light, colonial slave economies resembled less the commercial society from which they spun off than the precommercial stage the British had supposedly left behind.

Against this ideological background, the following passages that Wakefield wrote twenty years apart pinpoint the civilizational coordinates of slavery in his thought:

> Convict labor being a kind of slavery, the employer of convicts is a species of slave-driver, and his children are little slave drivers. As his slaves have more rights and more reason than the black slaves of Virginia, his position is more injurious to his character than that of the Virginian slave-owner . . . One can imagine a kind of master of downright slaves; but to drive men, half slaves and half freemen, *must* make the driver a brute . . . the injury done to the character of the master by our slave system is quite perfect. Is this not a great evil? (LS, 136)
>
> Negro slavery is detestable for the master who was not bred, born, and educated within hearing of the driving-whip. If I could find a stronger word than detestable, I would apply it to the life of a decent Englishman who has become a driver of convicts in Tasmania. . . . [The] political danger and social plague [of a degraded slave population] is tolerable, indeed, for those who are used to it, and to whom it is, moreover, a convenience in other respects; but the British capitalist is not used to it. (AC, 852–53)

Arresting the barbarizing expansion of the frontier by means of coerced labor gave rise to another form of civilizational relapse by turning the slave-owner into a despot equally egregious to the liberal English character. Wakefield was not alone in his apprehension about slavery. As Catherine Hall points out, an uneasy coexistence of material symbiosis and cultural revulsion marked the relationship between the West Indies and England. For the English, she remarks, "the wealthy planters represented forms of vulgarity, backwardness, and degeneracy that inverted the standards of English civility and culture," and the West Indies "a kind of outpost of the metropolis, an extension or perhaps an excrescence of the British self rather than a place entirely separate."[97] Here was another conundrum for spontaneous colonization: free labor in the colonies culminated in vagrant savagery, while bonded labor bred barbarous despotism. The inhabitants of settler colonies were free but not civilized (resembling the savages of American wilderness), while those of the slave colonies were relatively civilized but not free (akin to Asiatic despotisms). Whether they set sail to become homesteaders or planters, "something happened to Britons when they left the island shores."[98]

Systematic Colonization: Capital and Empire

If capitalist civilization and its liberal image were both to survive in the colonies, "free labor" had to be consummated as a juridical-economic form. It had to remain "free"—that is, the exclusive private property of the laborer, who could voluntarily alienate it through contracts. At the same time, it had to remain "labor"—that is, a commodity the purchase and employment of which yielded a profit. Wakefield's scheme of systematic colonization proposed to manage the tension between these two priorities by connecting the metropole and the colonies with imperial flows of labor, capital, and commodities. Properly administered, these imperial flows could relieve the pressure in the metropole by channeling excess labor and capital to the colonies without; however, letting them dissipate in the wilderness. Optimum economic pressure on both ends of the transfer could secure a free, reliable, and contented labor supply throughout Britain's imperial economy.

In Wakefield's view, labor was either free or not; all hybrid forms of labor control (indenture, apprenticeship, convict transportation) qualified as "virtual slavery." In this regard, he very much aligned himself with the liberal abolitionist sensibilities of his time that enshrined the labor contract as the mark of personal freedom and civil liberties.[99] Wakefield's ingenious solution to the colonial labor problem involved *indirectly coercing* free labor into the service of capital while maintaining a formally laissez-faire stance on labor recruitment. He contended that both capitalist relations *and* freedom could be achieved in the colonies by placing an artificially inflated price on public lands in order to prolong the period for which emigrants had to work as wage laborers to save enough to purchase land. The compulsion to work would issue not from the sound of master's lash or the sight of the gallows, but from the Malthusian fear of destitution and the Smithian desire to improve one's condition.

The cornerstone of Wakefield's policy measures was the mode of land disposal in the colonies. The manner in which individuals appropriated colonial land heavily influenced the prevalent forms of property, organization of labor, and, consequently, prospects of socioeconomic development. The "grants system" that had hitherto been adopted by European governments represented a "faulty mode of colonization" inasmuch as it made land accessible to people who would otherwise be wage laborers. Wakefield admitted that governments could not physically control the amount of fertile land available to settlers. They could, however, control the disposal of secure titles to that land. Unlike Locke, who had invoked natural law to derive landed property from the activity of laboring, Wakefield drew the line between "waste" and "property" by positive law. He defined "waste land" that constituted the object of colonization as "land that is not yet the property of individuals, but liable to becoming so through the intervention of government" (EA, 504). Assuming that no person would choose to settle and improve land without legal ownership of it, colonial dispersal could be preempted by restricting the amount of land the colonial government would legally sanction and protect as private property. From such restriction would follow social concentration, a constant workforce, division of labor, productivity, wealth, leisure, and refinement. Insofar as "government might, by restricting the amount of grants, establish and maintain the most desirable proportion between people and territory," Wakefield concluded, it "possesses the power to civilize its subjects" (LS, 158–59).

As the first measure, the grants system had to be replaced by the sale of colonial lands, which would give government a much more precise instrument of disposal.[100] This policy envisioned much stronger and exclusive preemptive crown rights over colonial lands. For civilized colonization to succeed, land "must not only be waste, but it must be *public property*, liable to be converted into private property for the end in view" (EA, 527; emphasis added). The "power of government over waste land must be exerted actively" in bestowing land titles, but "that power must be exerted negatively, in refusing titles to waste land," as well (EA, 538). The controlled sale of lands would operate like an "elastic belt" around the field of production, stretching outward when capital needed fresh areas of investment, and simultaneously maintaining a sizeable body of landless laborers who would work for the capitalists. By gradually expanding cultivation to marginal lands, it would ascertain that "the capital and labor possessed by the Colony at any given time, will be employed on those portions of land, which from quality or situation, can be most advantageously cultivated" (PC, 303). The gradual expansion of landed property would keep the land rents at a steady optimum.

Wakefield's proposal ran directly counter to the established Smithian perspective on the economics of colonization. Smith had condemned all sorts of government intervention in colonial settlement and trade as ineffectual at best and often pernicious.[101] He championed spontaneous colonization as the actual engine of colonial prosperity and pointed to the astonishing growth of Britain's North American colonies as the strongest case for a laissez-faire approach to colonization policy.[102] In North America, the abundance and fertility of the colonial land, coupled with low rents and low taxes, increased the profit margins of farming. This motivated each colonist "to render as great as possible a produce, which is thus to be almost entirely his own," and allowed him to pay high wages to his farm hands.[103] The combination of personal liberty, agricultural skill, and plenty of land paved the path to opulence.[104] Measured by a Smithian metric, Wakefield's proposal for a government-created scarcity of land appeared both illiberal and counterproductive.

Wakefield knew Smith's arguments on colonial prosperity rather well, as he had edited an annotated copy of the *Wealth of Nations*.[105] Wakefield criticized Smith for assuming, quite erroneously, the existence of functional land and labor markets in the colonies as metropolitan economists understood them. As we have seen, Wakefield contended that the severe shortage and inconstancy of labor rendered it so expensive that it ceased to be "labor" as the metropolitan economy understood it. Wakefield argued conversely that the overabundance of land rendered it a species of natural commons, "supplied, like air or water, in unlimited qualities," which was "not in any proportion to the market demand for land, but so as to prevent such a demand" (AC, 933). Wakefield agreed with Smith that the value of land, as measured in rents, arose not from natural fertility but from the competition for it (EA, 423). However, competition presupposed the scarcity of land. The facility with which land could be obtained in the colonies translated into the absence of such scarcity, vitiating colonial land markets. Wakefield analogized the profusion of colonial land ownership to inflationary monetary policy. Goaded by the confusion of abundant land with actual wealth, liberally granting colonial land to private persons was akin to flooding the economy with coin minted from a newly discovered gold mine (EA, 427). In the colonies, the "tragedy of the commons" issued not from the absence of private property but from its ubiquity.[106]

Against this background, Wakefield's "elastic belt," built from strong preemptive crown rights and public-property claims, represented the boundaries of the colonial territory to be cordoned off, negated as commons, and reconstituted as "property" with a market value.[107] In the colonies, commodity had not yet become the general social form that governed the conception, ownership, and transaction of land. Expressed in stadial terms, insertion of land into the relations of production as a commodity rather than a means of subsistence (or what Polanyi called "improvement" as opposed to "habitation") constituted the precondition of commercial society.[108] As Pocock reminds us, in the Enlightenment thought, "[t]here is no fourth [i.e., commercial] stage until land becomes purely a commodity."[109] Wakefield thereby countered both Lockean philosophical argument (labor) and Smithian economic reasoning (opulence) as adequate grounds for the free appropriation of land. He rebutted the former, in Benthamite fashion, by substituting positive law for natural law as the foundation of property, and the latter by demonstrating the need for government intervention to create land as a commodity and object of investment. This theoretical confrontation cast into relief the political, legal, and essentially nonmarket preconditions of the market in land.

Despite the liberal skepticism it occasioned, Wakefield's defense of a government grip on landed property intended nothing less than the enclosure and nurturing of a sphere in which the movement of land and labor could conform to the metropolitan laws of commodity and capital. Wakefield consummated this argument in a hypothetical scenario, wherein he fantasized about the physical production of land for the market:

> Suppose then, that Liebig should discover a process by which the water of the sea might be converted into fertile land, at a cost of, let us say forty shillings an acre. Suppose, further, that the state did not monopolize the exercise of this art, and allowed a free trade in it. Immense capitals would be invested in this trade. The quantity of sea converted into land would be as much as there was a prospect of being able to sell for the cost of production and a profit besides. (AC, 937)[110]

Costs that attended the production of land for sale at a profit (i.e., capitalist production) would be sufficient to align land relations with the market logic. "In the colonies" however, "there is no such cost of production. There, the whole good effect must be produced by a price imposed by the government, or not produced at all" (AC, 938). This price would help demarcate a capitalist enclave, sequestered from the unruly waste surrounding it, within which labor and land could find their market price. In the waste of the colonies, the production of land as a commodity through the exercise of juridico-political power unfolded openly and unentangled with English customary and common law. In Wakefield's fiction we find land to be literally a fictitious commodity, fabricated for sale on the market.[111]

Given that the overabundance of colonial land obviated a market price for it, the government had to sell public lands at a "sufficient price" that was artificial but not arbitrary. The price had to be "sufficient" to fulfill several social-utility functions at once. First and foremost, it had to be sufficiently high to make land financially accessible and appealing only to those colonists with the economic means and the intention to improve it. The obverse side of this objective was to bar people with meager resources from obtaining landed property and to force them into wage labor. The embryo of this idea appeared in *A Letter from Sydney*, where Wakefield advocated the imposition of "some considerable price on land" for the purpose of maintaining "a constant supply of the demand for well-paid labor" that would occasion "the greatest increase of wealth and civilization" (LS, 159–60).

Wakefield refined and reiterated this argument in the following two decades both theoretically (EA, 540–47; AC, 935–50) and in policy form (PC, 276–78). Over the same period, he encountered persistent skepticism regarding the possibility of ascertaining a sufficient price.[112] He responded to these criticisms by asserting the status of the sufficient price as the outcome of a multivariate calculus that had to factor in circumstantial data. What price was "sufficient"?

How soon was "too soon"? These questions depended on the "elements of calculation," such as the rate of population increase, volume of colonial emigration, wage levels and subsistence costs that determined the average rate of saving, and the nature of the soil and climate that impacted the size of economically viable farms.[113] Wakefield concluded:

> There is no price that would be suitable for the colonies generally: the price must needs vary according to peculiar natural and other circumstances in each colony: and in order to determine the price for each colony, practical proceedings of a tentative or experimental nature are indispensable . . . That it is so becomes very plain, when one considers what are the elements of a calculation made with a view of determining the sufficient price for any colony . . . to name a price for all the colonies, would be as absurd as to fix the size of a coat for mankind. (AC, 939–40)

Whether one could pinpoint a sufficient price for all colonies was an incidental question compared to its overall objective; namely, "so limiting the quantity of land, as to give the cheapest land a market value that would have the effect of compelling labourers to work for some considerable time for wages before they could become landowners" (AC, 935). "There is but one object of a price; and about that there can be no mistake. The sole purpose of a price is to prevent labourers from turning into landowners too soon" (AC, 939–40).

Wakefield's scientific-experimental conceptualization of the sufficient price was consonant with his utilitarian outlook on social and institutional design. If "the proportion between people and territory does, in new countries, depend altogether upon the will of the government" (LS, 159), then the sufficient price, as a "variable force, completely under the control of government," would be the most efficient instrument for calibrating the proportion between land and labor (AC, 935). In this capacity, sufficient price theory formulated the political and legal means of reproducing in the colonies the class of dispossessed laborers that the Parliamentary Enclosures (itself a massive juridico-political instrument) had been producing in the metropole. British political sovereignty that drove a wedge between labor and land in Britain was summoned reappear in the colonies as a barrier that prevented their reunion. The sufficient price, as two commentators have recently observed, constituted a "surreptitiously reintroduced form of primitive accumulation," a premeditated separation of labor from its conditions by extra-economic means in order to render it subservient to the priorities of capital.[114] In contrast to land, labor could be made to conform to the laws of supply and demand only when it existed abundantly relative to the amount of capital in a given field of employment, or in Marxian terms, when capital had at its disposal a reserve army of labor.[115] The elegance of the sufficient price resided in producing relative scarcity of land and relative superfluity of labor and therefore a capitalist market in both in one and the same stroke.

Wakefield's colonial reform program therefore aimed to promote not just settler colonialism (which had been underway since the 1810s) but *settler capitalism*, "a distinctive form of capitalist regime" that emerged from the "economic activities of European empires and . . . worldwide flows of strategic raw materials, manufactures, capital and labour."[116] Most relevant for Wakefield's reflections in this regard was Australia, where spontaneous colonization and labor shortage had driven settlers to engage in land-extensive practices of pastoralism on Crown lands, the sort of barbarous and primitive lifestyle that he despised. Sporadic settlement of the continent had also given rise to the Australian "squattocracy," which locked out alternative forms of land use, such as capitalist agriculture favored by urban-commercial colonial interests.[117] Within the colony, Wakefield's theory openly championed the cause of the urban and commercial classes by advocating a division of labor between town and country, reorganization of colonial agriculture along capitalist lines, and the deepening of colonial domestic markets.

Globally, the broader role that Wakefield envisaged for the reformed colonies was one of economic complementarity with the metropole. He built on Smith's thesis on the role of markets in stimulating the division of labor, productivity, and economic growth.[118] "In order to sell merchandise in a colony, it is necessary that the colony should *exist*" (EA, 505). Wakefield found the criticism of mercantilist monopolies on colonial markets justified, but he warned against throwing the baby out with the bathwater, for "the uses and abuses of colonization are very different things" (EA, 508). Correct imperial policy would require the government to promote the civilized settlement and orderly expansion in the colonies and at the same time allow them to trade freely with both the mother country and other nations. Relations of mutualism embedded in an international division of labor would naturally follow. The colonists

> would be growers of food and raw materials of manufacture for this country: we should buy their surplus food and raw materials with the manufactured goods. . . . Thus employment of capital and labor would be increased in two places and in two ways at the same time; abroad, in the colonies, by the removal of people and capital to fresh fields of production; at home, by the extension of markets, or the importation of good and raw materials. (AC, 806)

The outcome would be the augmentation of "population, wealth and greatness of the empire" (AC, 954).

In the end, Wakefield's vision carried the day, as urbanization, social concentration, and export orientation increasingly became concrete realities in Australia and New Zealand in the 1860s. They did so, however, with a great deal more chaos, conflict, and brutality than he projected, including the genocidal displacement of the Australian Aborigines and the subjugation of the Maori by settler militia and regular British troops through warfare (1845–72) and "lawfare" by the Native Land Court (1865).[119] The "great land grabs of the nineteenth century temperate zone," as Christopher Lloyd remarks, were propelled by the "settler-capitalist possibilities within a world market. The wealth to be had from commodity production and exports drove the rapacious alliances of the settler states and capitalist landed, mining, and financial classes in all the settler zones."[120]

Through a re-evaluation of the categories of political economy, Wakefield concluded, no doubt counterintuitively, that artificial land scarcity would foster colonial prosperity. The second theoretical challenge, the charge of illiberality, proved to be thornier. Wakefield's theory of colonization properly belonged to what Kale has labeled a system of "imperial labor allocation," which comprised an arsenal of imperial legal, financial, and military technologies through which "empire made labor accessible to suitably situated employers."[121] The slavery and indenture that had long been part of this arsenal, frequently in racialized forms, were inapplicable to the labor problem at hand. Wakefield's prospective emigrants represented "properly free" laborers: English, male, white, civilized, and in control of their own labor.[122] Indenturing, let alone enslaving them, was out of the question.[123] As Bell notes, the rhetoric of childhood and maturity marshaled to legitimate British rule in its dependencies in India could not be readily applied to settler colonies because the colonists were seen as "reproductions of the metropolitan archetype, as passing the minimum threshold of civilized life."[124] Their civil liberties, above all, their freedom of movement, right to own and sell property, and right to enter labor contracts could not be abridged. Colonial primitive accumulation—qua transoceanic relocation, preemptive dispossession, and proletarianization of emigrant labor—had to be achieved while respecting the inviolability of the labor contract and the principle of voluntarism.

If colonists' economic freedoms could not be infringed, their political freedoms were another story. Although the rhetoric of childhood could not be applied to individual settlers, Bell contends, it could be "applied to the colonies as a whole. It was the political institutions and socioeconomic systems of the nascent communities, that were coded as immature and in need of (some) guidance."[125] Wakefield's systematic colonization theory embodied this outlook. The hoped-for effects of colonization were to be produced by targeting, not the individual behaviors of colonial emigrants, but the legal and institutional environment that surrounded them—or, in Michel Foucault's words, through "a minimum of economic interventionism" and "maximum legal interventionism."[126] Systematic colonization found its key lever in the power to issue secure titles to colonial lands, which could be monopolized by the imperial state without directly encroaching on civil liberties. Fortunately for Wakefield, the institutional inventory of the British Empire contained an appropriate instrument for reforming economically stagnant and socially degenerate colonies. This was the status of Crown Colony, a mode of proconsular despotism that directly bound a colony to the Colonial Office through an appointed colonial governor whose authority overrode that of the colonial assemblies.[127] Although himself a principled advocate of colonial self-government (EA, 579–87; AC, 859–64, 880–81),[128] Wakefield perceived in untrammeled imperial sovereignty the means to implement the sufficient-price policy in a "uniform" and "permanent" manner as the decisive first move to curb the supply of cheap land.[129]

When Wakefield lambasted Crown Colonies, he did so not so much for "too much government" as for "misgovernment" that owed to colonial administrators' ignorance of political economy, and he complained of a general "paucity of government" in British colonies, especially at the initial stage of settlement. He drew a critical distinction between the founding of a new society and its reproduction and assigned a different governmental logic to each phase. "It is difficult, as impossible, to colonize well without plenty of government, as to work a steam engine without fuel . . . Intervention of government is more, and more constantly needed in the multifarious business of constructing society, than that of preserving it" (AC, 868). As we have seen, Wakefield perceived colonies to be chaotic spaces inhabited by barbarous and ungovernable people lacking settled rules, norms, or conventions. Accordingly, he defined the first and most fundamental function of imperial sovereignty to be to impose a legal order on the unruly frontiers of the empire and to fashion out of the disorderly multitude of colonists a discernible society. He wrote,

> The grand point for the colonies, as to government, is that they should always know what they might lawfully do, and what they might not. What the law permitted or forbade them to do would be of comparatively small importance. . . . I ask that the colonies should be governed, as a trespasser or vagrant is prosecuted in this country, that is to say, "according to law;" that they should be ruled even according to the law-martial of a man-of-war rather than left to the lawlessness of a pirate ship; that they should be *governed* by the imperial power instead of being the sport of the chapter of accidents. (AC, 902)

As Wakefield's emphatic embrace of "imperial power" and "law-martial" over "accidents" and "lawlessness" suggests, the authority of law backed by unqualified imperial power would provide the groundwork for second-order legal arrangements like property rights. Once the imperial state brought a colony within the fold of law, it could institute government as the sole source of legitimate property and engross all formally untitled land as exclusive crown territory. This would be followed by "opening the public waste to settlers by extensive surveys, and converting it into private property according to law" (AC, 868).[130] In short, only imperial sovereignty could provide the juridico-political preconditions of the right to life, liberty, and property through which capitalist civilization could be established in the colonies.

Crucially, Wakefield envisioned this exercise of unrestrained imperial power mainly in instrumental terms, as the enabling precondition of an essentially liberal strategy of promoting colonial emigration. Government "cannot force either capital or people to emigrate," Wakefield remarked emphatically, "the principal [*sic*] of laissez-faire must be strictly observed in this case" (AC, 824). However, government possessed "control over the *disposition* of people and capital" and could manipulate these dispositions into "*inducements* to emigration for various classes of people" (AC, 824–25, emphases mine). Wakefield drew inspiration from Bentham's utilitarian theory of human motivation, especially regarding the effect of property rights on human expectations and behavior. "Expectation is a chain that unites our present existence to our future existence," Bentham averred, and "the idea of property consists in an established expectation."[131] By the same token, state power could intervene at the level of institutional design to create expectations that would prompt individuals to act in line with the socioeconomic objectives of systematic colonization. After a comparative economic survey of Britain's colonies, Wakefield concluded that "in all these cases, people are attracted from a worse to a better proportion between land and people; from lower to higher profits and wages. That it should be so is consistent with the principles of human nature and political economy" (EA, 551).[132] To channel excess capital and labor to the colonies, government had to create the conditions of high profits and wages by regulating the ratio between capital, labor, and the field of employment.

Prospective colonial capitalists had to be assured of an abundant and pliable labor force, adequate economic infrastructure, and steady rents. "Certainty of obtaining labor in the new colony would be the strongest inducement to the migration of capitalists, ambitious to take part in laying the foundation of an empire" (EA, 577). Since a reliable labor supply did not naturally present itself in the colonies, it had to be ensured by administrative means. The sufficient price was the cost of such regulation, order, certainty, and "system" (EA, 556–57). "The sufficient price alone," however, provided "only for civilized, not for rapid colonization" (AC, 952). To expedite the process, Wakefield complemented the sufficient price with a plan for an "emigration fund," whereby the revenues from the sale of colonial lands would be spent on defraying the emigration costs of future workers, further increasing the labor-land ratio in the colonies (AC, 952–57; EA, 555). Additionally, revenues extracted from the taxation of colonial rents would be plowed back into the local economy by supplementing the emigration fund and financing infrastructural improvements that would raise land values, such as roads, ports, and towns (LS, 162).[133] Social status and the "right to a liberal popular Government" would constitute the social and political incentives compounding the economic ones (PC, 301).

Encouraging labor emigration would similarly rely on the promise of liberal wages, and more importantly, the prospects of ultimately becoming a landowner. This would rely in part on publicity efforts to remove the stigma that had attached to colonial emigration because of pauper shoveling and convict transportation. Wakefield promoted the publishing of poor emigrants' encouraging letters to their friends in England in order to popularize the "charms of colonization" among the laboring class (EA, 568–71; AC, 825, 828–29). The other dimension of the effort was economic. The sufficient price in each colony had to straddle a fine line, in that it ought to be sufficiently high to delay most settlers' plans to establish independent property, yet sufficiently low to keep these plans viable so as to motivate settlers to emigrate in the first place. "*No pains should be spared to teach the laboring classes to regard the colonies as the land of promise, which it should be their highest ambition to be able to reach.*" (LS, 100). In other words, the sufficient price functioned as the linchpin of a utilitarian calculus that neither indulged nor frustrated but harnessed the "passion to own land" and turned it into an inducement to accept wage labor in the colonies.

The ultimate promise of landownership has led some historians to paint Wakefield as a friend and advocate of the laboring class.[134] This interpretation confuses strategy and objective. The goal of creating a dispossessed working class that animated the theory of systematic colonization obviated the possibility of landownership for *all* laborers. Yet to encourage the emigration of laborers, the prospect of landownership had to be more than simply a myth, and it had to be possible for *some* laborers to rise to the rank of proprietors. An illustrative case is the recruitment efforts of the New Zealand Company, which Wakefield and his entourage founded in 1837, and which exhibited the dialectic tension between the myth of social mobility and the imperative of labor supply. James Belich remarks that the Company associates preferred "social sojourners," who emigrated to the colonies for the purpose of "bettering themselves," for such aspirations of social mobility formed the most formidable bulwark against worker dissent and rebellion. The dreadful scenario for the Company was the hardening of the colonial laborers into "social settlers" who not only embraced their working-class position but were also cognizant of its structural permanence and conflict with the capitalist class. "It was not classlessness," Belich concludes, "but class harmony that was the imperative."[135] Ideally, systematic colonization would resolve the economic problem of labor shortage without tipping it over into the political problem of labor militancy that blighted the metropole. Paradoxically, the promise of landownership was part of a totalizing strategy to keep it only a dream for the majority of colonists.

Furthermore, liberal strategies of systematic colonization incorporated a strong gender dimension. Wakefield boldly proclaimed that "without women, colonization could not succeed" (AC, 979). The twin objectives of relieving England of its excess population and populating the colonies would be most efficiently achieved by promoting the emigration of young couples, transferring not only bodies but also their fertility (LS, 164). Wakefield's blueprint for the colonization for South Australia stipulated that the recipients of emigration assistance "consist entirely of *young* married or marriageable persons *of both sexes in equal numbers*" (PC, 276). To this end, he advocated reserving the emigration fund to finance the passage of married couples or single women and denying it to single men (EA, 574). Another inducement for female emigration would be the promises of a bright future haloed by the middle-class ideals of womanhood and conjugality, prospects of marriage, domesticity, and respectability.[136] In the long run, the population growth spurred by this demographic policy would ameliorate the colonial labor problem. "If all the people who have removed from Europe to America had been young couples, just arrived at the age of puberty, slavery in north America must have long since died a natural death" (AC, 971). Gender balance would also reinstate the sexual division of labor that often disintegrated at the frontier, such that the male laborer would no longer have to "divide his labour between household cares and the work of production" and could dedicate "the whole of his time, attention, and labour, to the work of production" (EA, 562).[137] The second crucial outcome would be the civilizing impact of women and domesticity in their capacity to "sop up, civilize and anchor chaotic surplus males."[138] With Victorian bourgeois domesticity reincarnated in the colony, "[n]o man would have any excuse for dissolute habits . . . Every pair of immigrants would have the strongest motives for industry, steadiness, and thrift" (EA, 567).

It would be difficult to assail the voluntary emigration of free laborers as being illiberal. The same could not be said, however, of Wakefield's colonial land-disposal system. As Eric Richards notes, Wakefield's proposals for government intervention were formulated "in the teeth of the laissez-faire doctrines of the times."[139] By the early nineteenth century, the Smithian precept that private individuals were the best judges of their own interests and that the free pursuit of private interests advanced public good had become the *doxa* of classical political economy. Malthus, Ricardo, and especially McCulloch rebuked systematic colonization as a violation of individual liberty, insofar as it laid the heavy hand of the government on the most important business of choosing the location and the amount of land that a colonist wished to purchase. While this infraction of right indirectly implicated laborers, it pertained more immediately to wealthier settlers whose private decisions to buy land would under Wakefield's system be subject to such extraneous and suspiciously vague considerations as "land-labor ratio" and "degree of concentration." To these challenges, Wakefield's retort was to invoke the social irrationality of spontaneous colonization. His argument hinged on the opposition between short-term and long-term considerations and between apparent and actual interests. The "passion to own land" that spurred colonial emigration was a myopic impulse. Although independent landowner-ship served the proximate interests of individual colonists, the socioeconomic torpor and regression it occasioned impeded the advancement of the colony as a whole. "There is no business more entirely a man's own business than that of a settler picking new land for his own purpose," admitted Wakefield; "I would if possible open the whole of the waste land of a colony to intending purchasers" (AC, 982). Under such "perfect liberty of choice," however,

> the settlers would disperse themselves too much ... wander about the waste portions of the colony ... where, being distant from a market, and from all that pertains to civilization, they would fall into a state of barba-rism: instead of acquiring wealth as all colonists ought to do, the settlers would only raise enough produce for their own rude subsistence; and the colony, instead of exporting and importing largely, would be poor and stagnant. (AC, 982)

"In a word, there would be mischievous dispersion," concluded Wakefield, continuing, "but mischievous to whom? Mischievous, if at all, to the settlers themselves. The supposition then is, that the settlers would injure themselves in consequence of not knowing what was for their own advantage" (AC, 983). From this, Wakefield concluded that "the truism of our time, that in matters of private business the parties interested are sure to judge better than any govern-ment can judge for them, is an error, if the best of governments could determine as well as the settler himself the quality and position of land the most suitable to his objects" (AC, 982).

By interposing government between the colonists and their interests, Wakefield's defense of the sufficient price thus assumed an unmistakably pater-nalistic tone that cut against the liberal sensibility of classical political economy. His disagreement with the proponents of laissez-faire turned on the question of whether it was possible to adopt a totalizing standpoint from which one could transparently grasp the inner logic of economic processes. As I discussed in chapter 3, liberal economists denied the possibility of such a sovereign standpoint because of the tremendous socioeconomic complexity, and therefore opacity, of commercial-capitalist societies. By contrast, Wakefield's analysis, precisely because it started from an investigation of colonial economies, assumed a sovereign economic gaze. The complexity of the metropolitan economy might have obscured the fundamental principles governing the movement of labor, capital, and land, and the corresponding distribution of wages, profits, and rents. In the colonies, however, such complexity unraveled and laid bare the structural background conditions on which these economic principles rested. Social and technical division of labor could not arise spontaneously from the propensity to truck, barter, and exchange, as Smith had postulated. Without the separation of labor from the means of production, "capital," "labor," and "land" as classical political economy understood them would not exist. For Wakefield, then, the primacy of the juridico-political field in establishing capitalist relations and commercial society constituted the window through which the entire landscape of economic relations could be surveyed.

Marx therefore had a point in crediting Wakefield for discovering the "secret" of primitive accumulation in the colonies, the divorcing of direct producers from the means of production by the extra-economic force of the state. However, Wakefield himself was not willing to admit this secret explicitly. Although he diagnosed the "complete separation" between capitalists and workers as the prerequisite of the modern division of labor, and although he openly championed wage labor as the index of civilization, he spared the origins of this "complete separation" from the incisive economic analysis that he elaborated on the origins of colonial slavery. Instead, he buried it, much like Adam Smith had, in the misty recesses of time. Smith had argued that "the accumulation of stock must, in the nature of things, be previous to the division of labor" and predicated the accumulation of capital on the "parsimony" that saved the value created by labor.[140] The implied conclusion, according to Marx, was that a "diligent, intelligent, and frugal elite" accumulated wealth, while the profligate multitude "finally had nothing to sell but their skins."[141] Wakefield spun a different account of original accumulation, more in tune with his utilitarian leanings yet no less mythical and idyllic.

Wakefield conjectured that prior to their bifurcation into workers and capitalists, all individuals worked on their own land and stock in order to produce their own subsistence—not unlike, he added, the American settlers, Irish cottagers, or French peasants of his time. Far from triggering an unequal accumulation of stock (as Smith had suggested), this hypothetical scenario of independent producers culminated in a situation in which "all members of the society are supposed to possess equal portions of capital" (EA, 326). Such egalitarianism, however, "would not admit of much further improvement in the productive powers of industry" (EA, 326). Under these conditions, "no man would have a motive for accumulating more capital than he could use with his own hands," making it impossible to undertake any large-scale projects, such as roads or irrigation, that required the "employment of many hands and fixed capital" (EA, 326). In the absence of social cooperation and the division of labor, society would remain locked in a stationary paradigm of subsistence that would allow at best an economy of petty commodity production. Wakefield's message was clear. Pace Smith, spontaneous pursuit of short-term individual interests did not promote but inhibited social advancement and public utility. The separation of producers into workers and capitalists, which broke through social stasis and set accumulation in motion, had to be sought elsewhere.

In his alternative account, Wakefield carefully avoided the actual, historical emergence of the capitalist class division out of systems of self-provisioning, as this would bring him too close to the ongoing history of the state-led dispossession in the interests of the propertied—that is, to the very class antagonism and "bad blood" that he tried to eschew. Therefore, he opted to take refuge in a fiction:

> Mankind have adopted a . . . contrivance for promoting the accumulation of capital, and the use of capital when required, both in large masses and fixed shape: they have divided themselves into owners of capital and owners of labour. But this division was, in fact, the result of concert or combination of labour. The capitals of all being equal, one man saves *because* he expects to find others to work for him; other men spend *because* they expect to find some men ready to employ them; and if it were not for this readiness to cooperate, to act in concert or combination, the division of the industrious classes into capitalists and labourers could not be maintained. (EA, 326–27)

The conjecture that individuals would "concert" to their dispossession and therefore to dependent livelihood in order to promote capital accumulation has struck some as absurd.[142] Indeed, the fable in question posits rational and self-possessed individuals inhabiting a sort of natural state with equal freedoms to make use of their labor and stock. It then places these individuals in a social contract of dispossession to which they accede in full knowledge of the ends to be achieved (capital accumulation) and the means to achieve them (separation of labor from the instruments of labor). Instead of dismissing this fiction of contractual dispossession as absurd, I suggest considering it a fantasy that casts primitive accumulation in a liberal mold of consent and compact. Just as Locke's fiction of mankind's universal consent brought colonial land appropriations within the liberal ambit of his labor theory of private property (see chapter 2), Wakefield's myth of contractual dispossession effaced the elements of constitutive coercion, unfreedom, and inequality from the process that gave birth to "free labor."

The same ideological conundrum rose to an urgent pitch in Wakefield's paternalist justification of the system of colonial land disposal. His plans for establishing capitalism de novo in the colonies broached the issue of capitalism's illiberal origins. In defending the sufficient-price theory, Wakefield wrote, "[I]t is for the good of all that no individual should be allowed to injure other individuals by taking more than the right quantity of waste land" (EA, 537). The "right" quantity of wasteland clearly implied an overarching calculus in which it functioned as an adjustable variable for maximizing social utility.

> With the exception of the small proportion of the people who in the case supposed would be labourers for hire, every man would be palpably interested in making land dearer, even the labourers would have the same interest, though it would be a little more remote and therefore, perhaps, much less obvious. In all probability, therefore, we should pass a law for making land dearer. (AC, 938)

The same grounds of social utility, which made it an "injury" to engross more land than was in the greatest good of all, also authorized the dispossession of laborers by juridico-political means. However, a self-referential invocation of social utility to justify primitive accumulation would not simply be totalizing but, insofar as it came at the expense of individual liberty, profoundly illiberal. Using state power to create a class of propertyless laborers against their patent desire to be landowners and, at the same time, leave this power ideologically naked, would hardly appeal to prospective colonial laborers or the political economists of the time. Nor could it avoid the charge of being a despotic design to reduce laborers to a state of perpetual servitude.

To navigate this problem, Wakefield revisited the contractual fantasy of dispossession. The preemptive crown rights, restrictive land titles, and sufficient price represented "nothing but the enforcement of a *compact among all* who are interested in the disposal of waste land; and *agreement* that none shall be allowed to injure others, that the *greatest good* of all should be consulted" (EA, 537; emphasis added). By invoking a colonial contract of dispossession among "all who are interested," which obviously included landowners, the middle classes, and laborers, Wakefield not only reintroduced the principle of consent and, therefore, of liberty and volition; he once again appealed to the harmony of class interests. The voluntary self-division of mankind into capitalists and workers in the Old World, whose actual history was conveniently lost to liberal economists, repeated itself in the colonies. In both cases, the decision of the contracting parties was purportedly informed by a notion of common good keyed to the telos of productivity and capitalist civilization—a paradoxical notion of the common good that was at once transparent only to the enlightened political economist and yet somehow accessible to all, that was in conflict with the natural passion to own land yet powerful enough to override it through reasoned agreement. State-led proletarianization resolved this paradox in practice but at the cost of opening a rift in the theoretical fabric of Wakefield's avowed liberalism. His fantasy of contractual dispossession, not unlike Edmund Burke's "well-wrought veil" to be thrown on the ignominious beginnings of all property, covered over this rift. If, as John Locke proclaimed, "in the beginning, all the world was America," then in the colonies one returned to those beginnings, where the original sin of primitive accumulation stood naked.

Conclusion: The Empire of Liberty

Wakefield's theory of systematic colonization revealed, in Marx's words, that "before he [the laborer] spends his leisure time in surplus labor for others, compulsion is necessary."[143] For Wakefield, the key task was to devise a mode of *compulsion without coercion* that would preserve the capital-positing status of labor in the colonies without the need for recourse to forms of bondage that had become extremely controversial, if not unacceptable, in early Victorian Britain. The civilizational regress that he observed in the colonies marked the limits of the bourgeois modernity that imagined itself to be capitalist, industrial, and urban, as well as progressive, polished, and liberal. The perceived peasantization of colonists eroded the capitalist-urban pillar of civilization, and enforced servitude cut against its liberal-progressive commitments. The barbarism of capital accumulation by unfree labor rivaled the barbarism of free labor without capitalism. Wakefield set out to resolve this dilemma of competing barbarisms by, on the one hand, inducing the voluntary emigration of free proletarian labor from England and, on the other, creating the background conditions under which colonial labor would be pressed into the service of capital by the "silent compulsion of economic relations."[144] As theoretically ingenious as this proposal was, it had to admit the necessity of a heavy dose of juridico-political power in designing the institutional structure that would exert the impersonal and systemic force of material necessity on laborers. At that moment, when the constitutive violence of primitive accumulation glared most brightly, Wakefield conjured up his myths of contractual dispossession to imbue proletarianization with a liberal aura of deliberation, foresight, and consensus.

Scholars who are critical of Wakefield have pointed out the flaws in his comprehension of classical political economy, as well as the practical failure of his colonization schemes.[145] Such derisions bypass the significance of Wakefield's writings

in reimagining and reconfiguring the British Empire through an ideological reju-
venation of settler colonialism. Wakefield and the Colonial Reform Movement
spearheaded the reinvention Britain's "second settler empire" (Canada, Australia,
and New Zealand) in British political opinion as an economic and cultural totality, the very backbone of Britain's power, and the embodiment of the progressive Anglo-Saxon character. In Karen O'Brien's words, systematic colonization
"exerted a disproportionate influence upon the reconceptualization, in the first
half of the nineteenth century, of Britain's relationship with its colonies, of their
nature, economic purpose, and the kinds of imperial future they might bring."[146]
The ideological wave set in motion by the Colonial Reformers who dreamed
of "Better Britains" in the South Pacific would swell to a high watermark with
the ideal of "Greater Britain" in the last third of the nineteenth century.[147] For
Wakefield, Britain's settler empire was exceptional in embodying universal progressive principles that shone most brightly "in colonies peopled by the energetic
Anglo-Saxon race" (AC, 800). This and similar notions, once they took root in
the British political imagination, would sprout into grandiose visions of a British
imperial federation, an imperial commonwealth, or an "Anglo-world," that offered
a transitional model for a peaceful, cosmopolitan world order.[148] Wakefield's writings also offer a sort of "prehistory" of the idea of Greater Britain inasmuch as
they disclose the elements of imperial intervention and discipline that metropolitan thinkers thought were necessary to sufficiently civilize colonial emigrants
before they could be fully admitted to the expanded imagined community.

There is a broader implication for the study of liberalism and empire in this
last point. As I discussed in chapter 1, scholars in this field have mainly devoted
their attention to the civilizational hierarchies that ordered European thinkers'
view of non-European peoples and spaces. What Wakefield's disdain for barbarous settlers, as before him Burke's vitriol for barbarous Company agents, suggests is that metropolitan civilizational categories, their normative freight, and
the imperial interventions they authorized traversed the putative cultural divide
and extended to Britain's white subjects overseas. Understanding why metropolitan thinkers constructed certain Europeans in colonial contexts as savage
or barbarous requires more precise theoretical tools than hypostatized notions
of "cultural difference." Nor can explanations from cultural difference as such
account for the fluidity and variation in the markers of barbarism imputed to
Europeans overseas. Illuminating in this respect is the shift from Locke's tacit
and Burke's open embrace of British settlers in America as the imperial vanguard
of civilization to Wakefield's denigration of the same as "white savages" who
needed government intervention for social regeneration before they could be
properly admitted to a renewed British Empire.[149]

We can obtain a finer-grained picture of the interface between political
thought and empire by focusing on the shifting political and economic priorities

of imperial governance, because these agendas inflected certain colonial differences, embodied as much by Europeans as non-Europeans, with a civilizational charge and thereby sanctioned specific modes of imperial intervention. For instance, Burke believed that the commercial barbarism of India's plunderers had to be punished by the authority of Britain's imperial Parliament, whereas Wakefield deemed the executive power of the imperial state to be the appropriate instrument in the mission to civilize semi-savage settlers. To suggest this much is not to downplay racialized discourses and strategies of imperial domination but to highlight the modularity and mobility of their categorical building blocks within the space of empire. As the early Victorian fear of the mad, bad, and dangerous people indicates, one did not have to leave the metropole to encounter semi-savage multitudes, only visit a working-class neighborhood.[150] In the upper- and middle-class opinion, civilizing Britain's brown and black subjects was not entirely separate from civilizing its white subjects, both at home and in the colonies. Empire, to qualify Uday Mehta's thesis, was an engine that towed not only non-European societies "stalled in their past into contemporary time and history" but also those sections of the European self that could not keep up with the norms, discipline, and sensibilities of capitalist civilization.[151]

Wakefield did not merely advocate settler colonialism; he pressed for settler capitalism. His vision of a modern world order with a reinvigorated imperial Britain as its ballast was essentially capitalist. Capitalism was in turn symbiotic with colonization. The establishment of capitalist relations with the help of government intervention would liberate existing colonies from their barbarous stasis, and the acquisition and settlement of new colonies would save the metropole from the explosive concentration of capital and labor. In the vast expanses of the settler empire, capitalism could reach, borrowing from Bell, the "escape velocity" that would allow it to outpace a terminal crisis.[152] Wakefield admitted that colonization "must have a limit as to its duration. Of course it must; because the world is of limited extent." He nonetheless reassured his readers that

> even if a system of free migration were adopted in all new countries, so as to permit the population of the world [to] exert its utmost capacity of increase, still half a century must elapse before the pressure of population upon territory would be felt, at the same moment, all over the world; and perhaps in the course of fifty years we might discover a way to "new countries" in the moon, or, what appears quite as difficult, a means of checking population otherwise than by sin and sorrow. (LS, 164)

British imperial expansionism often brings to mind Cecil Rhodes and his hubristic, if melancholy, statement, "The world is nearly all parcelled out, and what there is left of it is being divided up, conquered and colonised. . . . I would annex the planets if I could."[153] Writing several decades earlier, at a time of profound crisis rather than of imperial self-confidence, Wakefield had already intuited that the salvation of Britain's capitalist civilization depended on its continuous expansion.

That the colonized "new countries" had been wrested from their original inhabitants by force did not bother Wakefield. By his time, liberalism had for the most part settled its scores with territorial expansion through the Lockean doctrine of occupation, which, as we have seen in the previous chapters, relied on arguments about the level of socioeconomic development for invalidating indigenous claims to land.[154] Similarly, nineteenth-century British liberals furthered the eighteenth-century ideal of a commercial empire and, by the middle of the century, could boast "the vision a global order based on free trade, peace, and progress in civilisation" as "Britain's contribution to the international history."[155] Wakefield's deft utilization of political economy contributed to the transvaluation of empire from being the antithesis of free trade (as Hume, Smith, and Bentham, among others, had variously held) into its enabling politico-legal foundation. He joined in the Enlightenment critique of the "old colonial system" only to enlist its theoretical resources in the cause of building a "new colonial system." With the ideological boundaries of property and trade within the empire settled along broadly liberal lines, Wakefield tackled the legal status of labor needed to transform the appropriated land and resources into commodities for the world market. Although his blueprint of imperial labor allocation disappointed in practice, his categorical embrace of free wage labor as the only labor regime compatible with capitalist civilization completed the ideological tripod on which the liberal image of capitalism stood. Britain's settler empire provided the stage on which Wakefield reconciled legal freedom and economic dependence and disavowed the illiberality of the primitive accumulation that engendered both. With this third ideological piece in place, the British Empire could consummate its liberal essence and become what it had always been. An empire of private property, free trade, and free labor. An empire of liberty.

Conclusion

Bringing the Economy Back In

The historical relationship between liberalism and capitalism has been one of uneasy union, fraught with ideological tensions and dependent on theoretical balancing acts for its continuation. This study has demarcated a specific strand of these tensions by foregrounding primitive accumulation and, especially, its colonial manifestations.[1] Primitive accumulation constituted the background conditions of capitalism as a social order and created the social forms around which liberal conceptions of capitalism developed. As merchants, planters, companies, and colonial states pressed ever expanding swathes of land and labor into the service of capital accumulation, classical political economists in Europe theorized the emergent global economic order as the advent of private property, free trade, and free labor. On the other hand, primitive accumulation also introduced a deep rift into liberal conceptions of capitalism by virtue of the extra-economic and at times extralegal force that drove the transformation and articulation (or what Marx called "subsumption") of production around the globe. Many of the same political economists also recognized the genetic ties that private property, market exchange, and free labor shared with their ugly cousins, namely, land seizures, commercial plunder, and slavery, which equally belonged to the family of capitalism. Not everyone who observed these ties disavowed them (recall Adam Smith's ambivalence), but those who did, like Locke, Burke, and Wakefield, proved critical in crafting a liberal image for the empire and its capitalist economy. In their writings we therefore find not simply the expression but, more importantly, the negotiation of the constitutive and contradictory relationship between liberalism, capitalism, and empire.

As an analytic framework, colonial capitalism generates systematic and contestable answers to two key questions in the study of liberalism and empire. The first question concerns the hierarchical evaluation of social difference in metropolitan thought. In her review of Domenico Losurdo's "counter-history" of liberalism, Jennifer Pitts has described liberalism as a "set of characteristic dispositions [that have] always been articulated in universal terms" yet have always already been inflected by "various circumstances."[2] Implied in this formulation is the task of constructing an account of how historical circumstances shaped and colored the "universal ambitions" of liberalism across specific imperial sites. Put more precisely, the problem is why liberal politics of universalism revolved around certain social practices and not others. The second question is one of historical change. In concluding her book *Alibis of Empire*, Karuna Mantena has called for a more sustained analysis of the link "between historical and conceptual transformation, between the external and internal sources of intellectual change."[3] Here the relevant task is to explain how particular signifiers of colonial difference and their normative valence varied over historical periods. The lens of colonial capitalism addresses both these questions—that is, the hierarchical evaluation of social difference and the changing structure of this hierarchy over time—by directing metropolitan thinkers' assessment of European and non-European practices to socioeconomic structures and transformations within the empire. Without abandoning attention to semantic contexts, this move entails stepping beyond these contexts and locating the ideas under study simultaneously at the institutional-ideological level of analysis. While this approach does not lay exclusive claim to theorizing the imperial context, it connects the socio-historical and the ideational planes of analysis in illuminating ways.

We can briefly explicate this point with regard to liberalism's internal variegation, more specifically, the cross-pollination of liberal ideas with diverse, even discordant, social and political philosophies. The scholarship on liberalism and empire has produced a detailed inventory of such cross-pollinations that have resulted from attempts to reconcile liberal universals with colonial particularisms. These include, among others, a stadial theory of human development that included yet infantilized the colonized,[4] a brand of cosmopolitan pluralism that tempered imperial arrogance and refused to judge non-Europeans,[5] and a fatalistic view of the colonized as being incapable of progress and therefore subject to the protective rather than the civilizing mission of the empire.[6] The prism of colonial capitalism can bring into view some of the uneven material dynamics that connect these different ideological expressions. Specifically, the extent to which colonial primitive accumulation *assimilated* (destroyed and reconstructed) or *articulated* (subordinated and managed) existing relations of production in the colonies serves as a useful heuristic. Settler capitalism in British "neo-Europes," which invariably entailed the extirpation or drastic marginalization of indigenous populations (as in America and Australasia), lent plausibility to the triumphalist narratives of universal progress qua the expansion of the market, civil society, life, liberty, and property—the cherished liberal patrimony of Anglophone imperialism.[7] By contrast, confronted by the demographic resilience, robust social structures, and the risk of social upheaval attendant on drastic capitalist transformation (as in Asia and Africa), colonizers opted for intensifying, leveraging, and occasionally inventing local structures of authority and exploitation for extracting remittable surplus, becoming convinced in the process that these "traditional" ways of life were hopelessly ingrained in the social code of the natives.[8] The deracination of Native Americans who refused to be "Red Lockeans" and the genocidal elimination of Australian aborigines— which prompted Herman Merivale to lament, "desolation goes before us"— were emplotted as the inexorable, if occasionally tragic, march of civilization.[9] By contrast, the failure of the Permanent Settlement of Bengal to create a class of capitalist farmers and improving yeomen was attributed to the intractable singularity of the Indian society, their village communities, their "castes of mind."[10] Put summarily, territorial imperialism and commercial imperialism each bred its own strain of liberal justification.[11] The uneven and heterogeneous development of global capitalism in imperial networks can thus provide a matrix for mapping the variegated dilemmas of liberalism and their entwinement with other social philosophies in specific socioeconomic contexts.

The perspective of colonial capitalism further complicates the interplay of liberal universals and colonial difference by disclosing that the civilizational hierarchies of the British imperial ideology, which contemporary commentators decode in terms of racial and cultural difference between the colonizer and the colonized, actually cut across this divide. As I argued in chapters 3 and 4, British settlers, planters, and company agents occupied a contradictory position in the British imagined community. On the one hand, they were an integral and indispensable part of the imperial polity as British subjects under a "coherent imperial constitution" and the economic pioneers of the empire who forged the networks through which British capital could expand, penetrate, and transform the colonies.[12] On the other hand, the same colonial entrepreneurs were variously derided by metropolitan thinkers as unruly, despotic, and barbaric. The ambiguous and shifting civilizational status of British colonial entrepreneurs complicates the assumption that discourses of civilization and savagery, stadial theories of progress, and ideologies of colonial difference exclusively targeted the colonizers' non-European others. Relying on race and culture as the primary operators of colonial difference offers little traction in attempts to explain, for instance, why the enclosing and improving settler who was hailed as the agent of civilization well into the eighteenth century was condemned as savage, uncivilized, and in need of some sort of imperial tutelage in the early nineteenth. Shifting dynamics of colonial capitalism in the British imperial formation can offer some answers to this and similar puzzles by embedding these specific instances of racialization in the relations of production, labor regimes, and social struggles.

In this respect, this line of inquiry extends Patrick Wolfe's fundamental insight about the inflection of racial dynamics in colonial settings by context-specific yet structural conditions of capital accumulation. As Wolfe remarks with respect to American settler capitalism, the demand for African labor and Native American land led to miscegenation laws that interpreted the racist "one-drop rule" to diametrically opposite effects for Africans and Native Americans. One drop of non-Native blood irreversibly compromised one's indigeneity and vitiated her claim to land, while one drop of African blood perpetually stamped one as black and bound her to labor.[13] The specific types of racial construction that received juridico-political sanction were the ones that made possible the slave-plantation complex—the combination of black labor and native land under the direction of white capital—that formed the backbone of the New World economy. Although, as Cedric Robinson reminds us, racialization neither began with nor was exclusive to the history of capitalism, examining imperial ideologies through the lens of racialization without a matching attention to the political economy of empire might obscure as much as it reveals.[14]

Beyond a reappraisal of liberal thought in the colonial-capitalist fold, the foregoing analysis is also an invitation to expand the boundaries of political theory by incorporating a range of questions that are conventionally relegated to political economy and social theory. As I briefly mentioned in chapter 1, a growing number of political theorists have reclaimed the notion of primitive accumulation from Marxian analysis in order to bridge political philosophy and social theory. One can point to a number of earlier, if overlooked, precedents for highlighting the political theoretical work that primitive accumulation can perform.[15] For instance, Partha Chatterjee frames primitive accumulation as the process that, by destroying the noncapitalist community, brings into existence the social constructs that liberal political theory treats as axiomatic: the individual with subjective rights, the totalizing politico-legal framework of the nation-state, and the market-cum-civil society as the domain of voluntary association.[16] In a similar vein, Hannah Arendt posited primitive accumulation, which she rephrased as "expropriation," at the threshold of modernity, the birth of the social, the rise of the society of laborers, and world alienation.[17] Finally, Max Weber resorted to the logic of primitive accumulation in explaining how the modern state acquired its signature feature, namely, the sovereign monopoly of legitimate violence.[18] What these formulations variously articulate is a constitutive link and even a structural analogy between, on the one hand, capitalism as an institutionalized system of exploitation of social labor and ecology and, on the other, the specific modality of political power encased in the modern state, both in its imperial and national variants.[19] There remains much work to be done in conceptualizing this constitutive link it in its historical and contemporary instantiations, which would entail a more sustained engagement with questions of exploitation, expropriation, and social reproduction.[20]

Although there are a myriad ways of bringing capitalism within the ambit of political theory, I believe a particularly fruitful avenue is to reconceptualize primitive accumulation through the nomenclature of "constituent power" that has been conceived and developed in the field of democratic theory.[21] The theoretical problem of founding a political order, the legitimacy of which necessarily originates outside the endogenous legal framework that it institutes, can apply with equal force to the origins of capitalism as a historically determinate social formation.[22] What is brought into existence in this case is not a body politic but a specific system of production and social reproduction, which nonetheless shares with the former a jagged process of founding punctuated by (to borrow Jason Frank's term) "constituent moments."[23] The contexts of colonial capitalism surveyed in this book, ranging from the English enclosures and the slave-plantation complex to the deindustrialization of India and settler colonialism in the Pacific, can be construed as locally sited yet globally networked constituent moments of global capitalism. These instances of subsumption of land and labor under capital gave rise to profound questions of legitimacy that are analogous to those explored by theories of political founding. This is because the extra-economic and extralegal force of primitive accumulation could not be justified with reference to a fully constituted capitalist economy with a liberal juridical framework precisely because primitive accumulation created the very conditions of a capitalist economy and did so precisely by violating liberal precepts.

Constituent moments of capitalism were therefore moments of ideological difficulty for metropolitan thought and especially liberalism, which invited justifications from legitimacy rather than legality. Illuminating in this vein, for instance, was Burke's insistence on having Warren Hastings, whom he called the "great criminal [who] has the law in his hands," tried at the bar of "natural, immutable and substantial justice" rather than by the British common law.[24] Although Burke's insistence has been interpreted as a strategic attempt to expedite the impeachment proceedings, it can also be construed as a sign of his conviction that the social upheavals in India overflowed the boundaries of the British legal framework. The political violence that cleft through the Indian economy and social institutions was of an order-founding and order-destroying magnitude— or what Carl Schmitt labeled *nomos* and *anadasmoi*.[25] It could therefore be captured and adjudicated only by the political power of the Parliament that would wield it in the name of transcendental and substantive principles, as opposed to positive or customary legal precepts. Likewise, when the "normal" conditions of capitalist reproduction threatened to implode in the colonies, Wakefield did not hesitate to call for the exercise of imperial executive fiat in the form of martial law—that is, a state of exception—for reinstating the specific juridico-political order in which production and exchange could conform to the dictates of capitalist civilization.[26] Locke's theoretical rendering of the private and unilateral land appropriation in America was undergirded in the first and last instances by a theological authority that commanded men to labor and subdue the earth for the benefit of mankind. In all three cases we find the denial (or the presumed absence) of a shared legal framework with the colonized redirecting the colonizers to their own substantive moral values for explaining colonial violence, and referring colonial conquest, dispossession, and bondage back to a purportedly universal normative order. At constituent moments of global capitalism, one finds the ideologues of the new order, to use Locke's famous phrase, appealing to heaven.[27]

In conclusion, situating the history of Western political thought in the history of European colonial empires ought to involve more than simply expanding the reach of familiar questions to new and unfamiliar contexts. Colonial empires were certainly structures of political domination and subordination, and they shaped metropolitan understandings of freedom, consent, legitimacy, inclusion, and pluralism. But they were more than political structures. They were also economic systems of expropriation and exploitation, of commandeering resources and managing labor, of organizing production and trade, of creating wealth, accumulating capital, and raising revenue. It was these agendas and priorities, rather than a principled commitment to globalizing liberal values and institutions, that reshaped the world. Liberalism was coeval with not just colonial empires but also with colonial capitalism, and mapping its entwinement with empire requires an account of empire's socioeconomic materiality.

This is not just a matter of scholastic rectitude. Historical continuities between the world of formal empires and our putative postcolonial present are most salient at the level of institutional-ideological structures that have evolved in tandem with the systemic shifts in the global capitalist economy, whether one conceives of these shifts in terms of hegemonic cycles or regulatory regimes.[28] The so-called crisis of liberalism in Europe and the United States—evidenced in Trump presidency, Brexit, the rise of Front National, and other forms of "illiberal democracy" elsewhere—cannot be thought independent of the structural as well as ideological crisis of neoliberalism as a regime of accumulation. Contemporary worries that the United States will abandon its hegemonic role in maintaining the liberal global order, compounded by the alarm over the growing popularity of the "Beijing Consensus" in Asia and Africa, belong to the increasingly fragile imagination of capitalism as being an essentially liberal and cosmopolitan economic system.[29] This liberal imagination is battered by global "expulsions" that traverse zones of austerity in Europe and North America, authoritarian capitalism in China, and offshore land acquisitions for commercial agriculture in Africa, which connect capital accumulation to new forms of expropriation and exploitation.[30] As this book attempts to show, political theory has much to contribute to the conceptualization, framing, and analysis of these issues that stamp our "colonial present." To do so in a grounded manner, however, requires a closer dialogue with political economy, social theory, and critical geography.

NOTES

Introduction

1. Adam Smith, *An Inquiry into the Nature and Causes of the Wealth of Nations*, ed. R. H. Campbell and A. S. Skinner, vol. 2 of the: Glasgow Edition of the Works and Correspondence of Adam Smith (Indianapolis, IN: Liberty Fund, 1981), 65 (hereafter cited as *Wealth of Nations*).
2. For an appraisal of this ambivalence, see Sankar Muthu, "Adam Smith's Critique of International Trading Companies: Theorizing Globalization in the Age of Enlightenment," *Political Theory* 36 (2008): 185–212; Emma Rothschild, "Adam Smith in the British Empire," in *Empire and Modern Political Thought*, ed. Sankar Muthu (Cambridge: Cambridge University Press, 2012), 184–98.
3. For a representative collection of essays, see Sankar Muthu, ed., *Empire and Modern Political Thought* (Cambridge, MA: Cambridge University Press, 2012).
4. James Tully, *Public Philosophy in a New Key*, vol. 2, *Imperialism and Civic Freedom* (Cambridge: Cambridge University Press, 2008), 200.
5. Paul Gilroy, "Multiculturalism and Postcolonial Theory," in *The Oxford Handbook of Political Theory*, ed. John Dryzek and Bonnie Honig (Oxford: Oxford University Press, 2006), 657.
6. James Tully, "Rediscovering America: The Two Treatises and Aboriginal Rights," in *An Approach to Political Philosophy: John Locke in Contexts* (Cambridge: Cambridge University Press, 1993), 137–76; Barbara Arneil, *John Locke and America: The Defence of English Colonialism* (Oxford: Clarendon, 1995); Uday Mehta, *Liberalism and Empire: A Study in Nineteenth-Century British Liberal Thought* (Chicago: University of Chicago Press, 1999); Bhikhu Parekh, "Liberalism and Colonialism: A Critique of Locke and Mill," in *The Decolonization of Imagination: Culture, Knowledge and Power*, ed. Jan Nederveen Peterse and Bhikhu Parekh (London: Zed, 1995), 81–98; Lynn Zastoupil, *John Stuart Mill and India* (Stanford, CA: Stanford University Press, 1994).
7. For an overview, see Duncan Bell, "The Dream Machine: On Liberalism and Empire," in *Reordering the World: Essays on Liberalism and Empire* (Princeton, NJ: Princeton University Press, 2016), 19–61.
8. For a critical diagnosis, see Andrew Sartori, "British Empire and Its Liberal Mission," *Journal of Modern History* 78 (2006): 623–42.
9. The most famous and controversial have been Niall Ferguson *Empire: The Rise and the Demise of the British World Order and the Lessons for Global Power* (New York: Basic Books, 2003); Ferguson, *Colossus: The Price of America's Empire* (New York: Penguin Press, 2004).
10. This orientation has a long lineage that extends at least back to the dependency theory, if not to earlier studies on capitalism and slavery. I am indebted to Jairus Banaji's sophisticated reconstruction of this theoretical perspective, above all, in his *Theory as History: Essays on Modes of Production and Exploitation* (Leiden: Brill, 2010) and, more recently, in "Merchant

Capitalism, Peasant Households, and Industrial Accumulation: Integration of a Model," *Journal of Agrarian Change* 16 (2016): 410–31.

11. Karl Marx, *Capital*, vol. 1, *Critique of Political Economy* (London: Penguin, 1976).

12. David Armitage, *The Ideological Origins of the British Empire* (Cambridge: Cambridge University Press, 2000), 173.

13. For a recent contextualist assessment of the uses and misuses of the term "liberalism," see Duncan Bell, "What Is Liberalism?," *Political Theory* 42, no. 6 (2014): 682–715.

14. Andrew Sartori, "From Statecraft to Social Science in Early-Modern English Political Economy," *Critical Historical Studies* 3 (2016): 181–214.

15. See, most recently, David Armitage, "John Locke: Theorist of Empire?," in *Foundations of Modern International Thought* (Cambridge: Cambridge University Press, 2013), 114–34.

16. Richard Bourke, *Empire and Revolution: The Political Life of Edmund Burke* (Princeton, NJ: Princeton University Press, 2015); Daniel O'Neill, *Edmund Burke and the Conservative Logic of Empire* (Oakland: University of California Press, 2016).

17. Duncan Bell, "John Stuart Mill on Colonies," *Political Theory* 38 (2010): 34–64; Tony Ballantyne, "The Theory and Practice of Empire-Building: Edward Gibbon Wakefield and 'Systematic Colonization,'" in *The Routledge History of Western Empires*, ed. Robert Aldrich and Kirsten McKenzie (London: Routledge, 2014), 89–101.

18. Karuna Mantena, *Alibis of Empire: Henry Maine and the Ends of Liberal Imperialism* (Princeton, NJ: Princeton University Press, 2010).

19. Charles Maier, *Among Empires: American Ascendancy and Its Predecessors* (Cambridge, MA: Harvard University Press, 2006), 55.

20. Ferguson, *Empire*; Michael Ignatieff, *Empire Lite: Nation-Building in Bosnia, Kosovo, and Afghanistan* (Toronto: Penguin, 2003).

21. Douglass C. North and Barry Weingast, "Constitutions and Commitment: The Evolution of Institutions Governing Public Choice in Seventeenth-Century England," *Journal of Economic History* 49 (1989): 803–32; Daron Acemoglu and James Robinson, *Why Nations Fail: The Origins of Power, Prosperity, and Poverty* (New York: Crown Business, 2012).

22. I dwell on this question at length in Onur Ulas Ince, "Bringing the Economy Back In: Hannah Arendt, Karl Marx, and the Politics of Capitalism," *Journal of Politics* 78 (2016): 411–26.

23. Frederick Cooper and Ann Laura Stoler, "Between Metropole and Colony: Rethinking a Research Agenda," in *Tensions of Empire: Colonial Cultures in a Bourgeois World*, ed. Frederick Cooper and Ann Laura Stoler (Berkeley: University of California Press, 1997), 1–56. On political economy as a species of political reflection, see Istvan Hont, introduction to *The Jealousy of Trade: International Competition and the Nation-State in Historical Perspective* (Cambridge, MA: Belknap Press of Harvard University Press, 2005).

Chapter 1

1. Onur Ulas Ince, "Primitive Accumulation, New Enclosures, and Global Land Grabs: A Theoretical Intervention," *Rural Sociology* 79 (2014): 104–31; and Ince, "Bringing the Economy Back In," 411–26.

2. Bell, "Dream Machine," 19.

3. For two excellent surveys of the literature on liberalism and empire and of the broader field of political theory of imperialism to which it belongs, see Jennifer Pitts, "Theories of Empire and Imperialism," *Annual Review of Political Science* 13 (2010): 211–35; and Bell, "Dream Machine."

4. "Postcolonial studies" is now an immense and highly heterogeneous field. For a useful overview of the formative debates in the field, see Ania Loomba, *Colonialism/Postcolonialism: The New Critical Idiom* (London: Routledge, 2005); and Ania Loomba, Suvir Kaul, Matti Bunzi, and Antoinette Burton, eds., *Postcolonial Studies and Beyond* (Durham, NC: Duke University Press, 2005). In this book I have above all benefited from an engagement with Dipesh Chakrabarty, *Provincializing Europe: Postcolonial Thought and Historical Difference* (Princeton, NJ: Princeton University Press, 2000); Partha Chatterjee, *The Nation and Its Fragments: Colonial and Postcolonial Histories* (Princeton, NJ: Princeton University Press, 1993); and Chatterjee, *The Black Hole of Empire: History of a Global Practice of Power*

(Princeton, NJ: Princeton University Press, 2012). A germinal collection of essays written in the spirit of the new imperial history is Kathleen Wilson, ed., *A New Imperial History: Culture, Identity and Modernity in Britain and the Empire, 1660–1840* (Cambridge: Cambridge University Press, 2004). For a succinct survey of the dominant trends in twentieth-century imperial historiography, see Richard Drayton, "Where Does the World Historian Write From? Objectivity, Moral Conscience, and the Past and Present of Imperialism," *Journal of Contemporary History* 46 (2011): 671–85.

5. Ferguson, *Colossus*; and Ferguson, *Empire*. See also Ignatieff, *Empire Lite*.

6. Armitage, "International Turn," 24.

7. Classic works in this vein are V. I. Lenin, *Imperialism: The Highest Stage of Capitalism* (New York: International, 1997); Rosa Luxemburg, *The Accumulation of Capital* (London: Routledge, 2003); John A. Hobson, *Imperialism: A Study* (Cambridge: Cambridge University Press, 2011); and Rudolf Hilferding, *Finance Capital: A Study of the Latest Phase of Capitalist Development* (London: Routledge, 1981).

8. For a lucid exposition on the spell of the linguistic turn in the social sciences and humanities, see Peter E. Gordon, "Contextualism and Criticism in the History of Ideas," in *Rethinking Modern European Intellectual History*, ed. Darrin McMahon and Samuel Moyn (Oxford: Oxford University Press, 2014), 32–55.

9. Jennifer Pitts, *A Turn to Empire: The Rise of Liberal Imperialism in Britain and France* (Princeton, NJ: Princeton University Press, 2005), 6; Mantena, *Alibis of Empire*, 8–9; Catherine Hall, *Civilising Subjects: Colony and Metropole in the English Imagination, 1830–1867* (Chicago: University of Chicago Press, 2002), 9–10.

10. Uday Mehta's work on liberalism and empire offers the most unequivocal condemnation of liberalism's complicity with imperialism, sharing in the postcolonial critique of the Enlightenment as a whole. Jennifer Pitts and Sankar Muthu have done much to challenge this catholic condemnation by reconstructing the anti-imperial streak in European Enlightenment thought, which, they argue, flared up for a resplendent if brief moment in the late eighteenth century. See Mehta, *Liberalism and Empire*; Uday Mehta, "Liberal Strategies of Exclusion," *Politics and Society* 18 (1990): 427–54. Sankar Muthu, *Enlightenment against Empire* (Princeton, NJ: Princeton University Press, 2003); Pitts, *Turn to Empire*.

11. Nicholas B. Dirks, introduction to *Colonialism and Culture*, ed. Nicholas Dirks (Ann Arbor: University of Michigan Press, 1992), 3. Most early twentieth-century Marxist analysis mentioned here evinced some sort of reductive teleology, notwithstanding its particular and enduring insights. For a twentieth-century reiteration, see Bill Warren, *Imperialism: The Pioneer of Capitalism* (London: Verso, 1980).

12. Sartori, "British Empire," 637. Sartori's essay provides what is in my opinion the most astute critique of the culturalism that is prevalent in the study of liberalism and empire. For an alternative materialist approach, see Andrew Sartori, *Liberalism in Empire: An Alternative History* (Berkeley: University of California Press, 2014). For a critical treatment of the kindred culturalist disposition in postcolonial studies, see Frederick Cooper, "Postcolonial Studies and the Study of History," in Loomba et al., *Postcolonial Studies and Beyond*, 401–22; and Ilan Kapoor, *The Postcolonial Politics of Development* (London: Routledge, 2008).

13. Drayton, "Where Does the World," 680.

14. Frederick Cooper, *Colonialism in Question: Theory, Knowledge, History* (Berkeley: University of California Press, 2005), 96.

15. The liberality of empire is further evidenced by the Anglo-American capacity to lament the violence that inevitably attends all empires. The bad conscience about the violent past of the empire reconfirms that the British imperialists were liberal at heart. For an exceptionally insightful critique of these discursive strategies, see Jeanne Morefield, "Empire, Tragedy, and the Liberal State in the Writings of Niall Ferguson and Michael Ignatieff," *Theory and Event* 11, no. 3 (2008), doi. 10.1353/tae.0.0014; and Jeanne Morefield, *Empires without Imperialism: Anglo-American Decline and the Politics of Deflection* (Oxford: Oxford University Press, 2014).

16. Pitt, "Theories of Empire," 220.

17. Duncan Bell, "Desolation Goes before Us," *Journal of British Studies*, 54, no. 4 (2015): 987–93, 989–90.

18. For a useful summary and nuanced vindication of the "social history of political thought," see Geoff Kennedy, "Capitalism, Contextualisation, and *The Political Theory of Possessive Individualism*," *Intellectual History and Political Thought* 1, no. 1 (2012): 228–51.

19. See especially Quentin Skinner, "Meaning and Understanding in the History of Ideas," *History and Theory* 8, no. 1 (1969): 3–53; Quentin Skinner, *Liberty before Liberalism* (Cambridge: Cambridge University Press, 1998); J. G. A. Pocock, *Politics, Language, and Time: Essays on Political Thought and History* (New York: Atheneum, 1971). The controversy is more expansive than the Macpherson-Skinner-Pocock exchange. Other interlocutors include social historians of political thought who proceed by embedding political ideas in contexts formed by property relations (Neal Wood, Ellen Meiksins Wood, and David MacNally), intellectual historians and philosophers who posit a liberal tradition originating in John Locke (Isaac Kramnick, Michael Zuckert, and Jeremy Waldron), and their historical contextualist detractors (John Dunn, James Tully, and Peter Laslett).

20. This description is necessarily brief and schematic. See the essays in James Tully, ed., *Meaning and Context: Quentin Skinner and His Critics* (Princeton, NJ: Princeton University Press, 1988); Richard Whatmore, *What Is Intellectual History?* (Cambridge: Polity, 2015), esp. 45–59; McMahon and Moyn, *Rethinking Modern*.

21. Moyn, "Imaginary Intellectual History," in McMahon and Moyn, *Rethinking Modern*, 115. For a context-sensitive model of long-range intellectual history, see David Armitage, "What's the Big Idea: Intellectual History and the Longue Durée," *History of European Ideas* 38, no. 4 (2012): 493–507.

22. Istvan Hont, *Politics in Commercial Society: Jean-Jacques Rousseau and Adam Smith* (Cambridge, MA: Harvard University Press, 2015), 6.

23. On the "strategy of containment," see Gordon, "Contextualism and Criticism," 34–37.

24. Such transhistorical interpretive moves fall prey to one or more of Skinner's famous mythologies of doctrine, coherence, and prolepsis. Skinner, "Meaning and Understanding." For a recent reiteration, see Bell, "What Is Liberalism?," 682–715.

25. Critical to linguistic contextualism is the Wittgensteinian notion of "language games" with their "own vocabulary, rules, preconditions and implications, tone and style." J. G. A. Pocock, "The Concept of a Language and the *Métier d'Historien*: Some Considerations on Practice," in *The Languages of Political Theory in Early-Modern Europe*, ed. Anthony Pagden (Cambridge: Cambridge University Press, 1990), 21.

26. On the mutations and complementarity of heterogeneous labor regimes in colonial circuits of capital, see Hilary Beckles, "The Concept of White Slavery in the English Caribbean during the Early Seventeenth Century," in *Early Modern Conceptions of Property*, ed. John Brewer and Susan Staves (New York: Routledge, 1995), 572–84; and Hilary Beckles, "The Hub of Empire: The Caribbean and Britain in the Seventeenth Century," in *The Oxford History of the British Empire*, vol. 1, *The Origins of Empire*, ed. Nicholas Canny (Oxford: Oxford University Press, 1998), 218–40.

27. On this point, I follow Steven Pincus, Robert Travers, and Sophus Reinert, who have recently called into question the influential interpretation, advanced most notably by J. G. A. Pocock, that early modern British political discourse was dominated by neo-republican or civic humanist language. J. G. A. Pocock, *The Machiavellian Moment: Florentine Political Thought and the Atlantic Republican Tradition* (Princeton, NJ: Princeton University Press, 1975); Steven Pincus, *1688: The First Modern Revolution* (New Haven, CT: Yale University Press, 2009); Robert Travers, *Ideology and Empire in Eighteenth-Century India: The British in Bengal* (New York: Cambridge University Press, 2007); Sophus Reinert, "The Empire of Emulation: A Quantitative Analysis of Economic Translations in the European World, 1500–1849," in *The Political Economy of Empire in the Early-Modern World*, ed. Sophus Reinert and Pernille Røge (New York: Palgrave MacMillan, 2013), 105–30.

28. I develop this argument in detail in "Primitive Accumulation" and in "Bringing the Economy."

29. Karl Marx, *Capital*, 1:873–76. Since Marx's elaboration, the usefulness of the term for a theory of capitalism has been hotly contested. Those who understand the term to mean a preliminary stockpiling of material resources, for example, Kenneth Pomeranz, call for abandoning the concept altogether, whereas others who emphasize the social-relational aspect of primitive accumulation, David Harvey and Saskia Sassen notable among them, have reworked the concept to

restore its contemporary relevance. Kenneth Pomeranz, *The Great Divergence: Europe, China, and the Making of the Modern World Economy* (Princeton, NJ: Princeton University Press, 2000); David Harvey, *The New Imperialism* (New York: Oxford University Press, 2003); Saskia Sassen, *Expulsions: Brutality and Complexity in the Global Economy* (Cambridge, MA: Harvard University Press, 2014). The recent spurt of scholarly interest in primitive accumulation has been dizzying. For an original take on primitive accumulation, see Massimo De Angelis, "Separating the Doing and the Deed: Capital and the Continuous Character of Enclosures," *Historical Materialism* 12 (2004): 57–87. A good overview of the extant literature can be found in Derek Hall, "Primitive Accumulation, Accumulation by Dispossession and Global Land Grab," *Third World Quarterly* 34, no. 9 (2013): 1582–1604. Scholars in the field of political theory have recently turned to primitive accumulation to recast old questions in a new light or to build bridges between political philosophy and social theory. See Glen Coulthard, *Red Skin, White Masks: Rejecting the Colonial Politics of Recognition* (Minneapolis: University of Minnesota Press, 2014); Robert Nichols, "Disaggregating Primitive Accumulation," *Radical Philosophy* 194 (2015): 18–28; Nikhil Singh, "On Race, Violence, and So-Called Primitive Accumulation," *Social Text* 34, no. 3 (2016): 27–50.

30. Marx, *Capital*, 1:915.

31. The notion of colonial capitalism here at bottom builds on than Sanjay Subrahmanyam's definition of "colonial empire" as "a particular kind of empire that is fundamentally characterized by the exploitative relations between an imperial core and a subject periphery." Yet it is also conceptually more capacious inasmuch as it extends beyond mere surplus transfer and encompasses coercive socioeconomic transformations in the colonies. The social-transformative as opposed to merely economic-extractive intension of colonial capitalism also distinguishes my analysis from Lisa Lowe's recent investigation of liberalism and empire, which collapses the material link between the two to the "colonial profits" that helped to build the European bourgeoisies and their liberal categories of development. In a sense, this accounting perspective simply inverts earlier claims that imperialism and colonialism were "unprofitable" and therefore "peripheral" to the development of capitalism in Europe. Sanjay Subrahmanyam, "Imperial and Colonial Encounters: Some Comparative Reflections," in *Lessons of Empire: Imperial Histories and American Power*, ed. Craig Calhoun, Frederick Cooper, and Kevin Moore (New York: New Press, 2006), 220; Lisa Lowe, *Intimacies of Four Continents* (Durham, NC: Duke University Press, 2015); Lance E. Davis and Robert A. Huttenback, *Mammon and the Pursuit of Empire: The Political Economy of British Imperialism* (Cambridge: Cambridge University Press, 1986); Patrick O'Brien, "European Economic Development: The Contribution of the Periphery," *Economic History Review*, 2nd ser., 35 (1982): 1–18. For a considered treatment of the institutional frame of analysis in the history of capitalist globalization, including the national, the imperial, and the global, see Cooper, *Colonialism in Question*, esp. 91–112.

32. Robin Blackburn, *The Making of the New World Slavery* (London: Verso, 1997), 567. For a similar analysis centered on the Atlantic, see Joseph Inikori, "Africa and the Globalization Process: Western Africa, 1450–1850," *Journal of Global History* 2, no. 1 (2007): 63–86. Recently, historians have challenged insular Atlantic histories, calling attention to interoceanic connections between the Atlantic and the Indian systems. See, for instance, Lauren Benton, "The British Atlantic in the Global Context," in *The British Atlantic World, 1500–1800*, ed. David Armitage and Michael Braddick (New York: Palgrave MacMillan, 2009), 271–89; H. V. Bowen, Elizabeth Mancke, and John Reid, eds., *Britain's Oceanic Empire: Atlantic and Indian Ocean Worlds, c. 1550–1850* (Cambridge: Cambridge University Press, 2015).

33. Jairus Banaji, "Islam, the Mediterranean, and the Rise of Capitalism," *Historical Materialism* 15 (2007): 47–74. On the European invention of armed trading and its intrusion into the relatively free and pacific commercial world of the Indian Ocean, see K. N. Chaudhuri, *Trade and Civilisation in the Indian Ocean: An Economic History from the Rise of Islam to 1750* (Cambridge: Cambridge University Press, 1985).

34. See, Patrick Wolfe, "Settler Colonialism and the Elimination of the Native," *Journal of Genocide Research* 8, no. 4 (2006): 387–404; Lorenzo Veracini, *Settler Colonialism: A Theoretical Overview* (Basingstoke, UK: Palgrave MacMillan, 2010); David Lloyd and Patrick Wolfe, "Settler Colonial Logics and the Neoliberal Regime," *Settler Colonial Studies* 6, no. 2

(2016): 109–18; Mahmood Mamdani, "Settler Colonialism: Then and Now," *Critical Inquiry* 41 (2015): 596–614; Nicholas Brown, "The Logic of Settler Accumulation in a Landscape of Perpetual Vanishing," *Settler Colonial Studies* 4, no. 1 (2014): 1–26.

35. For a trenchant criticism of Beckert's omission of Marxian antecedents, especially as furthered by pioneering theorists of capitalism and slavery such as Eric Williams, C. L. R. James, and Cedric Robinson, see Peter J. Hudson, "The Racist Dawn of Capitalism: Unearthing the Economy of Bondage," *Boston Review*, March 14, 2016, accessed May 7, 2016, http://bostonreview.net/books-ideas/peter-james-hudson-slavery-capitalism.

36. Sven Beckert, *Empire of Cotton: A New History of Global Capitalism* (London: Penguin, 2015), 36–37.

37. Such extra-economic coercion is, in Chakrabarty's formulation, "both originary/foundational (that is, historic) as well as pandemic and quotidian," which is also to suggest that primitive accumulation is not a concluded historical stage but has an inherent and continuous character as a capitalist strategy of reproduction, expansion, and crisis management. Chakrabarty, *Provincializing Europe*, 44. For a more detailed elaboration, see Ince, "Primitive Accumulation"; De Angelis, "Separating the Doing," 57–87.

38. Nancy Fraser, "Behind Marx's Hidden Abode," *New Left Review* 86 (2014): 66. On capitalism and ecology, see Jason Moore, *Capitalism in the Web of Life: Ecology and the Accumulation of Capital* (London: Verso, 2015). On modes of subjectification under capitalism, see Jason Read, *The Micro-Politics of Capital: Marx and the History of the Present* (Albany: State University of New York Press, 2003). On capital as political power, see Jonathan Nitzan and Shimshon Bichler, *Capital as Power: A Study of Order and Creorder* (New York: Routledge, 2009).

39. Milton Friedman, *Capitalism and Freedom* (Chicago: University of Chicago Press, 1962); Adam Smith, *Wealth of Nations*, 2:52.

40. Marx, *Capital*, 1:915.

41. Luxemburg, *Accumulation of Capital*, 351.

42. Fraser, "Behind Marx's Hidden Abode," 60, 64. For the capacious understanding of primitive accumulation as a social as opposed to simply an economic category, see Nichols, "Disaggregating Primitive Accumulation"; and Kalyan Sanyal, *Rethinking Capitalist Development: Primitive Accumulation, Governmentality and Post-Colonial Capitalism* (New Delhi: Routledge, 2007). Partha Chatterjee similarly defines primitive accumulation as "nothing else but the destruction of the precapitalist community, which, in various forms, had regulated the social unit of laborers with their means of production." Chatterjee, *Nation and Its Fragments*, 235.

43. For instance, Jason Read conjectures that for Marx, the "violent lawmaking power of primitive accumulation is merely privatized and brought indoors into the factory." Read, *Micro-Politics of Capital*, 28–29.

44. Fraser, "Behind Marx's Hidden Abode," 60, 64.

45. Werner Bonefeld, "Primitive Accumulation and Capitalist Accumulation," *Science and Society* 75, no. 3 (2011): 379–99, 396. For an original discussion of the domination of abstract labor in capitalism as a social formation, see Moishe Postone, *Time, Labor, and Social Domination: A Reinterpretation of Marx's Critical Theory* (Cambridge: Cambridge University Press, 1993).

46. The presumption of linearity underlies the troubled modernization theories that conceive of capitalist "transition" as the replication of the Euro-American economic experience.

47. On the fiscal-military state, see John Brewer, *The Sinews of Power: War, Money and the English State, 1688–1783* (New York: Alfred A. Knopf, 1989). On its historically developmentalist role, see Ha-Joon Chang, *Kicking Away the Ladder: Development Strategy in Historical Perspective* (London: Anthem, 2002).

48. Cooper, *Colonialism in Question*, 102.

49. On British imperial constitution, see Ken MacMillan, "Imperial Constitutions: Sovereignty and Law in the British Atlantic," 69–97, and Robert Travers, "Constitutions, Contact Zones, and Imperial Ricochets: Sovereignty and Law in British Asia," 98–129, both in Bowen, Mancke, and Reid, *Britain's Oceanic Empire*; Lauren Benton, *A Search for Sovereignty: Law and Geography in European Empires, 1400–1900* (Cambridge: Cambridge University Press, 2010).

50. Very useful in this regard is Chakrabarty's distinction between the "being" and "becoming" of capital, between its "universal logic" and the historically specific forms it assumes. The key

theoretical insight behind this distinction is Marx's discussion of the "real subsumption" and the "formal subsumption" of labor under capital's direction. Marx, *Capital*, 1:1019–38. For a rigorous analysis of the ways in which these two modalities are interrelated, see Jairus Banaji, "Modes of Production in a Materialist Conception of History," in *Theory as History: Essays on Modes of Production and Exploitation* (Leiden: Brill, 2010); Massimo De Angelis, *The Beginning of History: Value Struggles and Global Capital* (London: Pluto, 2007).

51. The powerful metanarrative of the "rise of the West" is vast genre that is as popular as it is social scientific, and as common among Marxists as it is dear to liberals. See, for instance, Douglass C. North and Robert P. Thomas, *The Rise of the Western World: A New Economic History* (Cambridge: Cambridge University Press, 1973); David Landes, *The Wealth and Poverty of Nations: Why Some Are So Rich and Some So Poor* (New York: Norton, 1998); Ellen Meiksins Wood, *The Origin of Capitalism: A Longer View* (London: Verso, 2002).

52. Nancy Fraser, "Expropriation and Exploitation in Racialized Capitalism: A Reply to Michael Dawson," *Critical Historical Studies* 3, no. 1 (2016): 163–78. For bold reappraisals that decenter the history of capitalism away from European agency and onto planetary processes of transmission and appropriation, see Alexander Anievas and Kerem Nisancioglu, *How the West Came to Rule: The Geopolitical Origins of Capitalism* (London: Pluto, 2015); James Blaut, *The Colonizer's Model of the World: Geographical Diffusionism and Eurocentric History* (New York: Guilford, 1993); John Hobson, *The Eastern Origins of Western Civilization* (Cambridge: Cambridge University Press, 2004).

53. Adrian Leonard and David Pretel, "Experiments in Modernity: The Making of the Atlantic World Economy," in *The Caribbean and the Atlantic World Economy: Circuits of Trade, Money and Knowledge, 1650–1914*, ed. Adrian Leonard and David Pretel (New York: Palgrave MacMillan, 2015), 8. The significance of the early modern Atlantic system for technological and organizational innovation is demonstrated in in a recent study by Nuala Zahedieh. Zahedieh's emphasis is as much on the technical advancements in colonial production as it is on their positive feedback effect on the metropolitan economy, above all, the reallocation of resources from craft production to manufactories employing low-skilled labor and machinery. Nuala Zahedieh, *Capital and the Colonies: London and the Atlantic Economy, 1660–1700* (Cambridge: Cambridge University Press, 2010), 230, 274, 279.

54. Carl Schmitt, *The Nomos of the Earth in the International Law of the Jus Publicum Europaeum* (New York: Telos, 2003).

55. Beckert, *Empire of Cotton*, 38.

56. Antony Anghie, *Imperialism, Sovereignty, and the Making of International Law* (Cambridge: Cambridge University Press, 2005). I am indebted to Adom Getachew for bringing this crucial yet frequently bypassed point to my attention.

57. Fraser, "Expropriation and Exploitation," 172; Singh, "On Race," 41. Also see Michael Dawson, "Hidden in Plain Sight: A Note on Legitimation Crises and the Racial Order," *Critical Historical Studies* 3, no. 1 (2016): 143–61. To give one example, in England the majority of the laboring population was subject to the Statute of Artificers, which bound apprentices to their masters but also provided them with recourse to common law and courts. By contrast, Barbados had a slave code (the first slave code in English history) to govern its black labor force, which was framed by and granted absolute prerogative to the white masters. Douglass Hay and Paul Craven, *Masters, Servants, and Magistrates in Britain and the Empire, 1562–1955* (Chapel Hill: University of North Carolina Press, 2004); Kenneth Morgan, *Slavery and the British Empire: From Africa to America* (Oxford: Oxford University Press, 2007).

58. Singh, "On Race," 41.

59. Saskia Sassen elaborates the methodological merits of focusing on "systemic edges" in analyzing the dispossessive and exclusionary logics of capitalism. The systemic edge represents "the site where general conditions take extreme forms," which in turn "makes visible larger trends that are less extreme and hence more difficult to capture." Sassen, *Expulsions*, 211.

60. Beckert, *Empire of Cotton*, 37.

61. Marx, *Capital*, 1:280.

62. Bell, "What Is Liberalism?," 684.

63. The major touchstones of this controversy are Pocock, *Machiavellian Moment*; C. B. Macpherson, *Political Theory of Possessive Individualism: Hobbes to Locke* (Oxford: Clarendon

Press, 1962); Leo Strauss, *Natural Right and History* (Chicago: University of Chicago Press, 1953); Isaac Kramnick, *Republicanism and Bourgeois Radicalism: Political Ideology in Late Eighteenth-Century England and America* (Ithaca, NY: Cornell University Press, 1990).

64. See Pincus, *1688*, 366–99; Hont, introduction to *Jealousy of Trade*; Donald Winch, *Classical Political Economy and Colonies* (Cambridge, MA: Harvard University Press, 1965); Sophus Reinert, *Translating Empire: Emulation and the Origins of Political Economy* (Cambridge, MA: Harvard University Press, 2011).

65. Jairus Banaji, "Globalizing the History of Capital: Ways Forward," *Historical Materialism* (forthcoming).

66. Jennifer Pitts, "Free for All," *Times Literary Supplement*, September 23, 2011.

67. Anthony Pagden, *Lords of All the World: Ideologies of Empire in Spain, Britain and France, c. 1500–c. 1800* (New Haven, CT: Yale University Press, 1995), 180.

68. See Christopher Berry, *The Idea of Commercial Society in the Scottish Enlightenment* (Edinburgh: Edinburgh University Press, 2013); Hont, *Jealousy of Trade*; and Hont, *Politics in Commercial Society*.

69. Armitage, *Ideological Origins*, 166.

70. Pincus, "Neither Machiavellian Moment nor Possessive Individualism: Commercial Society and the Defenders of the English Commonwealth," *American Historical Review* 103 (1998): 705–36, at 707–8.

71. Sophus Reinert's studies into the seventeenth- and eighteenth-century translations of political economic tracts provide a highly original mapping of the dissemination of this new political language among European political classes and lay publics. See Reinert, *Translating Empire*; and "Empire of Emulation," in Reinert and Røge, *Political Economy of Empire*.

72. P. J. Marshall, *The Making and Unmaking of Empires: Britain, India, and America, c. 1750–1783* (Oxford: Oxford University Press, 2005), 46.

73. Smith, *Wealth of Nations*, 2:34.

74. Christopher Bayly, *The Imperial Meridian: The British Empire and the World, 1780–1830* (London: Longman, 1989), 217–18.

75. Andrew Sartori, *Bengal in Global Concept History: Culturalism in the Age of Capital* (Chicago: University of Chicago Press, 2008), 51.

76. See, for instance, Siraj Ahmed, *The Stillbirth of Capital: Enlightenment Writing and Colonial India* (Stanford, CA: Stanford University Press, 2012).

77. Frederick Cooper, "Modernizing Colonialism and the Limits of Empire," in Calhoun, Cooper, and Moore, *Lessons of Empire*, 66.

78. Smith himself admitted how unrealistic his positive proposals would sound to his contemporaries. Ironically, however, his criticism of territorial empires would be appropriated by nineteenth-century rationalizations of commercial imperialism and indirect rule. See Andrew Fitzmaurice, *Sovereignty, Property and Empire, 1500–2000* (Cambridge: Cambridge University Press, 2014); Marc-William Palen, "Adam Smith as Advocate of Empire, C. 1870–1932," *The Historical Journal* 57, no. 1 (2014): 179–98.

79. P. J. Marshall, "A Free though Conquering People: Britain and Asia in the Eighteenth Century," in *A Free though Conquering People: Eighteenth-Century Britain and Its Empire*, Variorum Collected Studies 767 (Aldershot, UK: Ashgate, 2003), 1–21; and Marshall, *Making and Unmaking*.

80. Patrick K. O'Brien, "Inseparable Connections: Trade, Economy, Fiscal State, and the Expansion of Empire, 1688–1815," in *The Oxford History of the British Empire*, vol. 2, *The Eighteenth Century*, ed. P. J. Marshall (Oxford: Oxford University Press, 1998), 2:76.

81. Blackburn, *Making of New World Slavery*, 515; Sartori, "From Statecraft to Social Science," 181–214; Kenneth Morgan, "Mercantilism and the British Empire, 1688–1815," in *The Political Economy of the British Historical Experience 1688–1914*, ed. Donald Winch and Patrick O'Brien (Oxford: Oxford University Press, 2002), 165–92. For a recent iteration, see the exchange between Kevin H. O'Rourke and Jeffrey G. Williamson, "When Did Globalisation Begin?," *European Review of Economic History* 8 (2004): 109–17; and Dennis O. Flynn and Arturo Giráldez, "Born Again: Globalization's Sixteenth-Century Origins (Asian/Global versus European Dynamics)," *Pacific Economic Review* 13, no. 3 (2008): 359–87. An excellent collection of essays that reappraise mercantilism as philosophy, doctrine, and policy can be

found in Philip Stern and Carl Wennerlind, eds., *Mercantilism Reimagined: Political Economy in Early Modern Britain and Its Empire* (New York: Oxford University Press, 2014).

82. Mantena, *Alibis of Empire*, 4–5. Mantena contends that ethical imperialism was eclipsed in the 1860s by more expressly racialized modes of imperial justification and strategies of indirect rule. Anthony Pagden similarly rules out racial arguments as a viable fundament for the justification of imperial rule in this period. Anthony Pagden, "The Peopling of the New World: Ethnos, Race, and Empire in the Early-Modern World," in *Burdens of Empire: 1539 to the Present* (Cambridge: Cambridge University Press, 2015).

83. Chatterjee, *Black Hole*, 52.

84. On the "imperial commons," see Antoinette Burton and Isabel Hofmeyr, "The Spine of Empire? Books and the Making of an Imperial Commons," in *Ten Books That Shaped the British Empire: Creating and Imperial Commons*, ed. Antoinette Burton and Isabel Hofmeyr (Durham, NC: Duke University Press, 2014). It remains controversial to what extent the British public at large imagined themselves as belonging to an essentially imperial polity. For contrasting positions, see Hall, *Civilising Subjects*; and Bernard Porter, *The Absent-Minded Imperialists: Empire, Society, and Culture in Britain* (Oxford: Oxford University Press, 2004).

85. Sybille Fischer, *Modernity Disavowed: Haiti and the Cultures of Slavery in the Age of Revolution* (Durham, NC: Duke University Press, 2004), 38. For a kindred analysis of liberal strategies of "deflection," see Morefield, *Empires without Imperialism*. The term "incitement to discourse" is from Michel Foucault, *The History of Sexuality* (New York: Pantheon, 1978), notwithstanding Foucault's reservations against the symptomatic reading of texts as encryptions of deeper social and historical structures.

86. This line of argument is advanced in Pitts, *Turn to Empire*; and Marshall, "Free though Conquering People." For a critique of this position, see Karuna Mantena, "Fragile Universals and the Politics of Empire," *Polity* 38 (2006): 543–55.

87. Bayly, Imperial *Meridian*, 8–9.

88. Maier, *Among Empires*, 61.

89. Bernard Porter, *Empire and Superempire: Britain, America, and the World* (New Haven, CT: Yale University Press, 2006), 24, 44, 48, 53.

90. Richard Drayton, "Imperial History and the Human Future," *History Workshop Journal* 74 (2012): 156–72, esp. 168; Patricia Seed, *Ceremonies of Possession in Europe's Conquest of the New World, 1492–1640* (Cambridge: Cambridge University Press, 1995), 11. For a recent reiteration, see Fitzmaurice, *Sovereignty*, 8.

91. Duncan Bell, "Ideologies of Empire," in *Reordering the World*, 96.

92. See, generally, Fitzmaurice, *Sovereignty*.

93. Maier, *Among Empires*, 61, 64.

94. James Tully, *Strange Multiplicity: Constitutionalism in an Age of Diversity* (Cambridge: Cambridge University Press, 1995); and Tully, *Public Philosophy in a New Key*, vol. 2.

95. Mike Davis, *Late Victorian Holocausts: El Niño Famines and the Making of the Third World* (London: Verso, 2002).

96. Bonefeld, "Primitive Accumulation," 395.

97. On relating intellectual history and ideology, see Moyn, "Imaginary Intellectual History," in McMahon and Moyn, *Rethinking Modern*, 122–30. The theory of ideology based on the notion of necessary misrecognition is elaborated by Louis Althusser in "Ideology and Ideological State Apparatuses," in *Lenin and Philosophy, and Other Essays* (London: New Left Books, 1971).

98. Cooper, *Colonialism in Question*, 237.

99. On the link between capitalism and European conceptions of civilization, see Lowe, *Intimacies*; Thomas Holt, *The Problem of Freedom: Race, Labor, and Politics in Jamaica and Britain, 1832–1938* (Baltimore: Johns Hopkins University Press, 1992).

100. An orthogonal solution is presented by Duncan Ivison's coinage "proto-liberalism," which refers to seventeenth-century ideas we now associate with liberalism. Duncan Ivison, "Locke, Liberalism, and Empire," in *The Philosophy of John Locke: New Perspectives*, ed. Peter Anstey (New York: Routledge, 2003).

101. See, above all, Martti Koskenniemi, "Vitoria and Us: Thoughts on Critical Histories of International Law," *Rechtsgeschichte* 22 (2014), 119–38.

102. William H. Sewell, *Logics of History: Social Theory and Social Transformation* (Chicago: University of Chicago Press, 2005), 1–21, 318–72.

103. Sartori, *Liberalism in Empire*; Morefield, *Empires without Imperialism*. The concepts "logic of history" and "premise of provincialism" are borrowed respectively from Sewell, *Logics of History*, 10–11; and Gordon, "Contextualism and Criticism," 40–44.

104. Sartori, "British Empire," 624.

105. Sartori, *Bengal in Global Concept History*, 6.

106. Chakrabarty, *Provincializing Europe*, 63.

107. Hont, *Politics in Commercial Society*, 4.

108. Ellen Meiksins Wood, "The Social History of Political Theory," in *Ellen Meiksins Wood Reader*, ed. Larry Patriquin (Leiden: Brill, 2014), 143. For a systematic treatise adopting this methodological premise, see Ellen Meiksins Wood, *Citizens to Lords: A Social History of Western Political Thought from Antiquity to the Middle Ages* (London: Verso, 2008).

109. Kennedy, "Capitalism," 245.

110. Walter Benjamin, "Theses on the Philosophy of History," in *Illuminations: Essay and Reflections*, ed. Hannah Arendt (New York: Schocken, 1968), 255.

111. Walter Benjamin, quoted in Susan Buck-Morss, *The Dialectics of Seeing: Walter Benjamin and the Arcades Project* (Cambridge, MA: MIT Press, 1991), 292.

112. Sequestering the past from the present on the grounds of historical correctness can thereby militate, ironically, against one of the positive conclusions Skinner drew from the linguistic-contextualist approach—namely, that it can "show the extent to which those features of our own arrangements which may be disposed to accept as tradition or even "timeless" truths may in fact be the merest contingencies of our peculiar history and social structure." Skinner, "Meaning and Understanding," 53.

113. John Locke, *Two Treatises of Government*, ed. Peter Laslett (Cambridge: Cambridge University Press, 1988), 291.

114. James Wolfensohn, Annual Meeting Speech World Bank, October 1, 1996, http://web.worldbank.org, accessed May 16, 2015.

115. Fitzmaurice, *Sovereignty*, 19.

116. Michel Foucault, "Nietzsche, Genealogy, History," in *Language, Counter-Memory, Practice: Selected Essays and Interviews*, ed. Donald Bouchard (Ithaca, NY: Cornell University Press, 1977), 139–64.

117. Armitage, "What's the Big Idea?"

118. Anghie, Imperialism; Sundhya Pahuja, *Decolonising International Law: Development, Economic Growth, and the Politics of Universality* (Cambridge: Cambridge University Press, 2011).

119. The new institutionalist defense of "liberal" institutions for their inclusiveness and efficiency lacks Ferguson's brash imperialist bombast, but it is no less apolitical for that reason. In fact, Ferguson himself later expanded the scope of his pro-imperial stance to the Western civilization as a whole. Whatever their methodological choices and mode of presentation, both accounts similarly admit the place of illiberal, coercive methods in the history of global capitalism, only to cordon them off from the essentially liberal character and Western provenance of capitalism by casting them either as unfeasible economic strategies or as peripheral political expedients. See Acemoglu and Robinson, *Why Nations Fail*; Niall Ferguson, *Civilization: The West and the Rest* (London: Allen Lane, 2011); Niall Ferguson, *The Great Degeneration: How Institutions Decay and Economies Die* (London: Allen Lane, 2012).

120. On the notion of "constellation" as a conceptual apparatus of historical analysis, see Walter Benjamin, *The Origin of German Tragic Drama* (London: Verso, 1998), 34–35.

Chapter 2

1. Trailblazing colonial interpretations of Locke include James Tully, *An Approach to Political Philosophy: Locke in Contexts* (Cambridge: Cambridge University Press, 1993); Arneil, *John Locke and America*; and Mehta, *Liberalism and Empire*. For skeptical accounts, see

Vicki Hsueh, "Giving Orders: Theory and Practice in the Fundamental Constitutions of Carolina," *Journal of the History of Ideas* 63 (2002): 425–46; Hsueh, "Unsettling Colonies: Locke, 'Atlantis,' and the New World Knowledges," *History of Political Thought* 29 (2010): 295–319; and Armitage, "John Locke: Theorist of Empire?"

2. The *Two Treatises* are cited by treatise and section number, using *Two Treatises of Government: A Critical Edition with an Introduction and Apparatus Criticus*, ed. Peter Laslett (Cambridge: Cambridge University Press, 1960). All emphases are in the original unless stated otherwise.

3. This liberal-bourgeois interpretation of Locke dates at least back to Macpherson, in *Political Theory of Possessive Individualism*, if not to Strauss, *Natural Right and History*.

4. I borrow the term "possessive universalism" from George Caffentzis, *Clipped Coins, Abused Words, and Civil Government: John Locke's Philosophy of Money* (New York: Autonomedia, 1989).

5. The original insight behind this argument comes from Tully's *Approach to Political Philosophy*. For the most systematic treatment of this argument, see Barbara Arneil, "Trade, Plantations, and Property: John Locke and the Economic Defense of Colonialism," *Journal of the History of Ideas* 55 (1994): 591–609. Also see Ivison, "Locke, Liberalism," in Anstey, *Philosophy of John Locke*.

6. On "Atlantic history," see David Armitage and Michael Braddick, eds., *The British Atlantic World, 1500–1800* (New York: Palgrave MacMillan, 2009); J. H. Elliott, *Empires of the Atlantic World: Britain and Spain in America, 1492–1830* (New Haven, CT: Yale University Press, 2006); Thomas Benjamin, *The Atlantic World: Europeans, Africans, Indians, and Their Shared History, 1400–1900* (New York: Cambridge University Press, 2009); Elizabeth Mancke and Caroline Shammas, eds., *The Creation of the British Atlantic World* (Baltimore: Johns Hopkins University Press, 2005); Bowen, Mancke, and Reid, *Britain's Oceanic Empire*.

7. Kenneth R. Andrews, "The English in the Caribbean, 1560–1620," in *Westward Enterprise*, ed. Kenneth Andrews, Nicholas Canny, Paul Hair, and David Quinn (Detroit, MI: Wayne State University Press, 1979), 120. Also see Stuart B. Schwartz, "The Iberian Atlantic to 1650," in *The Oxford Handbook of the Atlantic World, 1450–1850*, ed. Nicholas Canny and Philip Morgan (Oxford: Oxford University Press, 2011), 147–64.

8. Elliott, *Empires of the Atlantic*, 113; Zahedieh, *Capital and the Colonies*; Nicholas Canny, "The Origins of Empire: An Introduction," in *Oxford History of the British Empire*, 131–32.

9. Nuala Zahedieh, "Economy," in Armitage and Braddick, *British Atlantic World*, 57–63; Zahedieh, "Overseas Expansion and Trade in the Seventeenth Century," in Canny, *Oxford History of the British Empire*, 1:402. Alison Games, *Migration and the Origins of the British Atlantic World* (Cambridge, MA: Harvard University Press, 1999); and Blackburn, *Making of the New World Slavery*, 250–51.

10. Michael Braddick, "The English Government, War, Trade, and Settlement, 1625–1688," in Canny, *Oxford History of the British Empire*, vol. 1; Elizabeth Mancke, "Empire and State," in Armitage and Braddick, *British Atlantic World*, 193–213; and MacMillan, "Imperial Constitutions," in Bowen, Mancke, and Reid, *Britain's Oceanic Empire*.

11. Joyce O. Appleby, *Economic Thought and Ideology in Seventeenth Century England*, (Princeton, NJ: Princeton University Press, 1978), 10–11, 31–2; J. H. Elliott, "The Seizure of Overseas Territories by the European Powers," in *Theories of Empire, 1450–1800*, ed. David Armitage (Aldershot: Ashgate Variorum, 1998), 148–49; Keith Wrightson, "Class," in Armitage and Braddick, *British Atlantic World*, 158; Zahedieh, *Capital and the Colonies*, 35, 126–27; and Blackburn, *Making of the New World Slavery*, 261–62.

12. Brewer, *Sinews of Power*; Patrick K. O'Brien and Philip Hunt, "The Rise of a Fiscal State in England, 1485–1815," *Historical Research* 66 (1993): 129–76; and Michael Braddick, *State Formation in Early Modern England, c. 1550–1700* (Cambridge: Cambridge University Press, 2000).

13. Appleby, *Economic Thought*, 26, 41, 51, 95; Also see Lars Magnusson, *Mercantilism: The Shaping of an Economic Language* (London: Routledge, 1994); and Michel Foucault, *Security, Territory, Population: Lectures at the College de France, 1977–1978*, ed. Michael Senellart (New York: Picador, 2007), 324–28.

14. David Armitage, introduction to *Theories of Empire*, ed. Armitage, xxvii. Also see Pincus, *1688*, 382, 389.

15. For the initial emulation of, and subsequent departure from, the Spanish model of coloniza-tion, see Pagden, *Lords of All the World*, 66–68, 127–28, 149; Elliott, *Empires of the Atlantic*, 9, 21–22; John Parry, "English in the New World," in Andrews et al., *Westward Enterprise*, 2–5. Elliott notes that the actual lines of separation between "good conquest" and "bad conquest," between conquest and settlement, and between English and Spanish patterns of coloniza-tion were not as stark as the English would have liked to believe. Elliott, "Seizure of Overseas Territories," 141–49; and Elliott, *Empires of the Atlantic World*, 24–28.

16. Carolina Shammas elegantly captures, with the phrase "commercialization of colonization," the process of reluctant turn to the cultivation of export crops in the wake of broken dreams of El Dorado, a point of broad agreement among the historians of the English Atlantic. See Caroline Shammas, "English Commercial Development and American Colonization, 1560–1620," in Andrews et al., *Westward Enterprise*, 151–74.

17. Elliott, "Seizure of Overseas Territories," 144–45; Elliott, *Empires of the Atlantic*, 105; Zahedieh, *Capital and the Colonies*, 214; and Allan Kulikoff, *Tobacco and Slaves: The Development of the Southern Cultures in the Chesapeake, 1680–1800* (Chapel Hill: University of North Carolina Press, 1986).

18. Elliott, *Empires of the Atlantic*, 106; Canny, "Origins of Empire"; Kenneth Morgan, *Slavery, Atlantic Trade, and the British Economy, 1660–1800* (Cambridge: Cambridge University Press, 2002); Morgan, *Slavery and the British Empire: From Africa to America* (New York: Oxford University Press, 2007); Blackburn, *Making of the New World Slavery*.

19. Leonard and Pretel, "Experiments in Modernity," in Leonard and Pretel, *Caribbean and the Atlantic*, 3. Also see Beckert, *Empire of Cotton*, 36–37.

20. Keith Wrightson, "Class," in Armitage and Braddick, *British Atlantic World*, 158; Leonard and Pretel, "Experiments in Modernity," in Leonard and Preel, *Caribbean and the Atlantic*, 10.

21. Benton, "The British Atlantic in the Global Context," in Armitage and Braddick, *British Atlantic World*, 276–77.

22. Beckles, "Hub of Empire," in Canny, *Oxford History of the British Empire*, 1:222. Also see, Zahedieh, "Economy," 62–65; Inikori, "Africa and the Globalization Process," 63–86, 73.

23. Jairus Banaji, "Globalizing the History of Capital: Ways Forward" (unpublished manuscript), 5, accessed June 15, 2016, https://www.academia.edu/22674507/Globalizing_the_his-tory_of_capital_Ways_forward.

24. Zahedieh, *Capital and the Colonies*, 216–17.

25. Michael Craton, "Property and Propriety: Land Tenure and Slave Property in the Creation of a British West Indian Plantocracy, 1612–1740," in *Early Modern Conceptions of Property*, ed. John Brewer and Susan Staves (New York: Routledge, 1995), 500–503. Also see Robert Weir, "Shaftesbury's Darling: British Settlement in the Carolinas at the Close of the Seventeenth Century," in Canny, *Oxford History of the British Empire*, 1:393–94.

26. Zahedieh, *Capital and the Colonies*, 274.

27. Zahedieh's *Capital and the Colonies* is the most comprehensive book-length account of the impact of Atlantic colonialism on England's long-term economic growth. Compare Pomeranz, *Great Divergence*.

28. Pincus, *1688*, 82.

29. Ibid., 87.

30. One could object to foregrounding land as the fulcrum of the Atlantic colonial constel-lation on the grounds that procuring labor, rather than land, posed the real challenge for those invested in colonialism and plantations. I admit that the "colonial labor problem" had its origins in the Atlantic, as attested by the explosion of the slave trade toward the end of the century. However, there are two reasons for concentrating on land in this period. The first has to do with colonial political economy. The colonial labor problem was a derivative, second-order problem entailed by the sudden availability of vast tracts of tropical land. The dearth of labor was not absolute but relative; that is, it was relative to the volume of workforce needed to cultivate a given amount of land (though the constant expansion of Europeans in the Caribbean and on the mainland rendered the labor problem chronic). As Joyce Appleby suggestively demonstrates, the dominant view in seventeenth-century England was one of *overpopulation*—that is, the *abundance* of idle hands that could be put to productive use. The second reason for restricting the focus on land in this chapter is the simple fact that,

as far Europeans' image of themselves was concerned, the eye of the controversy stood on American land appropriations rather than African enslavement. Robin Blackburn notes that despite some initial scruples, "competitive pressure, and the logic of Atlantic trade, made the slave trade widely acceptable—indeed, a commerce to be patronized by royalty, blessed by the clergy, and practiced by the aristocracy and gentry," and Kenneth Morgan concludes, "Negative perceptions of black Africans coupled with a virtually non-existent antislavery posture created the cultural outlook whereby European traders and New World settlers were morally untroubled in enslaving black human beings." The question of free and slave labor would have to wait until the early nineteenth century to assume the same proportions the colonial land problem had in the seventeenth century. Hence, chapter 4 of this book tackles the colonial labor problem in the immediate period around the abolition of slavery in the British Caribbean. Appleby, *Economic Thought*, 127–51; Blackburn, *Making of the New World Slavery*, 328–29; Morgan, *Slavery and the British Empire*, 23.

31. Elliott, "Seizure of Overseas Territories," 145.
32. Armitage, introduction to *Theories of Empire*, xv.
33. Pagden, *Lords of All the World*, 39–55; Pagden, "Dispossessing the Barbarian: The Language of Spanish Thomism and the Debate over the Property Rights of the American Indians," in Armitage, *Theories of Empire*; and Fitzmaurice, *Sovereignty*.
34. Anthony Pagden, "The Struggle for Legitimacy and the Image of Empire in the Atlantic to c. 1700," in Canny, *Oxford History of the British Empire*, 1:37–38. For the most comprehensive treatment of the crumbling of European civic history in the face of the encounter with America, see J. G. A. Pocock, *Barbarism and Religion*, vol. 4, *Barbarians, Savages, and Empires* (Cambridge: Cambridge University Press, 2005).
35. Anthony Pagden, "Conquest, Settlement, Purchase, and Concession: Justifying the English Settlement of the Americas," in *Burdens of Empire: 1539 to the Present* (Cambridge: Cambridge University Press, 2015), 122. Also see Richard Tuck, *Rights of War and Peace: Political Thought and International Order from Grotius to Kant* (Oxford: Oxford University Press, 1999); and Tuck, "The 'Modern' Theory of Natural Law," in *Languages of Political Theory in Early Modern Europe*, ed. Anthony Pagden (Cambridge: Cambridge University Press, 1987), 99–119.
36. James Tully, "Aboriginal Property and Western Theory: Recovering a Middle Ground," in Armitage *Theories of Empire*, 348. Also see Armitage, introduction to *Theories of Empire*, xxii.
37. Pagden, "Struggle for Legitimacy," 44–51; Seed, *Ceremonies of Possession*, 11.
38. John Brewer and Susan Staves, introduction to Brewer and Staves, *Early Modern Conceptions of Property*, 18.
39. Pagden, "Conquest," 123. For the forms and ideologies of colonization circulating between Ireland and the Americas in the seventeenth century, see Nicholas Canny, "The Permissive Frontier," in Andrews, et al., *Westward Enterprise*, 17–44.
40. Sartori, "From Statecraft to Social Science," 181–214.
41. For biographical accounts of Locke's professional involvement in England's colonial policy, see Maurice Cranston, *John Locke: A Biography* (New York: Longmans, Green, 1957), 153–57; and Roger Woolhouse, *John Locke: A Biography* (Cambridge: Cambridge University Press, 2006), 110–19, 361–63.
42. Armitage, "Theorist of Empire?," 7. Armitage adds, "[O]nly his rival on the Board of Trade, the career administrator Sir William Blathwayt, had a more comprehensive command of English colonial administration by that time."
43. For the revisionist accounts of Locke's position on liberalism, constitutionalism, and slavery informed by the discovery of his involvement in the *Fundamental Constitutions*, see Celia McGuiness, "The Fundamental Constitutions of Carolina as a Tool for Lockean Scholarship," *Interpretation* 17 (1989): 127–43; Hsueh, "Giving Orders"; Hsueh, "Unsettling Colonies"; James Farr, "Locke, Natural Law, and New World Slavery," *Political Theory* 36 (2008): 495–522; Farr, "So Vile and Miserable an Estate: The Problem of Slavery in Locke's Political Thought," *Political Theory* 14 (1986): 263–89; and David Armitage, "John Locke, Carolina, and the "Two Treatises of Government," *Political Theory* 32 (2004): 602–27; Armitage, "Theorist of Empire?"; and Weir, "Shaftesbury's Darling."
44. Cranston, *John Locke*, 155.

45. John Locke to Peter King, 4 Dec 1699 and 24 Jan 1701, in *John Locke: Selected Correspondence*, ed. Mark Goldie (Oxford: Oxford University Press, 2002), 281–82, 291.

46. Herman Lebovics, "The Uses of America in Locke's Second Treatise of Government," *Journal of the History of Ideas* 47 (1986): 567–81, 568, 578.

47. William Letwin observes a great discrepancy of clarity and sophistication between the first (1668) and second (1691) drafts of Locke's economic tract *Some Considerations of the Consequences of the Lowering of Interest, and Raising the Value of Money*, and contends that the vast improvement of the second draft over the first "can reasonably be attributed to his years of practice in the administration of the Carolinas and the Council for Trade and plantations." William Letwin, *The Origins of Scientific Economics: English Economic Thought, 1660–1776* (London: Methuen, 1963), 167–68.

48. E. J. Hundert, "The Making of Homo Faber: John Locke between Ideology and History," *Journal of the History of Ideas* 33 (1972): 3–22.

49. For Locke's historical involvement with the "Baconian improvers," see Neal Wood, *John Locke and Agrarian Capitalism* (Berkeley: University of California Press, 1984), chaps. 2 and 3; Patrick Kelly, "General Introduction: Locke on Money," in *Locke on Money*, ed. Patrick H. Kelly (Oxford: Clarendon Press, 1991), 100. For a more textual extrapolation of the Baconian influence in Locke's thought, see Thomas Pangle, *The Spirit of Modern Republicanism* (Chicago: University of Chicago Press, 1988), 166; Michael Zuckert, *Natural Rights and the New Republicanism* (Princeton, NJ: Princeton University Press, 1994), 203.

50. Wood, *John Locke*.

51. Armitage, "John Locke, Carolina," 611.

52. For Locke's position in Whig political economy, see Pincus, *1688*, 459. Also see Kelly, "General Introduction."

53. Fitzmaurice, *Sovereignty*, chap. 4.

54. On the exact coordinates of Locke's theory vis-à-vis Grotius and Pufendorf, as well as the Spanish humanists, compare Tuck, *Rights of War and Peace*; Arneil, *John Locke and America*; Pagden, *Lords of All the World*; and James Tully, "Framework of Natural Rights in Locke's Theory of Property," in *Approach to Political Philosophy*.

55. Robert Gray, in *A Good Speed to Virginia* (1609), quoted in Elliott, "Seizure of Overseas Territories," 148. For a discussion of internal critiques of English colonialism, see James Tully, "Rediscovering America: The Two Treatises and Aboriginal Rights," in *An Approach to Political Philosophy*; and Fitzmaurice, *Sovereignty*, chap. 3.

56. Tully, "Aboriginal Property," 350. Also see Sartori, *Liberalism in Empire*, 9–17.

57. Tully, "Rediscovering America"; Lebovics, "Uses of America"; Barbara Arneil, "The Wild Indian's Venison: Locke's Theory of Property and English Colonialism in America," *Political Studies* 44 (1996): 60–74; Vicki Hsueh, "Cultivating and Challenging the Common: Lockean Property, Indigenous Traditionalisms, and the Problem of Exclusion," *Contemporary Political Theory* 5 (2006): 193–214. Locke omitted accounts indigenous horticulture in his writings, even though he was well aware of it by virtue of the colonial reports, travel literature, and ethnographies in his library. Arneil, *John Locke and America*, 23–41. For Pocock, however, this does not pose a conundrum, since the Locke and Enlightenment anthropology in general assumed the use of heavy plows drawn by domesticated beasts of burden as the precondition of proper agriculture, which in turn made possible "the capacity for exchange, commerce, specialization and diversification" and the "step into humanity." J. G. A Pocock, "*Tangata Whenua* and Enlightenment Anthropology," in *The Discovery of Islands: Essays in British History* (Cambridge: Cambridge University Press, 2005), 208.

58. On Locke's parochial constitutionalism, see Tully, *Strange Multiplicity*, esp. chap. 3. For an expanded treatment of questions of constitutionalism, law, and rights in Locke's colonial forays, see Ivison, "Locke, Liberalism," in Anstey, *Philosophy of John Locke*; and Duncan Ivison, "The Nature of Rights and the History of Empire," in *British Political Thought in History, Literature and Theory, 1500–1800*, ed. David Armitage (Cambridge: Cambridge University Press, 2006).

59. The classical formulation of this claim can be found in Uday Mehta, *The Anxiety of Freedom: Imagination and Individuality in Locke's Political Thought* (Ithaca, NY: Cornell University Press, 1992); and Mehta, "Liberal Strategies of Exclusion," 427–54. For similar

interpretations of Locke's "monistic vision of good life," his provincial conception of reason, and his secularized Christian assumptions about the human soul, see Parekh, "Liberalism and Colonialism," 87–92; Arneil, *John Locke and America*, 200–211; Jakob de Roover and S. N. Balagangadhara, "John Locke, Christian Liberty, and the Predicament of Liberal Toleration," *Political Theory* 36 (2008): 523–49.

60. This section relies on the account developed in more detail in Onur Ulas Ince, "Enclosing in God's Name, Accumulating for Mankind: Money, Morality, and Accumulation in John Locke's Theory of Property," *Review of Politics* 73 (2011): 29–54.

61. C. B. Macpherson, "Locke on Capitalist Appropriation," *Western Political Quarterly* 4 (1951): 550–66; Macpherson, *Political Theory*; Hundert, "Making of Homo Faber"; Appleby, *Economic Thought*; Appleby, *Liberalism and Republicanism in Historical Imagination* (Cambridge, MA: Harvard University Press, 1992); Karen I. Vaughn, *John Locke, Economist and Social Scientist* (Chicago: University of Chicago Press, 1980); Vaughn, "The Economic Background to Locke's *Two Treatises of Government*," in *John Locke's* Two Treatises of Government: *New Interpretations*, ed. Edward J. Harpham (Lawrence: University Press of Kansas, 1992); N. Wood, *John Locke*; N. Wood, *Politics of Locke's Philosophy: A Social Study of* "An Essay Concerning Human Understanding," (Berkeley: University of California Press, 1983); Strauss, *Natural Right and History*; Pangle, *Spirit of Modern Republicanism*; Zuckert, *Natural Rights*; Zuckert, *Launching Liberalism: On Lockean Political Philosophy* (Lawrence: University Press of Kansas, 2002); and Peter C. Myers, *Our Only Star and Compass: Locke and the Struggle for Political Rationality* (Lanham, MD: Rowman and Littlefield, 1998).

62. See John Dunn, *The Political Thought of John Locke: An Historical Account of the Argument of the* Two Treatises of Government (London: Cambridge University Press, 1969); Karl Olivecrona, "Appropriation in the State of Nature: Locke on the Origin of Property," *Journal of the History of Ideas* 35 (1974): 211–30; Olivecrona, "Locke's Theory of Appropriation," *Philosophical Quarterly* 24 (1974): 220–34; James Tully, *A Discourse on Property: John Locke and His Adversaries* (Cambridge: Cambridge University Press, 1980); Tully, "Framework of Natural Rights"; Richard Ashcraft, *Locke's* Two Treatises of Government (London: Allen & Unwin, 1987); Ashcraft, *Revolutionary Politics and Locke's* Two Treatises of Government (Princeton, NJ: Princeton University Press, 1986); and Ashcraft, "The Politics of Locke's *Two Treatises of Government*," in Harpham, *John Locke's* Two Treatises of Government; Eldon Eisenach, "Religion and Locke's *Two Treatises of Government*," in Harpham, *John Locke's* Two Treatises; Alex Tuckness, "The Coherence of a Mind: John Locke and the Law of Nature," *Journal of the History of Philosophy* 37 (1999): 73–90; Matthew H. Kramer, *John Locke and the Origins of Private Property: Philosophical Explorations of Individualism, Community, and Equality* (Cambridge: Cambridge University Press, 1997); Kirstie M. McClure, *Judging Rights: Lockean Politics and the Limits of Consent* (Ithaca, NY: Cornell University Press, 1996); Kim I. Parker, *The Biblical Politics of John Locke* (Waterloo: Canadian Corporation for Studies in Religion, 2004).

63. Ashcraft, "Politics," 19.

64. For further discussion of the teleological aspect of Locke's philosophy, see Jeremy Waldron, *The Right to Private Property* (Oxford: Clarendon, 1988), 141; Waldron, *God, Locke, and Equality* (Cambridge: Cambridge University Press, 2002), 159; Ashcraft, *Locke's* Two Treatises, 38, 50, 135; and Ashcraft, "Politics," 19–25.

65. For similar passages see I. 41, 87, 88, and II. 6, 7, 16, 25, 26, 36, 37, 43, 44, 87, 171.

66. Waldron, *God, Locke, and Equality*, 160. On the morality of labor, also see Ashcraft, "Politics," 32–34; Tully, *Discourse on Property*, 116–21; Hundert, "Making of Homo Faber," 5; Parker, *Biblical Politics*, 136.

67. Ashcraft, *Locke's* Two Treatises, 134. Labor theory of appropriation is articulated in sections 27–36 in the *Second Treatise*.

68. The contrast between common waste and improved private property is developed in II. 36–37, 41–45. On the binary of waste and improvement, see Strauss, *Natural Right and History*, 243–44; Ashcraft, "Politics," 37–38; Pangle, *Modern Republicanism*, 163–65; Waldron, *Private Property*, 169–70, 221–22.

69. Parekh, "Liberalism and Colonialism," 84.

70. As a result, the "enough and as good" proviso is satisfied by the increase in the amount of available land, and where this is not possible, by the increase in the amount of available provisions, *prior to the invention of money*. Dispossession does not violate the "enough and as good" proviso insofar as the dispossessed is offered the opportunity to labor for a living wage. For a brief and cogent account of the way in which the spoilage limitation supplants the "enough and as good" limitation by way of subsistence, increased common stock, welfare, and charity, see Stephen Buckle, *Natural Law and the Theory of Property: Grotius to Hume* (Oxford: Clarendon, 1991), chap. 3; and Zuckert, *Natural Rights*, 255, 266–71.

71. Parekh, "Liberalism and Colonialism," 84.

72. Gertrude Himmelfarb, *The Idea of Poverty: England in the Early Industrial Age* (New York: Alfred A. Knopf, 1984), 27–28. Himmelfarb designates Locke, along with Josiah Child and Daniel Defoe, as a proponent of the "ethic of productivity," which she describes as being concerned with not individual but social salvation, less moralistic but more coercive, less subjective and more consequentialist than the "puritan ethic" classically analyzed in R. H. Tawney's *Religion and the Rise of Capitalism: A Historical Study* (New York: Harcourt Brace, 1926).

73. Tully, "Aboriginal Property," 351, 358. This point finds further, if more circuitous, support from the influence of Samuel Pufendorf on Locke's thought, acknowledged by Locke himself. Istvan Hont has offered a penetrating analysis of the intimate connection between Pufendorf's conjectures on spontaneous sociability engendered by cooperative material production and the Scottish Enlightenment notion of an autonomously evolving civil society. See Istvan Hont, "The Language of Sociability and Commerce: Samuel Pufendorf and the Theoretical Foundations of the 'Four-Stages Theory,'" in Pagden, *Languages of Political Theory*.

74. Hundert, "Making of Homo Faber," 573–74.

75. Strauss, *Natural Right and History*, 237; Ashcraft, "Politics," 38.

76. For a detailed discussion of the relation of money to spoilage limitation, see Waldron, *Private Property*, 207–9; and Waldron, *God, Locke, and Equality*, 171.

77. Tully, *Discourse on Property*, 150.

78. On money's centrality to unleashing the productive, transformative, and edifying powers of labor, and to introducing an element of future-orientation in acquisitive behavior, see Strauss, *Natural Right and History*, 240–49; Pangle, *Modern Republicanism*, 163–66; Zuckert, *Natural Rights*, 268–69. On Locke's ideas on "hand-to-mouth existence," as emblematized by the seventeenth-century English poor, see Appleby, *Economic Thought*, 83; and Hundert, "Making of Homo Faber," 19–20.

79. Most importantly, the much-debated right to charity espoused in the *First Treatise* (I. 42) remains in force, and it operates even more efficiently since there is now a larger common stock from which to dispense charity. As Ian Shapiro puts it, somewhat bluntly, "Locke formulated an early version of the trickle-down justification for unlimited private accumulation." Ian Shapiro, "The Workmanship Ideal and Distributive Justice," in *Early Modern Conceptions of Property*, ed. John Brewer and Susan Staves (New York: Routledge, 1995), 36n4. The issue of charity in Locke has been a major node of contention, particularly inasmuch as it has been made into a bulwark against unlimited accumulation (see, e.g., Tully, *Discourse on Property*, esp. chap. 6). While it is the case that for Locke charity is an enforceable right that gives the destitute a minimal entitlement to others' economic surplus, this functions as a limit to accumulation only insofar as the economy is a "zero-sum-game." However, a "positive-sum-game" qua increased common stock is precisely what subtends Locke's theory of property. Consequently, charity as a right to surplus under conditions of extreme want, especially when prequalified with work obligations, is quite compatible with Locke's accumulative worldview. This position can be most readily gleaned from Locke's "An Essay on the Poor Law," in *Locke: Political Essays*, ed. Mark Goldie (Cambridge: Cambridge University Press, 1997). For a comprehensive discussion of the idea of charity as an enforceable right, see John Simmons, *The Lockean Theory of Rights* (Princeton, NJ: Princeton University Press, 1992), esp. 307–54; and Waldron, *God, Locke, Equality*, 170–87. For an account of Locke's vision of political economy as a positive-sum game based on labor, efficiency, and commerce, see Steven Pincus, *1688*, chap. 12.

80. Caffentzis, *Clipped Coins*, 118–19. Also evocative is Pangle's expression "dynamic individualism," which underlies the "goal of unlimited accumulation of exchangeable value . . . in a society suffused with the Lockean spirit." Pangle, *Modern Republicanism*, 168–69.

81. Tully, "Aboriginal Property," 352–53.
82. See Ross Corbett, "The Extraconstitutionality of Lockean Prerogative," *Review of Politics* 68 (2006): 428–81; Iain Hampsher-Monk and K. Zimmerman, "Liberal Constitutionalism and Schmitt's Critique of the Rule of Law," *History of Political Thought* 28 (2007): 678–95; Clement Fatovic, *Outside the Law: Emergency and Executive Power* (Baltimore: John Hopkins University Press, 2009), chap. 2.
83. Matthew Connelly, "The New Imperialists," in in Calhoun, Cooper, and Moore, *Lessons of Empire*, 32.
84. Fitzmaurice, *Sovereignty*, 109; emphasis added.
85. Tully, "Aboriginal Property," 357.
86. Ashcraft, *Locke's* Two Treatises, 139; "Politics," 30; Tully, *Discourse on Property*, 147–50. Also see Parker, *Biblical Politics*, 136–37; McClure, *Judging Rights*, 171.
87. Macpherson, *Possessive Individualism*, 210; Appleby, *Liberalism and Republicanism*, 60; Vaughn, "Economic Background," 125, 134.
88. Caffentzis is perhaps first to recognize the exclusion of money from both natural law and the social contract. Nonetheless, he concludes by subsuming it under "philosophical law" or "the law of fashion," which misses the theological significance of money by reducing its use to a matter of habit. See Caffentzis, *Clipped Coins*, 68–72, 144–50.
89. This is paralleled by Locke's use of the term "earth," which denotes not a particular geography but the entire world. Locke otherwise specifies America, England, Spain, and so on.
90. John Locke, "Some Considerations of the Consequences of the Lowering of Interest, and Raising the Value of Money," in Kelly, *Locke on Money*, 233. This also suggests that the assumption of universality espoused earlier in the *Second Treatise* is neither accidental nor temporary. Curiously enough, the recent appraisals of Locke's theory of money also seem to have missed this point, even when they train their attention on the connection between Locke's writings on money and his epistemology. See, Daniel Carey, "Locke's Species: Money and Philosophy in the 1690s," *Annals of Science* 79 (2013): 357–80; Douglass Casson, "John Locke, Clipped Coins, and the Unstable Currency of Public Reason," *Etica and Politica* 18 (2016): 153–80.
91. Kelly tries to resolve this conundrum by construing the term "universal" as "analogous to its use in the term 'universal truth,' i.e. everyone on having the advantages of gold and silver as the medium of exchange explained to him, necessarily consents to their adoption." Kelly, "General Introduction," 88. This interpretation fails to explain how the status of a consensual practice can be akin to "universal truth" unless it is already contained in the natural order of human reality, which redirects one to the domain of natural law.
92. "The promises and bargains for truck, &c. between the two men in the desert island, mentioned by *Garcilasso de la Vega*, in his history of *Peru*; or between a *Swiss* and an *Indian*, in the woods of *America*, are binding to them, though they are perfectly in a state of nature, in reference to one another: for truth and keeping of faith belongs to men, as men, and not as members of society" (II. 14).
93. In the *Second Treatise*, Locke includes the right to inheritance as an innate right on par with natural right to life and liberty. "Every man is born with a double right: first, a right of freedom to his person, which no other man has a power over, but the free disposal of it lies in himself. Secondly, a right, before any other man, to inherit with his brethren his father's goods" (II. 190).
94. Pocock, *Barbarism and Religion*, 4:173.
95. I have hinted at this earlier with reference to the Locke's comparison of American and English land in terms of their yields assessed in pounds and pennies (II. 43).
96. Sartori, "From Statecraft to Social Science."
97. For a more recent reiteration of this argument, see Ivison, "Nature of Rights."
98. Tully, *Strange Multiplicity*, 77.
99. For Grotius's argument that sovereign power over vacant territory exhausts claims to original appropriation by first occupancy, see Hugo Grotius, *The Rights of War and Peace* (New York: M. Walter Dunne: 1901), 89–92.
100. For the argument that European jurists developed the modern notion of sovereignty precisely by denying it to non-European peoples, see Anghie, *Imperialism*.

101. Pocock, "*Tangata Whenua*," 203–12; and Pocock, *Barbarism and Religion*, 4:172–73.

102. In *A Letter Concerning Toleration*, Locke makes it evident that he considers property in money to be on the same legal footing as property in land and other goods. He explicitly enumerates money among the "civil interests" to be protected by the laws of the land, "the Possession of outward Things, such as Money, Lands, Houses, Furniture, and the like." John Locke, *A Letter Concerning Toleration*, ed. James Tully (Indianapolis, IN: Hackett, 1983), 26.

103. Istvan Hont, "Adam Smith's History of Law and Government as Political Theory," in *Political Judgment: Essays for John Dunn*, ed. Richard Bourke and Raymond Geuss (Cambridge: Cambridge University Press, 2009), 131–71.

104. For the convolution of the experiential grasp of the law of nature, see McClure, *Judging Rights*, 180–81. For an insightful political analysis of the function of the early modern liberal state in managing "frictions" between property-owning individuals, see Foucault, *Security, Territory, Population*, 342–53.

105. On the function of commonwealth as such as opposed to specific governments, see Alex Tuckness, "Punishment, Property, and the Limits of Altruism: Locke's International Asymmetry," *American Political Science Review* 102 (2008): 467–79, esp. 472.

106. Mehta, "Liberal Strategies," 61–62. For a critique, see Bell, "Dream Machine."

107. Mehta, "Liberal Strategies," 61–62.

108. Mehta, *Liberalism and Empire*, 16, 57; Mehta, "Liberal Strategies," 63–70. More generally, see Mehta, *Anxiety of Freedom*.

109. Mehta, *Liberalism and Empire*, 18–25, 30–31, 48, 77.

110. Mehta, *Liberalism and Empire*, 108, 127. By embedding Locke in a tradition stretching from Newton back to Euclid, Mehta partakes in the tendency to treat abstraction "as a kind of 'original sin' of the West." Sartori, "British Empire," 625.

111. John Locke, *Some Thoughts concerning Education, with introduction, notes, and critical apparatus*, ed. John W. Yolton and Jean S. Yolton (Oxford: Clarendon, 1989), sect. 45.

112. Caffentzis deserves credit for being, to my knowledge, the first interpreter to discover this connection. See Caffentzis, *Clipped Coins*, esp. 70–71.

113. McClure, *Judging Rights*, 176. This is also in line with Locke's eschewal of other, equally complex manifestations of social abstraction among Native Americans, such as symbolic exchange and wampums, as a proper solution to the limits of natural economy.

114. Karen Vaughn notes that the purpose of "hoarding" that Locke leaves unexplored in the *Two Treatises* is clarified as "productive investment" in *Some Considerations*. This is why, Locke maintains in that pamphlet, people are willing to "buy the use of money" by paying interest. Vaughn, "Economic Background," 138.

115. John Locke, *An Essay Concerning Human Understanding, with an introduction, critical apparatus and glossary*, ed. Peter H. Nidditch (Oxford: Clarendon Press, 1975), bk. 2, chap. 11, para. 10–11.

116. This conception has led Charles Taylor to famously label Locke's idealized subject as the "punctual self." Charles Taylor, *Sources of the Self: The Making of the Modern Identity* (Cambridge, MA: Harvard University Press, 1989), chap. 9.

117. Zuckert, *Natural Rights*, 283.

118. Waldron, *God, Locke, and Equality*, 75.

119. Locke, *Essay*, bk. 1, chap. 3, para. 9, and chap. 4, para. 8.

120. John Locke, *Letter Concerning Toleration*, 43. Further corroborating this point, Armitage notes that "in 1669 the authors of the *Fundamental Constitutions* had specified that "Idollatry Ignorance or mistake gives us noe right to expell or use [the Natives of Carolina] ill," and that article remained in all later versions of the *Fundamental Constitutions*. Armitage, "John Locke, Carolina," 618.

121. Armitage, "Theorist of Empire?," 119, 120.

122. Locke, "Draft B" of the *Essay*, para. 50, quoted in Armitage "Theorist of Empire?," 121.

123. I owe this insightful formulation to Sibylle Fischer's unpublished essay, "When Things Don't Add Up: The Consequences of an Enslaved Enlightenment," presented at Cornell University in 2008.

124. Chakrabarty, *Provincializing Europe*, 43.

125. Patrick Wolfe, "Race and Trace of History," in *Studies in Settler Colonialism: Politics, Identity, and Culture*, ed. Lionel Bateman and Fiona Pilkington (New York, NY: 2011), 275.

126. See Sartori, *Liberalism in Empire*.

127. In an insightful recent essay, Sartori argues that early modern transoceanic commerce furnished political-economic analysis in England with the model for imagining "commercial society." Finding its original concrete reference in the economic relations of the Atlantic, the concept of commercial society was only later applied to an examination of domestic economies. Sartori, "From Statecraft to Social Science."

128. For an examination of this connection around the problem of "wasted" land and labor, see Marc Neocleous, "War on Waste: Original Accumulation and the Violence of Capital," *Science and Society* 75 (2011): 506–28, esp. 515; As Marc Neocleous has recently argued, this accumulative logic and its normative metric construes America and the commons as "waste land" and Native Americans and the English poor as "waste persons," authorizing a righteous "war on waste" through expropriation, enslavement, and transportation. Neocleous, "War on Waste," 506–28. On Locke's position on impressment and colonial transportation, see Sarah Pemberton, *Locke's Political Thought and the Oceans: Pirates, Slaves, and Sailors* (New York: Lexington, 2017)

129. John Locke, *Some Considerations*, quoted in Edward J. Harpham, "Class, Commerce, and the State: Economic Discourse and Lockean Liberalism in the Seventeenth Century," *Western Political Quarterly* 38 (1985): 565–82.

130. Tully, "After the Macpherson Thesis," in *An Approach to Political Philosophy*, 87–88.

131. Edward Andrew, "Possessive Individualism and Locke Doctrine on Taxation," *Good Society* 21 (2012): 151–68, 155.

Chapter 3

1. The interpretive variance owes in no small part to the diversity of imperial contexts and problems that Burke addressed over three decades and on three continents. Coupled with Burke's stature as a practical statesman, this has led some interpreters, such as J. G. A. Pocock and P. J. Marshall, to abandon the search for a coherent image of Burke's political thought. See J. G. A. Pocock, "Burke and the Ancient Constitution," in *Politics, Language, and Time*; P. J. Marshall, "Edmund Burke and India: The Vicissitudes of a Reputation," in *Politics and Trade in the Indian Ocean World*, ed. Rudrangshu Mukherjee and Lakshmi Subramanian (Oxford: Oxford University Press 1998).

2. On shared custom, see Iain Hampsher-Monk, "Edmund Burke and Empire," in *Lineages of Empire: The Historical Roots of British Imperial Thought*, ed. Duncan Kelly (Oxford: Oxford University Press, 2009). On providence and imperial duty, see P. J. Marshall, introduction to *The Writings and Speeches of Edmund Burke*, vol. 7, ed. Peter J. Marshall (Oxford: Clarendon, 1981); and Marshall, "Burke and Empire," in *Hanoverian Britain and Empire: Essays in Memory of Philip Lawson*, ed. Richard Connor, Clyve Jones, and Stephen Taylor (Woodbridge, UK: Boydell, 1981).

3. Mehta, *Liberalism and Empire*; Pitts, *Turn to Empire*.

4. Sara Suleri, *The Rhetoric of English India* (Chicago: University of Chicago Press, 1992); Nicholas Dirks, *The Scandal of Empire: India and the Creation of Imperial Britain* (Cambridge, MA: Belknap Press of Harvard University Press, 2006).

5. Frederick Whelan, *Edmund Burke and India: Political Morality and Empire* (Pittsburgh: University of Pittsburgh Press, 1996); Margaret Kohn and Daniel I. O'Neill, "A Tale of Two Indias: Burke and Mill on Empire and Slavery in the West Indies and America," *Political Theory* 34 (2006): 192–228; Daniel O'Neill, *The Burke-Wollstonecraft Debate: Savagery, Civilization, Democracy* (University Park: Pennsylvania State University Press, 2007).

6. Daniel O'Neill, *Edmund Burke and the Conservative Logic of Empire* (Oakland: University of California Press, 2016); Richard Bourke, *Empire and Revolution: The Political Life of Edmund Burke* (Princeton, NJ: Princeton University Press, 2015).

7. All of the primary texts cited are from *The Writings and Speeches of Edmund Burke*, ed. Paul Langford (Oxford: Clarendon Press, 1981), cited as *W&S* followed by volume and page numbers. All emphases are in the original, unless stated otherwise.

8. As I detail below, the distinction between civil and political liberties is critical to grasping Burke's liberalism. Burke advocated the equal right of all British subjects to freedom from arbitrary government and the freedom to dispose of their property and labor, but openly denied them an equal right to exercise political power. His was a vision of market equality and freedom existing within the framework of social and political hierarchies.

9. Ahmed, *Stillbirth of Capital*.

10. H. V. Bowen, *The Business of Empire: The East India Company and Imperial Britain, 1756–1833* (Cambridge: Cambridge University Press, 2006); Philip Stern, *The Company-State: Corporate Sovereignty and the Early Modern Foundations of the British Empire in India* (Oxford: Oxford University Press, 2011).

11. The only open confrontation with the Mughals in 1689–1690, spurred by the aggressive territorial vision of its Tory governor, Josiah Child, ended with the humiliating seizure of Bombay by Mughal forces.

12. K. N. Chaudhuri, *Asia before Europe: Economy and Civilisation of the Indian Ocean from the Rise of Islam to 1750* (Cambridge, 1990); and David Washbrook, "South Asia, the World System, and World Capitalism," *Journal of Asian Studies* 49 (1990): 479–508.

13. Ahmed, *Stillbirth of Capital*, esp. chap. 6.

14. H. V. Bowen, "Britain in the Indian Ocean Region and Beyond: Contours, Connections, and the Creation of a Global Maritime Empire," in Bowen, Mancke, and Reid, *Britain's Oceanic Empire*, 53.

15. P. J. Marshall, *Making and Unmaking*, 224.

16. For contrasting positions on the "drain theory," see P. K. O'Brien, "European Economic Development, 1–18; and Irfan Habib, *Essays in Indian History: Towards a Marxist Perspective* (London: Anthem, 2002), esp. 259–335.

17. Banaji, "Islam, the Mediterranean," 47–74, at 53. Also see Flynn and Giráldez, "Born Again," *Pacific Economic Review* 13 (2008): 359–87.

18. Banaji, "Islam, the Mediterranean," 65; emphases in the original.

19. Giovanni Arrighi and Jason Moore, "Capitalist Development in World Historical Perspective," in *Phases of Capitalist Development: Booms, Crises and Globalizations*, ed. Robert Albritton, Makoto Itoh, Richard Westra, and Alan Zuege (New York: Palgrave Macmillan, 2001).

20. On real and formal subsumption, see Karl Marx, *Capital*, 1:1019–38. Banaji notes, that the "subsumption of labour into merchant capital is thus irreducible to any single formula" and comprises "a variety of enterprises from putting-out networks and peasant agriculture to slave plantations and factories in the modern sense." Banaji "Islam, the Mediterranean," 67.

21. Karl Marx, *Grundrisse: Foundations of the Critique of Political Economy* (London: Penguin, 1993), 510.

22. For deindustrialization of Indian textile production, see Hameda Hossain, *The Company Weavers of Bengal: The East India Company and the Textile Production in Bengal, 1750–1813* (Delhi: Oxford University Press, 1988). For the Permanent Settlement, see Ranajit Guha, *A Rule of Property for Bengal: An Essay on the Idea of Permanent Settlement* (Durham, NC: Duke University Press, 1996); and Eric Stokes, *English Utilitarians and India* (Oxford: Clarendon Press, 1959). For the commercialization of agriculture, see Rajat Datta, *Society, Economy, and the Market: Commercialization in Rural Bengal, c. 1760–1800* (New Delhi: Manohar, 2000).

23. J. H. Elliott, "The Seizure of Overseas Territories by the European Powers," in *Theories of Empire, 1450–1800*, ed. David Armitage (Aldershot: Ashgate Variorum, 1998), 150. On the commerce in the Indian Ocean prior to European incursion, see Chaudhuri, *Asia before Europe*.

24. Beckert, *Empire of Cotton*, 42–43.

25. Beckert, *Empire of Cotton*, 43–44.

26. Sartori, *Bengal in Global Concept History*, 57. Postcolonial Indian historiographers have extensively investigated the subjugation of the peasant labor in India to capital accumulation through the proliferation and intensification of unfree forms of labor. See Gyan Prakash, *Bonded Histories: Genealogies of Servitude in Colonial India* (Cambridge: Cambridge University Press, 1990); Jairus Banaji, "The Fictions of Free Labour: Contract, Coercion, and the So-Called Unfree Labour," *Historical Materialism* 11 (2003): 69–95. Also see, Kenneth

Pomeranz and Steven Topik, *The World That Trade Created: Society, Culture, and the World Economy, 1400–the Present* (Armonk, NY: M. E. Sharpe, 1999).

27. For an excellent discussion of "vertical concentration" as a strategy of mercantile capitalism in the colonies, see Jairus Banaji, "Merchant Capitalism, Peasant Households, and Industrial Accumulation: Integration of a Model," *Journal of Agrarian Change* 16 (2016): 410–31.

28. Ahmed argues that eighteenth-century Enlightenment thinkers targeted Britain's Indian empire for its disastrous military-fiscalism that wove together war, territorial expansion, monopoly trade, and tribute extraction in the subcontinent. By decimating Bengal's economy, Ahmed maintains, the Company rule in fact spelled the preemption of capitalist development in India rather than its onset. Ahmed's textual analysis is penetrating but it shares with the postcolonial scholars whom he criticizes the idealized Smithian conception of capital as a peaceful market phenomenon. I addressed the pitfalls of this position in chapter 1.

29. Sartori, "British Empire," 642. Also see David Washbrook, "India, 1818–1860: The Two Faces of Colonialism," in *Oxford History of the British Empire*, vol. 3, *The Nineteenth Century*, ed. Andrew Porter (Oxford: Oxford University Press, 1999).

30. Karl Marx, *Capital: A Critique of Political Economy*, vol. 3 (London: Penguin, 1991), 448.

31. Bourke, *Empire and Revolution*, 635. For a contrasting view that prioritizes Britain's constitutional order, see Sartori, *Liberalism in Empire*, 26.

32. On the inaccuracy of the distinction between "settler colonies" and "imperial dependencies" as well as the supposed "authoritarian turn" in the mid-eighteenth century, see Robert Travers, "Contested Despotisms: Problems of Liberty in British India," in *Exclusionary Empire: English Liberty Overseas, 1600–1900*, ed. Jack P. Greene (Cambridge: Cambridge University Press, 2010), 196, 219.

33. Burke himself shared these anxieties, as observed by almost every Burke scholar. Nonetheless, he did not despair, for he thought it possible to arrest the destructive tendencies of empire by maxims of welfare, justice, and parliamentary oversight. See Marshall, "Burke and Empire," 290–91. For a useful overview of the general anxiety over the Indian empire until the 1790s. See Marshall, "Free though Conquering People."

34. See Marshall, "Burke and Empire," 297; and Marshall, "Edmund Burke and India," 256–57; Whelan, *Edmund Burke and India*, 6, 257.

35. On Burke's views on empire as trusteeship, see William Bain, *Between Anarchy and Society: Trusteeship and the Obligations of Power* (Oxford: Oxford University Press, 2003), chap. 2; Richard Bourke, "Liberty, Authority, and Trust in Burke's Idea of Empire," *Journal of the History of Ideas* 3 (2000): 453–71.

36. Travers notes that eighteenth-century English political thought was not entirely unfamiliar with such constitutional entanglements between distant and alien geographies. A complex web of imperial jurisdiction and a "coherent imperial constitution" was believed to tie together the distant parts of the empire. Travers, "Contested Despotisms," in Greene, *Exclusionary Empire*, 200–201. In his inaugural speech at the impeachment, Burke maintained that the quasi-sovereign powers that devolved on the Company from the British Crown and the administrative powers granted to the company by the Mughal emperor created a web of interconnected and overlapping jurisdictions in Bengal (*W&S*, 6:281–82). See Marshall, introduction to *Writings and Speeches*, 7:25–27; Marshall, "Edmund Burke and India," 256, 261–63; and Marshall, "Burke and Empire," 290–96. Also see David Bromwich, introduction to *On Empire, Liberty and Reform: Speeches and Letters*, ed. David Bromwich (New Haven, CT: Yale University Press, 2000), 13, 16; Whelan, *Edmund Burke and India*, 236, 271, 278.

37. By the time the East India Company drew Burke's attention and, shortly thereafter, his wrath, Adam Smith had already supplied a catholic critique of chartered trading companies. Smith had inveighed against chartered companies on two major counts: driven by the necessity for immediate profit, they lacked the broad political vision required for good government, such that they impoverished their dominions instead of investing in their long-term prosperity; second, they lacked the principle of "authority" that would legitimize their rule and had only brute force and despotism available as an instrument of rule. Smith, *Wealth of Nations*, 72–76; Muthu, "Adam Smith's Critique," 185–212. Similarly, for Burke, local customs, values, and institutions were, in Hampsher-Monk's words, the "tools of the politician's trade," without which the only resort was to violence. Burke, "Speech on Fox's India Bill,"

386–87; and Iain Hampsher-Monk, introduction to *The Political Philosophy of Edmund Burke*, ed. Iain Hampsher-Monk (New York: Longman, 1987), 36. Also see Travers, *Ideology and Empire*; Travers, "Ideology and British Expansion in Bengal, 1757–72," *Journal of Imperial and Commonwealth History* 33 (2005): 7–27.

38. MacMillan, "Imperial Constitutions," in Bowen, Mancke, and Reid, *Britain's Oceanic Empire*, 84; Marshall, *Making and Unmaking*, 8–9; and Bourke, *Empire and Revolution*, 350, 365.

39. For instance, Marshall attributes to Burke a "premodern" conception of empire that is concerned with "honor and reputation rather than with power and profit, which would be incidental benefits." Marshall, "Burke and Empire," 297. Strikingly, analyses of Burke's political economic thought rarely incorporate the importance he accords to imperial commerce. Such analyses predominantly focus on his criticism of the East India Company from a laissez-faire perspective or on the corrupting effects of imperial revenue on domestic politics. See, among others, Hampsher-Monk, introduction to *Political Philosophy*; C. B. Macpherson, *Burke* (New York: Hill and Wang, 1980); Donald Winch, *Riches and Poverty: An Intellectual History of Political Economy in Britain, 1750–1834* (Cambridge: Cambridge University Press, 1996), chaps. 7 and 8; J. G. A. Pocock, "Political Economy of Burke's Analysis of the French Revolution," in *Virtue, Commerce, History: Essays on Political Thought and History, Chiefly in the Eighteenth Century* (Cambridge: Cambridge University Press, 1985); Jerry Muller, *The Mind and the Market: Capitalism in Modern European Thought* (New York: Alfred A. Knopf, 2002), chap. 5.

40. Robert Travers, "British India as a Problem of Political Economy: Comparing James Steuart and Adam Smith," in *Lineages of Empire: The Historical Roots of British Imperial Thought*, ed. Duncan Kelly (Oxford: Oxford University Press, 2009), 39.

41. Marshall, *Making and Unmaking*, 226.

42. Reinert, "Empire of Emulation," in Reinert and Røge, *Political Economy of Empire*.

43. Hont, introduction to *Jealousy of Trade*, 7–8. On Burke's economic reason of state, see Francis Canavan, *The Political Economy of Edmund Burke: The Role of Property in His Thought* (New York: Fordham University Press, 1995), 122; Winch, *Riches and Poverty*, 210. O'Neill sees Burke's free trade arguments with America and Ireland as reluctant concessions aimed to hold the empire together. O'Neill, *Edmund Burke*, 59, 82, 137.

44. By the same token, Hont continues, the confinement of murderous intensity to colonial spaces left "Europe's intracontinental trade" unaffected. Hont, introduction to *Jealousy of Trade*, 17.

45. Edmund Burke and William Burke, *An Account of the European Settlement in Americas* (London: Printed for J. Dodsley, 1757), 128–29.

46. Twelve years after this speech, and in an unusually close examination of the political arithmetic of the British economy, Burke would note that out of a total of 10.5 million pounds of British balance of trade in 1796, a staggering four million pounds (nearly 40%) was in the East and West Indies trade (*W&S*, 9:384).

47. The necessity of an imperial political vision was previously asserted by Burke on the American question. See *Address to the Colonists* (*W&S*, 3:285), for Burke's views on improving the English constitution in order to accommodate the increase in dominions and population.

48. H. V. Bowen, "British Conceptions of Global Empire, 1756–83," *Journal of Imperial and Commonwealth History* 26 (1998), 1–27; Travers, "Constitutions, Contact Zones," in Bowen, Mancke, and Reid, *Britain's Oceanic Empire*.

49. O'Neill, *Edmund Burke*, 33.

50. P. J. Marshall, *Problems of Empire: Britain and India, 1757–1813* (London: Allen and Unwin, 1968), 30. See, for instance, Burke's "Speech on State of East India Company" and "Speech on Bengal Judicature Bill," both delivered in 1781 (*W&S* 5). Although Burke was critical of the Company's dealings with the local rulers, he nonetheless defended its independence from government.

51. The Select Committee investigated the conflict of jurisdiction between the Council of Bengal and the Supreme Court of Bengal, the latter having been formed by North's Regulating Act in 1773 in order to curtail the abusive practices of the Company servants in India. In the course of his inquiries, Burke was heavily influenced by the information provided by Philip Francis, a recalled member of the Council of Bengal, an inveterate enemy

of Warren Hastings, and an English Physiocrat whose plans for India would shape Burke's drafting of the Fox's India Bill.

52. Emma Rothschild, "Global Commerce and the Question of Sovereignty in the Eighteenth Century Provinces," *Modern Intellectual History* 1 (2004): 3–26, 11. Also see Travers, "British India," in Kelly, *Lineages of Empire*.

53. Marshall, *Problems of Empire*, 59–60.

54. Pitts, *Turn to Empire*, 96.

55. Bourke, *Empire and Revolution*, 828.

56. Pocock, *Barbarism and Religion*, 4:7. On the British preconceptions of Asiatic despotism and their impact on the practices of imperial governance in India, see Travers, "Contested Despotism"; and Travers, "Ideology and British Expansion."

57. For a meticulous discussion of the Greek-Roman dichotomy in the British political imaginary and its implications for empire building, see Armitage, *Ideological Origins*.

58. Bowen, *Business of Empire*, 15.

59. The East India Company had been resorting to extraordinary means of raising revenue, one of which was to engage in "subsidiary alliances" whereby the Company troops would be deployed for "protecting" local rulers in return for a fee. In addition to this racketeering scheme, the Company also engaged in mercenary operations by lending British troops to its local "allies" for their military campaigns.

60. Burke's bundling of the national reputation, Company interests, and the well-being of the natives is an enduring theme in his works on India and reappears almost identically in his "Speech on Pitt's India Bill" (*W&S*, 5:457).

61. Hampsher-Monk's introduction to *Political Philosophy of Edmund Burke* offers an exemplary formulation of this interpretation. Marshall, Bromwich, and Whelan pursue the same line of explanation. See Marshall, "Edmund Burke and India," "Edmund Burke and India," and the introductions to the *Writings and Speeches*, vols. 5, 6, and 7; Bromwich, introduction to *On Empire*; Whelan, *Edmund Burke and India*, esp. chap. 2.

62. Burke's portents were somewhat vindicated as the King used Fox's India Bill as an excuse to dismiss the Fox-North coalition, and Pitt's electoral victory in 1784 was indebted to considerable support by the India interests. Paul Benfield, a merchant who made his fortune in Madras, in part by funding local wars through expensive loans, was for Burke the embodiment of the corrupt Indian wealth in British politics.

63. Burke's anxious diagnosis of the Indian influence goes back to 1783, even before the Indian influence would help Pitt strip the Rockinghamites of the governmental seat. In "Speech on Fox's India Bill," the returned Company servants "loaded with odium and with riches" were depicted as a pestilence that infiltrated the body politic of the English elite: "they marry into your families; they enter into your senate; they ease your estates by loans; they raise their value by their demand" (*W&S*, 5:443, 403). Two years later, back in parliamentary opposition, Burke is more explicit in his indictment of Paul Benfield, who had "no fewer than eight members in the last parliament"; ministers of the Pitt administration; and Henry Dundas, a "prosecutor turned protector" for securing political protection for the Indian delinquents (*W&S*, 5:541–52). In a masterful passage during the impeachment proceedings, he cautions the House, "[T]oday the Commons of Great Britain prosecute the delinquents of India. Tomorrow, the delinquents of India will be the Commons of Great Britain" (*W&S*, 7:63). The same idea is repeated in *Reflections on the Revolution in France*, where the continual greatness of the House is predicated on keeping "the breakers of law in India from becoming the makers of law in England" (*W&S*, 8:96).

64. Marshall, introduction to *Writings and Speeches*, 7:4–35.

65. Bromwich, introduction to *On Empire*, 29. Also see Whelan, *Edmund Burke and India*, esp. 14 and 275–91.

66. Bourke, *Empire and Revolution*, 653.

67. P. J. Cain and A. G. Hopkins, *British Imperialism: Innovation and Expansion, 1688–1914* (New York: Longman, 1993).

68. See Macpherson, *Burke*; Pocock, "Political Economy"; Muller, *Mind and the Market*; Himmelfarb, *Idea of Poverty*; Corey Robin, "Edmund Burke and the Problem of Value," *Raritan* 36 (2016): 82–106. For a more skeptical approach to Burke's commercial allegiances

see Bromwich, introduction to *On Empire*; Hampsher-Monk, introduction to *The Political Philosophy*; Winch, *Riches and Poverty*. On this point, I broadly agree with Macpherson, Muller, and Himmelfarb that by the late eighteenth century, the fundamental features of a capitalist economy were more or less in place in England, and Burke's defense of the existing political economic system was therefore tantamount to a defense of the commercial-capitalist economy.

69. Donald Winch, "Science and the Legislator: Adam Smith and After," *Economic Journal* 93 (1982): 501–20.

70. Himmerfarb, *Idea of Poverty*, 27–28.

71. For the genealogy of this Whig political economic vision, see Pincus, *1688*, esp. chap. 12. The Whig political economy to which Burke subscribed viewed labor, rather than land, as the principal source of economic value. The assumption of labor's potentially unlimited capacity to create value made it possible for the first time to think of international trade as a positive-sum game. Burke criticized zero-sum conceptions of trade in a letter to a friend. "It is in the interest of the commercial world that wealth should be found everywhere. I know that it is but too natural for us to see our own *certain* ruin in the *possible* prosperity of other people. . . . Trade is not a limited thing; as if the objects of mutual demand and consumption could not stretch beyond the bounds of our Jealousies." Burke, *Two Letters from Mr. Burke to Gentlemen in the City of Bristol*, quoted in Muller, *Mind and the Market*, 115.

72. True to his Whig heritage, Burke hitched improvement in land to the prospect of drawing profit from it. "Every law against property is a law against industry," and such laws in Ireland were tantamount to proclaiming, "Thou shalt not improve." In Ireland, Ascendancy policies culminated in unproductive tenants reluctantly working the land of absentee landlords, leaving the agricultural lands unimproved and the public miserable (*W&S*, 9:476–77).

73. Comparing Burke's "Economical Reform" to Locke's journal entry "Understanding" offers one a view of the Baconian undercurrents that connected the two political theorists-cum-statesmen. For Locke's Baconian allegiances, see chapter 2 of this study.

74. Burke expressed the duty of the politician through an artistic analogy: "People are the masters. They have only to express wants at large and in gross. We are the expert artists; we are the skillful workmen, to shape their desires into perfect form, and to fit the utensil to the use" (*W&S* 3:547). In *Letter to a Noble Lord*, the good governance of the economy, or in Burke's words, "true oeconomy" or "higher oeconomy . . . is a distributive virtue, and consists not in saving, but in selection." It has "larger views. It demands a discriminating judgment and a sagacious mind" (*W&S*, 9:162). These words corroborate Pocock's observation that Burke's definition of virtue was based more on the management of public revenue than martial prowess, which made him a defender of the commercial society and the Whig aristocratic government that promoted it. See Pocock, "Political Economy," 209.

75. Smith, *Wealth of Nations*, 1:284–85.

76. See Albert Hirschman, *The Passions and the Interest* (Princeton, NJ: Princeton University Press, 1997), esp. 41, 53–62.

77. Burke elaborated an early account of this transformation in his aborted project, *An Abridgment of English History*. For a recent discussion of this work and its relevance for Burke's political philosophy, see Richard Bourke, "Edmund Burke and the Politics of Conquest," *Modern Intellectual History* 4 (2007): 403–32.

78. It has been suggested that Burke's economic reform policies aimed at curbing Crown influence, just as his advocacy of free trade with America targeted the revenue that the Crown could derive from duties on commerce. See, Hampsher-Monk, introduction to *Political Philosophy*, 19–20. While certainly plausible, this argument misses the broader principle and scope of Burke's economic argument, which he extended to the nobility as a whole. The nobility had to compensate for their "luxury and even their ease" by paying "contribution to the public; not because they are vicious principles, but because they are unproductive" (*W&S* 9:349). Although he did not explicitly refer to Smith, Burke's ideas on political economy, and particularly his assessment of revenue management, echoed the Smithian dichotomy between capital and revenue. Compare Burke's "Speech on Economical Reform" to the *Wealth of Nations*, 1:277–90.

79. The legal enclosure of common lands consolidated large tracts of private property that had been in the making since the fifteenth century and entrenched capitalist relations in

agriculture. See Michael Perelman, *Classical Political Economy: Primitive Accumulation and the Social Division of Labor* (London: Rowman and Allenhend, 1984), chaps. 2–4.

80. Unfortunately, Burke left no substantial tract or speech on the English enclosures. The only relevant remarks, which are mostly made in passing, can be found in his unpublished letters entitled "Mnemon to the *Public Advertiser*" (*W&S*, 2:75–87). Burke's position in these letters is not very clear, though it seems broadly in line with his economic reform proposals, with additional concerns with the rights of the poor and equity of the process. For a brief discussion, see Canavan, *Political Economy*, 118–19.

81. Burke stated his positive stance on the expansion of wage labor in his examination of the British economy in the first half of the 1790s. "An improved and improving agriculture, which implies a great augmentation of labor, has not yet found itself at a stand . . . An increasing capital calls for labor: and an increasing population answers to the call. Our manufactures augmented for both the foreign and domestick consumption . . . have always found the laborious hand ready for the liberal pay" (*W&S*, 9:353).

82. Robin, "Edmund Burke," 94.

83. Robin, "Edmund Burke," 83.

84. Burke's admonition of government intervention extended to credit markets. He criticized the regulation of the interest rate as tantamount to "a tax on that particular species [i.e., monied] property. In effect, it would be the most unjust and impolitick of all things, unequal taxation. It would throw upon one description of persons in the community, that burthen which ought by fair and equitable distribution to rest upon the whole" (*W&S*, 9: 346–47).

85. Burke resorted to providential language in explaining this unhappy state: "[I]t is the common doom of man that he must eat his bread by the sweat of his brow" (*W&S*, 3:355). Famine is explained in the same vein, as the decision of the benign and wise disposer to "with-hold the necessaries of life" (*W&S*, 9:137).

86. The natural entitlement of the capital owner to a profit on his capital was restated in Burke's defense of the monied property. "The monied men have a right to look to advantage to in the investment of their property. To advance their money, they risk it; and the risk is to be included in the price" (*W&S*, 9:346–47). This is obviously a far cry from the condemnation of usury in the Classical-Christian conception of moral economy, and opens to question the classical-traditionalist image that some have attributed to Burke. See, above all, Bromwich, introduction to *On Empire*, 20, 37.

87. Burke's natural chain of subordination in agriculture, though it used the language of natural law and the great chain of being, in fact captured the capitalist triad of landlord-tenant-laborer that had by the late eighteenth century dominated the south of England. Burke himself was at the top of the chain with a moderately sized estate that he rented out to tenant farmers.

88. See Robin, "Edmund Burke."

89. Freedom of contract and the juridical equality of the contracting parties also held valid for the financial transactions between the state and the citizens. In Burke's view, public debt, too, should ideally have conformed to the principles of a bargain. "Compulsion destroys the freedom of a bargain . . . the moment that shame, or fear, or force, are directly applied to a loan, credit perishes" (*W&S*, 9:347). Of course, Burke had in his sights the French revolutionary government's irregular borrowing practices, which bordered on taxation under the guise of "voluntary contributions." Insofar as it remained purely commercial, Burke did not seem to have a problem with the eighteenth-century novelty of public debt, which for Pocock marks *the* momentous transformation of the state-citizen relationship, and the distinctive feature of the commercial society. See J. G. A Pocock, "The Mobility of Property and the Emergence of Eighteenth Century Sociology," in *Virtue, Commerce, History: Essays on Political Thought and History, Chiefly in the Eighteenth Century* (Cambridge: Cambridge University Press, 1985), 109–12.

90. The language Burke used to describe the motives behind government intervention is worth attention. As opposed to the "reasonable" principle of self-interest that animated commercial actors, government intervention was driven by the "*zealots* of the *sect* of regulation" (*W&S*, 9:126, emphasis mine). What is equally striking is Burke's treatment of "pity," especially for the poor, as a kind of enthusiasm: "When we talk of the poor, that moment our reason quits us. Pity is one of the noblest of the Passions. So is zeal, but zeal and pity are still passions, and

extremely apt to blind good men" (W&S, 9:129n2). These passages lend considerable support to the argument that in political economy Burke was a thoroughly bourgeois subject.

91. The biographical and intellectual connection between Burke and the Scottish Enlightenment
is demonstrated in O'Neill, *Burke-Wollstonecraft Debate*, chap. 2.

92. Nicholas Phillipson, "Language, Sociability, and History: Some Reflections on the
Foundations of Adam Smith's Science of Man," in *Economy, Polity, and Society: British
Intellectual History, 1750–1950*, ed. Stefan Collini, Richard Whatmore, and Brian Young
(Cambridge: Cambridge University Press, 2000), 70. Burke parted ways with the Scottish
philosophers, however, on the direction of the causal chain. Whereas Adam Smith, William
Robertson, John Millar, and Adam Ferguson looked to the commercial mode of subsistence
to extrapolate polished manners and civil institutions, Burke prioritized the attenuating
impact of organized religion and prescriptive hierarchy on manners. Only after a certain
level of refinement was achieved could the relations characteristic of commerce take hold.
See Pocock, "Political Economy" 196–99, 210; Winch, *Riches and Poverty*, 176–79; O'Neill,
Burke-Wollstonecraft Debate, chaps. 1 and 2.

93. Burke expressed the distinction between civil and political liberties most unambiguously in
the *Reflections*, where he designated property, employment, inheritance, and patrimony to
be "amongst the direct original rights of men in civil society," while denying "power, authority, and direction" to all members of a commonwealth. (W&S, 8:110).

94. David Hume, *Essays Moral, Political, Literary*, ed. Eugene Miller (Indianapolis, IN: Liberty
Classics, 1987), 70.

95. Ironically, as Travers notes, the designation of civil liberties as distinct from and more fundamental to political liberties would furnish the late eighteenth- and nineteenth-century
empire builders with the notion of "despotism of law," a rather convenient ideological construct for governing an alien people in a distant province without political accountability
yet without the odium of arbitrary government. Travers, "Constitutions, Contact Zones,"
in Bowen, Mancke, and Reid, *Britain's Oceanic Empire*, 120; Travers and "British India,"
154–55.

96. Here, I am paraphrasing Muller's designation of hereditary aristocracy and organized religion as the "noncontractual basis of commercial society" in Burke's account. Given that the
Scottish stadial theory did not credit social contract theories, the "noncommercial basis of
commercial society" is a more apt moniker. Muller, "Edmund Burke," 137–38.

97. On "politicization of commerce," see Bourke, *Empire and Revolution*, 559.

98. There was no greater debasement of justice for Burke than allowing one to be a judge in one's
own case. The moment that government or its agents became a party to the contracts which
they also enforced, the general law of equality was irretrievably destroyed. This was the case
not only in how the Company ran its operations in India, but also how it managed its internal government. Former Company servants involved in delinquencies in India later became
members of the Court of Directors that was supposed to inspect the Indian delinquents
(W&S, 5:202–3, 219). "The vote is not to protect the stock, but the stock is bought to obtain
the vote," in order to protect corrupt agents, their corrupt networks of patronage, and their
illegitimate dealings in India (W&S, 5:437). A more detailed discussion of the principle of
impartial arbitration in Burke's moral philosophy can be found in Bromwich, introduction
to *On Empire*.

99. *Eleventh Report on the Select Committee*, though it apparently deals with the conflict between
Hastings and Francis in the Council of Bengal, is replete with references to the expropriation
and humiliation of the Indian nobility. This report, drafted mainly by Burke, contains the
bulk of the material that would fuel Burke's later speeches on India.

100. *Ninth Report of the Select Committee* was the most comprehensive tract Burke ever wrote on
the political economy of the Indian dominions.

101. On this occasion, Burke reiterated the recipe of a light and prudent government that he had
prescribed for the administering the economy of the American colonies, which he argued
would encourage enterprise and industry, promote prosperity, and secure a solid revenue
base for the state (W&S, 3:163, 280–81).

102. "The difference in favor of the first conquerors is this; the Asiatic conquerors very soon
abated of their ferocity, because they made the conquered country their own. They rose

or fell with the rise or fall of the territory they lived in. . . . But under the English government the order is reversed. The Tartar invasion was mischievous, but it is our protection that destroys India. It was their enmity, but it is our friendship" (*W&S*, 5:401–2).

103. An exemplary account can be found in the "Speech on the Sixth Article of Impeachment" (*W&S*, 6:37–59).

104. Burke's argument prefigured the early twentieth-century drain theory articulated by nationalist Indian political economists, most notably Dadabhai Naoroji. See Manu Goswami, *Producing India: From Colonial Economy to National Space* (Chicago: University of Chicago Press, 2004).

105. The Parliament not only came to the financial rescue of the Company, it also granted it exemption from the tea tax that its colonial competitors had to pay.

106. Ahmed, *Stillbirth of Capital*, 142.

107. In a *farman* proclaimed in 1717, Emperor Farrukhsiyar had granted the Company exemptions from export duties. Originally intended as a corporate exemption from export duties, the Emperor's grant had in the hands of Company servants turned into privileges in private inland trading at the expense of local competitors.

108. This theme was particularly pronounced among the French *philosophes*. For François Raynal and Dennis Diderot, the frontier was synonymous with the decay of civility, a space that rendered colonists "dissolute, unlocated, and hence uncivilized." Charles Talleyrand described settlers as "individuals without industry, without leaders, without customs." See Pagden, *Lords of All the World*, 165–68. Strikingly, Pagden notes, the French philosophers believed that only the English were immune to the degenerative tendencies of the frontier. Burke's studies and efforts about India perhaps represent the first critique of the *English frontier* that matches its French counterpart in empirical expanse and theoretical depth. Chapter 4 spends considerable time unpacking this trope in the writings of Edward Gibbon Wakefield.

109. Burke cited the American colonists' particularly fierce sentiments of liberty as a cause for reconciliation instead of heavy-handed subordination. In their weaker habits of subordination, the colonists bore a faint resemblance to ancient barbarians and contemporary savages who were thought to have an untamed and ferocious notion of freedom. See O'Neill, *Edmund Burke*, chap. 2; Bourke, *Empire and Revolution*, chaps. 6 and 9.

110. On isolation, alienation, and aggression in India, see Jon E. Wilson, "Anxieties of Distance: Codification in Early Colonial Bengal," *Modern Intellectual History* 4 (2007): 7–23; and Wilson, *The Domination of Strangers: Modern Governance in Eastern India 1780–1835* (Basingstoke, UK: Palgrave MacMillan, 2008), chaps. 2 and 3.

111. Pocock argues that eighteenth-century exponents of commercial society defined their modern civilization by contrasting it with a rude, unpolished, and bellicose depiction of the citizens of ancient Greco-Roman republics. See Pocock, "Mobility of Property," 114–15; and Pocock, "Political Economy" 195–96. Indeed, Burke did not hide his dislike for the Britons' "warlike ancestors" and their "barbarous, vulgar distinctions" (*W&S*, 3:282).

112. This is the argument adopted by Bourke, "Edmund Burke," and *Empire and Revolution*, 559, 628, 647.

113. Chatterjee, *Black Hole*, 57.

114. Hume had admitted that free governments were more oppressive toward their conquered provinces than despotic ones, although he had refrained from extending the implications to a discussion of modern commercial societies. Smith had carried Hume's observation further, contending that citizens of liberal commercial societies treated their slaves much more brutally than those of absolutist monarchies. Hume, *Essays*, 33–34; Smith, *Wealth of Nations*, 2:38–39. Also see Onur Ulas Ince, "Between Commerce and Empire: David Hume, Colonial Slavery, and Commercial Incivility," *History of Political Thought* (forthcoming).

115. Alexander Dow, *The History of Hindostan* (1779), quoted in Chatterjee, *Black Hole*, 58.

116. The "ambivalence" of eighteenth-century Enlightenment thought regarding the violent history yet cosmopolitan promise of "global commerce" has been explored most systematically in Sankar Muthu, "Conquest, Commerce, and Cosmopolitanism in Enlightenment Political Thought," in *Empire and Modern Political Thought*, ed. Sankar Muthu (Cambridge: Cambridge University Press, 2012); and Jennifer Pitts, "The Global in Enlightenment Historical Thought," in *A Companion to Global Historical Thought*, ed. Prasenjit Duara, Viren Murthy,

and Andrew Sartori (Chichester, UK: Wiley, 2014), 184–96. Partaking in this ambivalence, Richard Bourke remarks, "Burke could argue that although *doux commerce* had descended into conquest and belligerence in Asia, it had facilitated enlightenment and liberality in Britain." Bourke, *Empire and Revolution*, 840.

117. Siraj Ahmed, "The Theater of Civilized Self: Edmund Burke and the East India Trials," *Representations* 78 (2002): 28–55, 45. Ahmed argues that this vision was ultimately a theatrical ploy to conjure up a semblance of moral nationhood for the British to behold and emulate, as Burke had concluded toward the end of the impeachment that the national character had been hopelessly corrupted by the dependence on the trade and finance of the Indian empire.

118. Whelan, *Edmund Burke and India*, 275–97.

119. One can also adduce Burke's attempt to prove that Muslim and Hindu laws were in fact just laws on par with the English common law (*W&S*, 6:352–67). In a rhetorical tour de force in his speech in the opening of impeachment, Burke proclaimed, "I would as willingly have him [Hastings] tried upon the law of Koran, or the Institutes of Temarlane, or upon the Common Law or the Statue Law of this Kingdom" (*W&S*, 6:365).

120. Mehta, *Liberalism and Empire*, 41–42, 132–44, 175.

121. This is the position elaborated in Pitts, *Turn to Empire*, chap. 3, esp. 71–77.

122. Bell, "Dream Machine," 33.

123. O'Neill, *Edmund Burke*, 1–2. Also see Daniel O'Neill, "Rethinking Burke and India," *History of Political Thought* 30 (2009): 492–523; Kohn and O'Neill, "Tale of Two Indias."

124. On Burke's views on Native Americans and Africans, see O'Neill, *Edmund Burke*, 64–87.

125. On this score, Bourke remarks that the major trouble with the Indian empire was that "instead of pursuing a course of civilizing conquest, the Company had become mired in expropriating usurpation . . . thus compromising the national honor along with domestic reason of state." Bourke, *Empire and Revolution*, 538.

126. E. Burke and W. Burke, *Account of the European Settlement*, 2:127–28.

127. Burke's position on this matter was entirely consistent with the political economy of settler expansion and commercial agriculture in North America, which depended on the combination of American land and African labor, requiring the subordinate retention of Africans (enslaved or otherwise disciplined) and extirpation of American natives. Wolfe, "Settler Colonialism," 387–404, esp. 377–78.

128. The intellectual attempts to salvage Burke from aggressive imperialism and exclusion constitute a broad church. For a comprehensive summary and, in my opinion, a persuasive critique, see O'Neill, *Edmund Burke*, chap. 1.

129. On the "incivility" of West Indian slave societies and the West Indian interest in British politics, see Christopher Brown, "Politics of Slavery," in Armitage and Braddick, *British Atlantic World*, 232–51; Craton, "Property and Propriety," in Brewer and Staves. *Early Modern Conceptions of Property*.

130. O'Neill maintains that Burke judged the civilizational status of non-European societies based on the presence or absence of hereditary nobilities and organized religion (see generally O'Neill, *Edmund Burke*). By this metric, India and Ireland (especially the Indian and Irish nobilities), attracted Burke's sympathy, while Africans and Native Americans (together with the Irish poor and Indian *ryots*) received at best his high-handed paternalism. Keen to establish his conservative-imperialist Burke against cosmopolitan and anti-imperial representations, O'Neill glosses over Burke's economic liberalism. Crucially, what is lost sight of is the variable of "socioeconomic complexity" that structured Burke's conception of civilizational progress.

131. For excellent recent treatments, see Istvan Hont, *Politics in Commercial Society*; Berry, *Idea of Commercial Society*.

132. J. G. A. Pocock, introduction to *Reflections on the Revolution in France*, by Edmund Burke, ed. J. G. A. Pocock (Indianapolis, IN: Hackett, 1987), xv.

133. Smith, *Wealth of Nations*, 1:77.

134. On the historical origins and the geographic scope of the language of commercial society in early modern English political discourse, see Pincus, "Neither Machiavellian Moment"; and Sartori, "From Statecraft to Social Science," 181–214.

135. Michel Foucault, *The Birth of Biopolitics: Lectures at the College de France, 1978–1979*, ed. Michael Senellart (New York: Palgrave MacMillan, 2008), 279–81.

136. Hampsher-Monk, introduction to *Political Philosophy*, 35.

137. Macpherson, *Burke*, 50.

138. Bromwich, introduction to *On Empire*, 36–37.

139. This skepticism was not exclusively or even distinctively Burkean. The primacy of psychological moral sense over the faculty of abstract reason was an epistemological tenet shared widely by the Scottish Enlightenment philosophers. O'Neill, *Burke-Wollstonecraft Debate*, 33–34.

140. See above all O'Neill, *Edmund Burke*. It is worth noting the parallels between Robertson's and Burke's analyses of India's civilizational status. Robertson, with whom Burke had the most intellectual affinity among the Scottish Enlightenment philosophers, had depicted India as an ancient and commercial society, though recently languishing under the Mughal rule. See Robertson's appendix to *An Historical Disquisition Concerning the Knowledge which the Ancients Had of India* (London: Strahan and Cadell, 1791).

141. Pocock, "Mobility of Property," 121.

142. For an early observation of the parallels between France and India, see Regina Janes, "Edmund Burke's Flying Leap from India to France," *History of European Ideas* 7 (1986): 509–27.

143. Jeanne Morefield, *Empires without Imperialism: Anglo-American Decline and the Politics of Deflection* (Oxford: Oxford University Press, 2014).

144. O'Neill highlights Burke's strategy of "blaming the settler colonists and other administrators of empire at the periphery" for the failures of empire. Although O'Neill does a remarkable job in reconstructing Burke's indictment of the Protestant Ascendancy for the formation of the United Irishmen, he overlooks Burke's earlier exercise of this strategy in India. O'Neill, *Edmund Burke*, 156–57, 174.

145. Ince, "Between Commerce and Empire," forthcoming; Ince, "Adam Smith, Settler Colonialism, and Cosmopolitan Overstretch" (unpublished manuscript).

146. Adam Smith, quoted in Himmelfarb, *Idea of Poverty*, 66.

147. Only by neglecting Burke's political economy can O'Neill argue that "Edmund Burke developed a theoretical defense of the British imperial project wholly outside the theoretical parameters and assumptions of liberalism." O'Neill, *Edmund Burke*, 169. For the institutional conditions of global commerce as a theoretical problem in the eighteenth-century, see Emma Rothschild "Adam Smith in the British Empire," in *Empire and Modern Political Thought*, ed. Sankar Muthu (Cambridge: Cambridge University Press, 2012); and Hont, *Jealousy of Trade*.

148. Pitts, *Turn to Empire*.

149. O'Neill, *Edmund Burke*, 173.

Chapter 4

1. Duncan Bell, "John Stuart Mill on Colonies," *Political Theory* 38 (2010): 34–64.

2. Bell, "Dream Machine." Also see Wolfe, *Settler Colonialism and the Transformation of Anthropology: The Politics and Poetics of an Ethnographic Event* (London: Casse, 1999), 1.

3. By contrast, recent critical studies in law, political economy, and imperial history have shown more interest in Wakefield's writings. See, for instance, Gabriel Piterberg and Lorenzo Veracini, "Wakefield, Marx, and the World Turned Inside Out," *Journal of Global History* 10 (2015): 457–78; Marc Neocleous, "International Law as Primitive Accumulation; Or, the Secret of Systematic Colonization," *European Journal of International Law* 23 (2012): 941–62; Ballantyne, "Theory and Practice of Empire-Building," in Aldrich and McKenzie, *Routledge History of Western Empires*; and Ballantyne, "Remaking the Empire from Newgate: Wakefield's *A Letter from Sydney*," in *Ten Books That Shaped the British Empire: Creating an Imperial Commons*, ed. Antoinette Burton and Isabel Hofmeyer (Durham, NC: Duke University Press, 2014), 29–49.

4. Winch, *Classical Political Economy*, esp. part 2; Donald Winch, "Classical Economics and the Case for Colonization" in *Great Britain and the Colonies, 1815–1855*, ed. A. G. L. Shaw (London: Methuen, 1970); Bernard Semmel, *Rise of Free Trade Imperialism: Political*

Economy, the Empire of Free Trade and Imperialism, 1750–1850 (Cambridge: Cambridge University Press, 1970), esp. chaps. 4 and 5; and Semmel, "The Philosophic Radicals and Colonialism" in Shaw, *Great Britain*, 77–92.

5. In advancing the arguments of this chapter, I am indebted to J. G. A. Pocock's expert treatment of the Enlightenment categories of savagery and civilization. Pocock, *Barbarism and Religion*, vol. 4; and Pocock, *The Discovery of Islands: Essays in British History* (Cambridge: Cambridge University Press, 2005). For excellent examinations of these civilizational categories in Wakefield's colonization theory, see Erik Olssen, "Wakefield and the Scottish Enlightenment, with Particular Reference to Adam Smith and His Wealth of Nations," in *Edward Gibbon Wakefield and the Colonial Dream: A Reconsideration*, ed. Philip Temple (Wellington, UK: Friends of the Turnbull Library, 1997); Olssen, "Mr. Wakefield and New Zealand as an Experiment in Post-Enlightenment Practice," *New Zealand Journal of History* 31 (1997): 197–218; Pat Moloney, "Savagery and Civilization: Early Victorian Notions," *New Zealand Journal of History* 35 (2001): 153–76.

6. Bell, "Dream Machine," 43.

7. Settler colonialism as a distinct subfield of study has been flourishing. See, among others, Wolfe, "Settler Colonialism," 387–404; Veracini, *Settler Colonialism*; and Coulthard, *Red Skin, White Masks*.

8. See, above all, the essays in Istvan Hont and Michael Ignatieff, eds., *Wealth and Virtue: The Shaping of Political Economy in the Scottish Enlightenment* (Cambridge: Cambridge University Press, 1983); Winch, *Riches and Poverty*; and Himmelfarb, *Idea of Poverty*.

9. Boyd Hilton, *A Mad, Bad, and Dangerous People? England 1783–1846* (Oxford: Clarendon, 2006), 573.

10. Ibid., 8–9. On Parliamentary Enclosures, see G. E. Mingay, *Parliamentary Enclosure in England: An Introduction to Its Causes, Incidence, and Impact, 1750–1850* (London: Longman, 1997).

11. Hilton, *Mad, Bad, and Dangerous*, 23. Also, see Charles Kindleberger, *Manias, Panics, and Crashes: A History of Financial Crises* (New York: Basic, 1978).

12. Winch, *Riches and Poverty*, 246–47; Semmel, *Rise of Free Trade*, 51–54.

13. A. G. L. Shaw, introduction to *Great Britain*, 11–13. Also see Edward Kittrell, "Development of the Theory of Colonization in English Classical Political Economy," *Southern Economic Journal* 31 (1965): 189–206; G. S. L. Tucker, "The Application and Significance of Economic Theories of the Effect of Economic Progress on the Rate of Profit, 1800–1850," in Shaw, *Great Britain*, 132; Semmel, *Rise of Free Trade*, chap. 4; Semmel, "Philosophic Radicals," 79–80; Winch, *Classical Political Economy*, 79–81; and Winch, "Classical Economics," 97–99.

14. For a useful overview of the orthodox-heterodox debate about overproduction, its causes, and possible remedies, see Bernard Semmel, *Liberal Ideal and the Demons of Empire: Theories of Imperialism from Adam Smith to Lenin* (Baltimore: Johns Hopkins University Press, 1993), chap. 2.

15. For Wakefield's biography, see Philip Temple, *A Sort of Conscience: The Wakefields* (Auckland, NZ: Auckland University Press, 2002).

16. Piterberg and Veracini, "Wakefield, Marx," 461. On poverty and criminality in London, see Peter Linebaugh, *The London Hanged: Crime and Civil Society in the Eighteenth Century* (New York: Verso, 2003).

17. Edward G. Wakefield, *Facts Relating to the Punishment of Death in the Metropolis*, in *The Collected Works of Edward Gibbon Wakefield*, ed. M. F. Lloyd Prichard (London: Collins, 1968), 266. All citations are to this edition; individual works are abbreviated as follows: *A Letter from Sydney* (LS); *Plan of Company to be Established for the Purpose of Founding a Colony in Southern Australia* (PC); *England and America* (EA); *A View of the Art of Colonization* (AC). All emphases are in the original, unless stated otherwise.

18. Ballantyne, "Theory and Practice," 91.

19. Because of his tarnished reputation, Wakefield published most of his works anonymously. However, many influential thinkers and policymakers knew of Wakefield's authorship. Ballantyne, "Remaking the Empire," 40.

20. For the series of colonization societies and colonial land companies founded by Wakefield, see Prichard, introduction to *Collected Works*, 29–43.

21. Ballantyne, "Remaking the Empire," 33.
22. For an authoritative study of the Philosophic Radicals, see Elie Halévy, *The Growth of Philosophic Radicalism* (London: Faber and Faber, 1952).
23. A longer list of subscribers to Wakefield's principles of colonization can be found on the member list of the Provisional Committee of the South Australian Land Company (13 of the 23 members being MPs), in "Appendix III" to *England and America*, in *Collected Works*, ed. Prichard, 615.
24. Semmel, "Philosophic Radicals," 77–78.
25. Duncan Bell, "John Stuart Mill on Colonies," *Political Theory* 38 (2010): 34–64. Furthermore, Wakefield participated in the Durham Mission to Canada and composed the parts of the Durham Report on the management of public lands (1839); drafted and lobbied for the passing of the bill that created South Australia as a British province (1834); and served as witness before parliamentary select committees regarding the management of colonial waste lands (1836), New Zealand (1840), and Australia (1841).
26. See, for instance, Michael Turnbull, *New Zealand Bubble: Wakefield Theory in Practice* (Wellington, UK: Price Milburn, 1959); John Miller, *Early Victorian New Zealand: A Study of Racial Tension and Social Attitudes, 1839–1852* (London: Oxford University Press, 1958); Peter Stuart, *Edward Gibbon Wakefield in New Zealand: His Political Career, 1853–4* (Wellington, UK: Price Milburn, 1971); and Douglass Pike, *Paradise of Dissent* (London: Longmans, 1957).
27. Examining the prelude to the economic crisis of 1825–26, Boyd Hilton remarks, "The reduction of interest on government debt, and a shortage of opportunities for domestic investment in the period between the canal and railway building eras, fortuitously deflected all this extra capital into foreign loans and joint-stock ventures overseas." Boyd Hilton, *Corn, Cash, Commerce: The Economic Policies of the Tory Governments 1815–1830* (Oxford: Oxford University Press, 1977), 204–5.
28. On Malthus's exclusion of moral questions from economic policy, see David McNally, *Against the Market: Political Economy, Market Socialism, and the Marxist Critique* (London: Verso, 1993), chap. 3; Himmelfarb, *Idea of Poverty*, chaps. 4 and 5. On the moralization of English middle-class attitudes on the plight of the poor, see Susan Thorne, "The Conversion of Englishmen and the Conversion of the World Inseparable: Missionary Imperialism and the Language of Class in Early Industrial Britain," in Cooper and Stoler, *Tensions of Empire*, 238–62; Saree Makdisi, *Making England Western: Occidentalism, Race, and Imperial Culture* (Chicago: Chicago University Press, 2014).
29. On Wakefield's account, Adam Smith had incorrectly assumed that the division of labor would spontaneously grow wherever the natural propensity to exchange found expanded markets. Wakefield argued that social and technical division of labor presupposed "some anterior improvement," namely, the formation of a class of wage laborers (EA, 326).
30. Organization of productive labor in wage form offered an index of modern civilization. As I detail, for Wakefield, wage labor articulated prosperity and freedom in a singular way that neither commercial slave labor nor commodity-producing peasant labor could. We shall also see, however, that Wakefield's celebration of the existence of the working class was matched only by his prevarication about its historical origins in forcible dispossession.
31. Wakefield used the terms, "field of employment," "field of production," and "field of investment" interchangeably. I will be referring to this notion simply as "the field" in the rest of the chapter.
32. For instance, differential capital-labor-field ratios yielded high profits and high wages in America, high profits and low wages in Bengal, high wages and low profits in postwar France, and low profits and low wages in postwar England (EA, 375).
33. For a similar remark, see Karl Marx, *Capital*, 1:637, where Marx observed that mechanized agriculture had not yet expelled agricultural workers in America because of the expanding frontier.
34. The simple expression of the field of employment was "demand for capital" indicated by the interest rate. Interest rates were unusually low in mid-1820s. Hilton, *Corn, Cash*, chap. 8; Winch, "Classical Economics," 97.
35. What Wakefield perceived to be speculation in fact belonged to a broader shift in the composition the British economy in which commerce and finance claimed an increasing share.

From the 1830s onward, the British current account relied on "invisible earnings" from credit and capital exports rather than on a trade surplus in manufactures. See P. J. Cain, "Economics and Empire: The Metropolitan Context," in Porter, *Oxford History of the British Empire*, 3:34–35; P. J. Cain and A. G. Hopkins, "The Political Economy of British Expansion Overseas, 1750–1914," *Economic History Review* 33 (1980): 463–90, 466; Hilton, *Mad, Bad, and Dangerous*, 12–13. See more broadly, Cain and Hopkins, *British Imperialism*; A. R. Dilley, "The Economics of Empire," in *The British Empire: Themes and Perspectives*, ed. Sarah Stockwell (Oxford: Blackwell, 2008).

36. Hilton, *Mad, Bad, and Dangerous*, 573–74.

37. Ibid., 31.

38. Ibid., 580–81.

39. Richard Brown, *Chartism* (Cambridge: Cambridge University Press, 1998).

40. Eric Hobsbawm and George Rudé, *Captain Swing* (New York: Norton, 1975); Edward G. Wakefield, *Swing Unmasked, or, The Causes of Rural Incendiarism* (London: Effingham Wilson, 1831).

41. Hilton notes a certain middle-class callousness toward mass poverty, which stemmed in part from the new orthodoxy of the market forces, competition, and the minimal state. Hilton, *Mad, Bad, and Dangerous*, 21, 585.

42. Holt, *Problem of Freedom*, 76.

43. As Bernard Semmel accurately points out, Wakefield and other Philosophic Radicals anticipated most of what are now considered to be the exclusive province of Marxist analysis, such as crises of overaccumulation, social polarization, and class conflict, over a decade before Marx came to England. Semmel, *Liberal Ideal*, 31.

44. On this point, see Winch, *Classical Political Economy*, chap. 6; Semmel, *Rise of Free Trade*, chaps. 3 and 4; and Kittrell, "Development of the Theory."

45. Breaking with Ricardian animosity toward the British landed classes, Wakefield maintained that the Repeal would also benefit them through product diversification under an expanded domestic market (thanks to rising real wages) and consequently higher rents (EA, 420–23). Ricardo had proclaimed that "the interest of the landlord is always opposed to the interest of every other class in the community." David Ricardo, *An Essay on the Influence of a Low Price of Corn on the Profits of Stock* (London: John Murray, 1815). In early nineteenth century the promise of the "big loaf" had become a discursive nodal point around which working-class discontent coalesced with the industrialists' assault on the Corn Laws. For a focused treatment of Wakefield's rent theory and the Corn Laws, see Edward Kittrell, "Wakefield and Classical Rent Theory," *American Journal of Economics and Sociology* 25 (1966): 141–52.

46. Cain, "Economics and Empire," 34.

47. This proposal actually presaged the establishment of Hong Kong. Wakefield remarked, "[I]f there be any foreign restriction on the foreign demand for English manufactured goods, restrictions which it is in the power of the English government to remove, interference for that purpose is a proper office, a bounden duty, of government" (EA, 430). The liberal imperialist endorsement of establishing free trade by the military-diplomatic means was already in place in the early 1830s. The Colonial Reformers, in addition to being free traders, were also supporters of the Opium Wars.

48. For instance, *Plan of a Company* (1830) stipulated free trade for the prospective Australian colony not only with the mother country but also with the rest of the world. See Lionel Robbins, *Robert Torrens and the Evolution of Classical Economics* (London: MacMillan, 1958), chaps. 6 and 7.

49. Semmel, *Liberal Ideal*, 32.

50. Semmel, "Philosophic Radicals," 87.

51. James Belich, *Replenishing the Earth: The Settler Revolution and the Rise of the Anglo-World, 1783–1939* (Oxford: Oxford University Press, 2009) downplays Wakefield's role in reviving British settler colonialism. For a response, see Ballantyne, "Theory and Practice" and "Remaking the Empire."

52. Kent Fedorowich, "The British Empire on the Move, 1760–1914," in *The British Empire: Themes and Perspectives*, ed. Sarah Stockwell (Oxford: Blackwell, 2008), 70.

53. Karen O'Brien, "Colonial Emigration, Public Policy, and Tory Romanticism, 1783–1830," in *Exclusionary Empire: English Liberty Overseas, 1600–1900*, ed. Jack P. Greene (Cambridge: Cambridge University Press, 2010), 161.

54. Fedorowich, "British Empire," in Stockwell, *British Empire*, 72–73.

55. K. O'Brien, "Colonial Emigration," in Greene, *Exclusionary Empire*, 161–62.

56. Winch, *Classical Political Economy*, 51–57; Shaw, introduction to *Great Britain*, 5–7.

57. Charles Buller, 1843 Parliamentary Speech.

58. For a comparison of the Wilmot-Horton's and Wakefield's colonization plans, see R. N. Ghosh, "Colonization Controversy: R. J. Wilmot-Horton and the Classical Economists," *Economica* 31 (1964): 385–400.

59. I borrow the term "frontier pathology" from Olssen, "Wakefield and New Zealand," 205.

60. Olssen, "Wakefield and the Scottish Enlightenment," 54–58. Also see Pocock, *Barbarism and Religion*, vol. 4, chaps. 9 and 10.

61. Moloney, "Savagery and Civilization," 153.

62. In fact, the expropriation and exploitation of the non-Europeans was more ruthless when the Europeans sincerely believed in the propriety and morality of their actions and affirmed their self-conception through them. Pocock neatly encapsulates this logic in his investigation of the British encroachment upon Maori territory in New Zealand: "[T]hough the ideology of agriculture and savagery was formed to justify this expropriation, it also articulated things which the Pakeha [British settlers] very deeply believed about themselves . . . They were not only expropriators, and this made it easier for them to deny that expropriation was what they were doing." Pocock, "*Tangata Whenua*," 214–15.

63. Indigenous people appeared to the promoters of colonization and settlers to be a temporal anomaly, destined for "elimination" either by assimilation or eradication by the inexorable advance of civilization. Wolfe, "Settler Colonialism"; Duncan Bell, "Desolation Goes before Us," *Journal of British Studies* 54 (2015): 987–93; Patrick Brantlinger, *Dark Vanishings: Discourse on the Extinction of Primitive Races, 1800–1930* (Ithaca, NY: Cornell University Press, 2003). On settler mythscapes, see Bell, "Dream Machine," 42, 28. Wakefield wrote, "If you had been a colonist, or architect of society, you would feel, as well as Bacon knew by means of his profound insight into the human nature, that colonization is a heroic work . . . the life of a settler, when colonization prospers, is a perpetual feast of anticipated and realized satisfaction" (AC, 827–28).

64. Moloney, "Savagery and Civilization," 171. Also see Olssen, "Wakefield and New Zealand," 205–11, and "Wakefield and the Scottish Enlightenment," 52, 58.

65. Wakefield often overstated the ease with which land could be purchased, cleared, and settled by workers without substantial means. Eric Richards notes that "laborers generally did not obtain land quickly; access to land was constrained much more by the economies of scale and the capital requirements of pastoralism." Eric Richards, "Wakefield and Australia," in Temple, *Edward Gibbon Wakefield*, 95.

66. Nonetheless, in the postscript to *A Letter from Sydney*, Wakefield seriously considered using Chinese indentured labor in the colonization of South Australia and New Zealand, reflecting the broader tendency to view the Pacific as "a labor reserve for indentured servitude." Donald Denoon and Marivic Wyndham, "Australia and the Western Pacific," in Porter, *Oxford History of the British Empire*, 3:553. When his predictions based on systematic colonization theory failed to materialize in New Zealand in 1850s, Wakefield did not hesitate to push for promoting the immigration of Chinese indentured workers. Prichard, introduction to *Collected Works*, 67.

67. Pocock, "*Tangata Whenua*," 211–12.

68. Ibid., 201–2.

69. Ironically, the social concentration argument was also wielded by the *opponents* of emigration, who saw in the social density of Britain the potential for a further division of labor, an increased productivity, and a solution to poverty. See Edward Kittrell, "Wakefield's Scheme of Systematic Colonization and Classical Economics," *American Journal of Economics and Sociology* 32 (1973): 87–111

70. Wakefield's anxieties about the subversive impact of letting colonists do as they wished had a much older genealogy. Early modern mercantilist debates exhibited grave concern

over the potential "abuse" of liberties by the masterless men spawned by the English enclosures. See Joyce O. Appleby, "Ideology and Theory: The Tension between Political and Economic Liberalism in Seventeenth-Century England," *American Historical Review* 81 (1976): 499–515.

71. The predominant controversy about labor in the seventeenth and eighteenth centuries was how to get laborers to work for more than what was enough to satisfy their basic needs. Put baldly, the laboring poor were not quite "laboring." One seventeenth-century commentator complained that if "two days pay will keep them a week," the lazy English workers would choose to loiter for the remaining five days. Another reproached them for being "too proud to beg, too lazy to work, when 'tis either too hot or too cold, and will choose their own time and wages, or you may do the work yourself." Appleby, *Economic Thought*, 146.

72. One significant merit of Wakefield's theory was to posit the problem from which Marx extrapolated the crucial antithesis between individual private property and capitalist private property. Individual property in the conditions of labor served as the basis of relative economic independence; whereas capitalist property emerged from the destruction of individual property and the subjection of the dispossessed to the imperatives of capital accumulation. Marx, *Capital*, 1:927–31.

73. Wakefield followed the distinction that Smith drew in the *Wealth of Nations* between the expenditure of income as "revenue" as opposed to "capital." Smith, *Wealth of Nations*, 1:277–90.

74. Marx, *Capital*, 1:931.

75. On "capital-positing labor," see Rakesh Bhandari, "The Disguises of Wage Labor: Juridical Illusions, Unfree Conditions and Novel Extensions," *Historical Materialism* 16 (2008): 71–99.

76. Marx, *Capital*, vol. 1, chaps. 13 and 14. As with labor, so was with land. Limited chances to market the produce of land, or in Wakefield's terms, to transform "plenty" into "value," severed the Ricardian cord between rents and the natural fertility of the soil. Wakefield explained differentials in rent by a tract of land's access to social factors of production (labor, manure, and other inputs), connection to transportation infrastructure (roads, ports), and proximity to towns and markets (LS, 161–62; EA, 413–16). Deriving the value of land from its natural fertility would be possible only "[i]f nature had provided markets in waste countries, or if mankind could fly, easily carrying great weights through the air" (EA, 414–15). Here, too, Wakefield crossed paths with Marx, who would later disparage Ricardo for seeking "refuge in organic chemistry" in explaining falling profits. Karl Marx, *Grundrisse: Foundations of the Critique of Political Economy* (London: Penguin, 1993), 754.

77. Moloney, "*Savagery and Civilization*," 153.

78. See Madhavi Kale, *The Fragments of Empire: Capital, Slavery, and Indian Indentured Labor Migration to the British Caribbean* (Philadelphia: University of Pennsylvania Press, 1998), esp. chap. 2. For the increasing centrality of the ideology of "free labor" to the hegemony of the British middle classes after 1832, as well as its dialectical relationship to the abolitionist discourse, see David Brion Davis, *The Problem of Slavery in the Age of Revolution, 1770–1823* (Ithaca, NY: Cornell University Press, 1975), 349–60.

79. Kale writes, "On the one hand, indentured migration was represented as a new system of slavery . . . On the other hand, it was defended as a form of free labor especially suited to distinctively imperial conditions, where natural resources and labor were not always coincident." Kale, *Fragments of Empire*, 173–74.

80. Ibid., 44–48.

81. Adam Smith, *Lectures on Jurisprudence*, ed. R. L. Meek, D. D. Raphael, and P. G. Stein, vol. 5 of *The Glasgow Edition of the Works and Correspondence of Adam Smith* (Indianapolis, IN: Liberty Fund, 1982), 179.

82. Hamish Maxwell-Stewart, *Closing Hell's Gates: The Life and Death of a Convict Station* (Crows Nest, UK: Allen & Unwin, 2008); Lucy Frost and Hamish Maxwell-Stewart, *Chain Letters: Narrating Convict Lives* (Carlton South, AUS: Melbourne University Press, 2002).

83. Eric Williams, *Capitalism and Slavery* (Chapel Hill: University of North Carolina Press, 1944), 9–16. Also see Marcus Rediker, Cassandra Pybus, and Emma Christopher, eds., *Many Middle Passages: Forced Migration and the Making of the Modern World* (Berkeley: University of California Press, 2007).

84. On settler capitalism in Australia, see Donald Denoon, *Settler Capitalism: The Dynamics of Dependent Development in the Southern Hemisphere* (Oxford: Oxford University Press, 1983); Philip McMichael, *Settlers and the Agrarian Question: Foundations of Capitalism in Colonial Australia* (Cambridge: Cambridge University Press, 1984).

85. Andrew Porter, "Trusteeship, Anti-Slavery and Humanism," in Porter, *Oxford History of the British Empire*, 3:204.

86. David Brion Davis points to the surge in slave populations in the Western Hemisphere as an indication of the "immense profitability of slave labor" in the half-century before the emancipation, around the same time classical economists and humanitarians took refuge in the "comforting illusion that slave labor was inefficient, unprofitable, and an impediment to economic growth." Davis, *Problem of Slavery*, 61.

87. Henry Taylor, "Paper on the proposed emancipation of slaves presenting the advantages and disadvantages of a number of plans for effecting the abolition of slavery" (1833), quoted in Holt, *Problem of Freedom*, 123.

88. Holt, *Problem of Freedom*, 123.

89. Ibid., 143, 146. As Kale aptly notes, what was lacking in the postemancipation Caribbean was not labor, but labor that yielded a surplus. Kale, *Fragments of Empire*, 55–60.

90. Holt, *Problem of Freedom*, 146. For an overview of the colonial labor problem in the Caribbean and the dilemmas of emancipation, see Gad Heuman, "The British West Indies," in Porter, *Oxford History of the British Empire*, vol. 3. Heuman emphasizes that imperial policymakers realized that abolishing slavery without "casting the West Indies in barbarism" hinged on retaining the plantation economy without slave labor. Heuman, "British West Indies," 474.

91. Lord Glenelg's dispatch to West Indian governors, quoted in Holt, *Problem of Freedom*, 74. Wakefield did not believe the West Indies to be immanently susceptible to barbarization because he considered the apprenticeship system to be a practical continuation of slavery (EA, 486).

92. Pocock, "Mobility of Property," 107–9, 114–15; and Popcock "*Tangata Whenua*," 206.

93. Pocock, "Mobility of Property," 121.

94. Pocock, *Barbarism and Religion*, 4:6.

95. Davis, *Problem of Slavery*, 82, 254, 349. The abolitionist cause did not imply a catholic sympathy for the laboring classes. Although the antislavery movement was certainly instrumental in "making a sincere humanitarianism an integral part of class ideology," it also offered a "highly selective response to the exploitation of labor," "isolating specific forms of human misery, allowing issues of freedom and discipline to be faced in a relatively simplified model." Davis, *Problem of Slavery*, 402–3, 455–58, 464–68.

96. The abolition of slavery belonged to a broader genus of institutional reforms targeting prisons, police, and poor relief in the 1830s and 1840s, which built on the modern techniques of disciplinary power. See Michel Foucault, *Discipline and Punish: The Birth of the Prison* (New York: Vintage, 1995).

97. Catherine Hall, "What Did a British World Mean to the British?," in *Rediscovering the British World*, ed. P. Buckner and R. D. Francis (Calgary: University of Calgary Press, 2005), 26, 28.

98. Hall, "What Did a British World Mean," in Bruckner and Francis, *Rediscovering*, 27

99. By the end of the eighteenth century, the laborer's consent to enter into a wage contract with the employer was the juridical sign of freedom, regardless of whether or not the laborer was in practical bondage. One illustrative case was the question, broached in *Knight v. Wedderburn*, of whether Scottish colliers and salters who were bound to mines for life were slaves. The court decided that because the miners received "high wages," their lifetime bondage represented not legal slavery but "commercial regulation." The decision demonstrated "the importance of wages as a symbol of exchange and voluntarism even in a situation of nearly absolute subordination." Davis, *Problem of Slavery*, 489–92. A similar case would be made by the critics of "gradual abolition." Against proposals to allow slaves to work one day of the week for wages in order to buy their freedom, critics like Lord Grey held that wages and slavery were mutually exclusive. Holt, *Problem of Freedom*, 47.

100. This was one area in which Wakefield's efforts bore fruit. With the adoption of Ripon Land Regulations in 1831, the sale of colonial lands replaced the land-grant system in Canada, the West Indies, and Australasia.

101. The earliest formulation of this position was arguably Locke's theory of the value-creating powers of labor in transforming the natural common into the common stock of mankind, which I discuss in chapter 2.

102. Smith wrote, "plenty of good land, and liberty to manage their own affairs their own way, seem to be the two greatest causes of the prosperity of all new colonies." Smith, *Wealth of Nations*, 2:28.

103. Ibid., 2:23.

104. See Thomas Hopkins, "Adam Smith on Economic Development and the Future of the European Atlantic Empires," in Reinert and Røge, *Political Economy of Empire*.

105. Adam Smith, *An Inquiry into the Nature and Causes of the Wealth of Nations . . . with a commentary by the author of "England and America,"* ed. Edward Gibbon Wakefield (London, Charles Knight: 1835–1840).

106. The term "tragedy of the commons" was coined and popularized by Garret Hardin, "The Tragedy of the Commons, *Science* 162 (1968): 1243–48.

107. Moloney observes that the association of property with exchangeable value was a strikingly constant tenet across the competing (Lockean, Scottish, and Utilitarian) theories of property in the colonization of New Zealand. Moloney, "Savagery and Civilization," 163–66.

108. Karl Polanyi, *The Great Transformation: The Political and Economic Origins of Our Time* (Boston: Beacon, 2001), chap. 3.

109. Pocock, *Barbarism and Religion*, 4:173n.

110. Justus von Liebig was a natural scientist who specialized in biological and agricultural chemistry. Ricardo had earlier argued, "If with every accumulation of capital we could tack a piece of fresh fertile land to our Island, profits would never fall." David Ricardo, "Essay on Profits," in *The Works and Correspondence of David Ricardo*, vol. 4, ed. Pierro Sraffa (Cambridge: Cambridge University Press, 1952), 18.

111. On fictitious commodities, see Polanyi, *Great Transformation*, chap. 6.

112. Prichard, introduction to *Collected Works*, 23–24.

113. True to his claim to utilitarian science, Wakefield did not entrust such a technically sophisticated manner to colonial governors, who were "always a sailor or a soldier" and "as fit to manage a great work of public economy as Adam Smith was fit to navigate a ship or command a regiment" (EA, 534). Wakefield's suggestion that the British government commission a political economist for each colony may sound fanciful, but it was consistent with the scientific-utilitarian underpinnings of his project (LS, 165).

114. Piterberg and Veracini, "Wakefield, Marx," 473.

115. On the function of the reserve army of labor in capital accumulation, see Marx, *Capital*, 1:792.

116. Christopher Lloyd, "The Emergence of Australian Settler Capitalism in the Nineteenth Century and the Disintegration/Integration of Aboriginal Societies," in *Indigenous Participation in Australian Economies*, ed. Ian Keen (Canberra: ANU Press, 2010), 26.

117. Christopher Lloyd, "Institutional Patterns of the Settler Societies: Hybrid, Parallel, and Convergent," in *Settler Economies in World History*, ed. Christopher Lloyd, Jacob Metzer, Richard Such (Ledien: Brill, 2012). Also see McMichael, *Settlers*.

118. Smith's favorable assessment of the colonization of North America was grounded in his assumption that there was a positive correlation between markets and the division of labor. Smith, *Wealth of Nations*, 1:350.

119. Patricia Burns, *The Fatal Success: A History of the New Zealand Company* (Auckland, NZ: H. Reed, 1989); M. P. K. Sorrenson, "The Politics on Land," in *The Maori and New Zealand Politics*, ed. J. G. A. Pocock (Auckland, NZ: Blackwood and Janet Paul, 1965); James Belich, *Making Peoples: A History of the New Zealanders, from Polynesian Settlement to the End of the Nineteenth Century* (Honolulu: University of Hawaii Press, 1996), chaps. 5–11.

120. Lloyd, "Emergence," 29.

121. Kale, *Fragments of Empire*, 5–6, 159.

122. Ibid., 111–13.

123. As Lloyd notes, even convicts had rights and could not be enslaved. Wolfe holds that differences of legal status notwithstanding, convict labor in settler societies structurally mirrored chattel slavery in plantation societies. Lloyd, "Emergence," 27; Wolfe, *Settler Colonialism*, 2.

124. Bell, "Dream Machine," 43.

125. Ibid.
126. Michel Foucault, *The Birth of Biopolitics: Lectures at the College de France, 1978–1979*, ed. Michael Senellart (New York: Palgrave MacMillan, 2008), 167.
127. Peter Burroughs, "Imperial Institutions and the Government of Empire," in Porter, *Oxford History of the British Empire*, vol. 3, 179–97. Also see Ann Laura Stoler, "On Degrees of Imperial Sovereignty," *Public Culture* 18 (2006): 125–46.
128. Wakefield's proposed plan for colonizing South Australia stipulated that the colony would be a crown colony until its adult male population reached 10,000, taken as an indication of the economic maturity he felt was requisite for self-government (PC, 277).
129. A case in point is Lord Glenelg's 1836 dispatch to all West Indian colonial governors, which virtually stipulated that Wakefield's theory be implemented to maintain capitalist civilization in the postemancipation West Indies. Holt, *Problem of Freedom*, 74–75.
130. This task could also proceed through public-private partnerships. Wakefield suggested "colonizing companies seated in the mother-country" as "very effective instruments of the state in promoting the emigration of capital and labour, because properly-empowered and properly-restrained instruments" (AC, 991).
131. Jeremy Bentham, *The Theory of Legislation* (New York: Harcourt, Brace, 1931), 110–11.
132. Wakefield observed the same "natural" inclinations in Chinese merchants, whose penchant for higher profits drove them to smuggling. His call for founding a free trade emporium on an island off the coast of China was similarly aimed at manipulating these inclinations to the benefit of British economic interests (EA, 453–58).
133. On Wakefield's reflections on land rents, see Kittrell, "Wakefield and Classical Rent."
134. John Martin, "A Small Nation on the Move: Wakefield's Theory of Colonisation and the Relationship between State and Labour in the Mid-Nineteenth Century," in Temple, *Edward Gibbon Wakefield*.
135. Belich, *Making Peoples*, 300–302.
136. Raewyn Dalziel, "Men, Women, and Wakefield," in Temple, *Edward Gibbon Wakefield*, 81–83.
137. Wakefield's conception of division of labor implicitly included women's labor as a condition of productivity but denied such labor itself any productive quality. Ibid., 83–84.
138. Belich, *Making Peoples*, 334. To this end, colonial entrepreneurs followed the Tory myths of the moral integrity of rural population into the English countryside, which they combed for single women who could be convinced to emigrate. Ibid., 334–36. Also see Fedorowich, "British Empire," 78.
139. Richards, "Wakefield and Australia," 97.
140. Smith, *Wealth of Nations*, 1:237–38, 281–82.
141. Marx, *Capital*, 1:873.
142. Marx did not spare Wakefield in his withering disdain for classical political economists. Michael Perelman likewise dismisses Wakefield's conjecture as outrageous and absurd. Marx, *Capital* 1:934; Michael Perelman, *The Invention of Capitalism: Classical Political Economy and the Secret History of Primitive Accumulation* (Durham, NC: Duke University Press. 2000), chap. 10.
143. Marx, *Capital*, 1:651.
144. Ibid., 1:899.
145. Turnbull, *New Zealand Bubble*; Tucker, "Application and Significance."
146. K. O'Brien, "Colonial Emigration," 164.
147. Duncan Bell, *The Idea of Greater Britain: Empire and the Future of World Order, 1860–1900* (Princeton, NJ: Princeton University Press, 2007).
148. Duncan Bell, "Imagined Spaces: Nation, State, and Territory in the British Colonial Empire, 1860–1914"; and Bell, "The Project for a New Anglo Century: Race, Space, and Global Order," both in *Reordering the World*, 166–81 and 182–210, respectively.
149. A similar case could be made about the changing metropolitan attitudes toward colonial slave ownership from the seventeenth to the eighteenth centuries. While this question lies outside the scope of this book, for some preliminary remarks see Ince, "Between Commerce and Empire," forthcoming.
150. See Thorne, "Conversion of Englishmen"; Makdisi, *Making England Western*.

151. Mehta, *Liberalism and Empire*, 82.

152. Duncan Bell, "Escape Velocity: Ancient History and the Empire of Time," in *Reordering the World*, 119–47.

153. Cecil Rhodes, *The Last Will and Testament of Cecil John Rhodes*, ed. William T. Stead (London: Review of Reviews, 1902), 190.

154. Even Smith, the inveterate critic of imperial conquest, did not see the Native American practices of cultivation as amounting to "agriculture proper" and therefore having advanced beyond the stage of savagery. Smith, *Lectures on Jurisprudence*, 5:54.

155. Anthony Howe, "Free Trade and Global Order: The Rise and Fall of a Victorian Vision," in *Victorian Visions of Global Order: Empire and International Relations Nineteenth-Century Political Thought*, ed. Duncan Bell (Cambridge: Cambridge University Press, 2007).

Conclusion

1. A recent line of research has emphasized the neo-republican critiques of capitalism as a structure of domination in the workplace and beyond. See, above all, Alex Gourevitch, *From Slavery to Cooperative Commonwealth: Labor and Republican Liberty in Nineteenth Century* (Cambridge: Cambridge University Press, 2014); William Clare Roberts, *Marx's Inferno: The Political Theory of Capital* (Princeton, NJ: Princeton University Press, 2016); Steven Klein, "Fictitious Freedom: A Polanyian Critique of the Republican Revival," *American Journal of Political Science*, online publication, July 4, 2017, doi.10.1111/ajps.12317.

2. Jennifer Pitts, "Free for All," *Times Literary Supplement*, September 23, 2011, 8.

3. Mantena, "Fragile Universals," 543–55, at 551.

4. Chakrabarty, *Provincializing Europe*; Mehta, *Liberalism and Empire*.

5. Pitts, *Turn to Empire*; Pitts, "Empire, Progress, and the Savage Mind," in *Colonialism and Its Legacies*, ed. Jacob T. Levy and Iris Marion Young (New York: Lexington, 2011), 21–52; Muthu, *Enlightenment against Empire*; Muthu, "Diderot's Theory of Global (and Imperial) Commerce: An Enlightenment Account of 'Globalization,'" in Levy and Young, *Colonialism*, 1–20. It is worth noting that even Uday Mehta, who furnished the most totalizing critique of liberal imperialism, acknowledges liberalism's internal variability, discerning a redeeming potential in the "cosmopolitanism of sentiment" that marks "this other liberalism." Mehta, *Liberalism and Empire*, 20, 43.

6. Hall, *Civilising Subjects*; Mantena, *Alibis of Empire*.

7. For an encompassing account on "neo-Europes," see Belich, *Replenishing the Earth*.

8. See, among others, David Washbrook, "Law, State, and Agrarian Society in Colonial India," *Modern Asian Studies* 15 (1981): 649–721; Frederick Cooper, *Decolonization and African Society: The Labor Question in French and British Africa* (Cambridge: Cambridge University Press, 1996); Ann Laura Stoler, *Capitalism and Confrontation in Sumatra's Plantation Belt, 1870–1979* (Ann Arbor: University of Michigan Press, 1995).

9. Ronald Takaki, *Iron Cages: Race and Culture in Nineteenth-Century America* (New York: Alfred A. Knopf, 1979); Herman Merivale, *Lectures on Colonies and Colonisation*, vol. 2 (London: Longman, 1842), 152.

10. Nicholas Dirks, *Castes of Mind: Colonialism and the Making of Modern India* (Princeton, NJ: Princeton University Press, 2001). Also see Goswami, *Producing India*.

11. Fitzmaurice, *Sovereignty*.

12. Travers, "Contested Despotisms," in Greene, *Exclusionary Empire*; B. R. Tomlinson, "Economics and Empire: The Periphery and the Imperial Economy," in Porter, *Oxford History of the British Empire*, vol. 3, 53–74.

13. Patrick Wolfe, "Land, Labor, and Difference: Elementary Structures of Race," *American Historical Review* 106 (2001): 866–905.

14. Cedric Robinson, *Black Marxism: The Making of the Black Tradition* (Chapel Hill: University of North Carolina Press, 1983). Also see Anibal Quijano, "Coloniality of Power, Eurocentrism, and Latin America," *Nepantla: Views from the South* 1 (2000): 533–80.

15. Nichols, "Disaggregating Primitive Accumulation," 18–28; Coulthard, *Red Skin, White Masks*; Gavin Walker, "Primitive Accumulation and the Formation of Difference: On Marx and Schmitt," *Rethinking Marxism* 23 (2011): 384–404; William Clare Roberts, "What Was

Primitive Accumulation? Reconstructing the Origin of a Critical Concept," *European Journal of Political Theory*, online publication, October 11, 2017, doi.10.1177/1474885117735961.

16. Following Kalyan Sanyal, Chatterjee contends that primitive accumulation not only institutes the conditions of liberal bourgeois civil society, but also creates alongside it dispossessed masses who are abandoned by capital, and whose livelihood exists outside the formal economy and jurisdiction of civil society. Partha Chatterjee, *The Lineages of Political Society: Studies in Postcolonial Democracy* (New York: Columbia University Press, 2011); Sanyal, *Rethinking Capitalist Development*.

17. Hannah Arendt, *Origins of Totalitarianism* (New York: Harcourt, Brace, 1973), 145–48.

18. Max Weber, *The Theory of Social and Economic Organization* (New York: Oxford University Press, 1947), 329–41; H. H. Gerth and C. Wright Mills, *From Max Weber: Essays in Sociology* (New York: Oxford University Press, 1946), 196–244. Also see Mara Loveman, "The Modern State and the Primitive Accumulation of Symbolic Power," *American Journal of Sociology* 110 (2005): 1651–83.

19. James Scott, *Seeing like a State: How Certain Schemes to Improve the Human Condition Have Failed* (New Haven, CT: Yale University Press, 1998).

20. I develop this point in more detail in Ince, "Bringing the Economy Back In," 411–26.

21. As I argue elsewhere, one way of incorporating theories of constituent power into the analysis of capitalism is to differentiate primitive accumulation into instances of "capital-positing" and "capital-preserving" violence operating at different structural moments of capitalist reproduction. The main inspiration behind this reformulation are Walter Benjamin's reflections on "law-making" and "law-preserving" extralegal violence. See Walter Benjamin, "Critique of Violence," in *Reflections: Essays, Aphorisms, Autobiographical Writings*, ed. Peter Demetz (New York: Harcourt, Brace, 1978); Onur Ulas Ince, "Between Equal Rights: Primitive Accumulation and Capital's Violence," *Political Theory*, online publication, December 18, 2017, doi.10.1177/0090591717748420.

22. Political founding as an explicit problem of political theory can be traced back to Jean-Jacques Rousseau's *Social Contract*. Some prominent twentieth-century reappraisals of the problem include Carl Schmitt, *The Crisis of Parliamentary Democracy* (Cambridge, MA: MIT Press, 1985); Claude Lefort, *Democracy and Political Theory* (Minneapolis: University of Minnesota Press, 1988); John Rawls, *Political Liberalism* (New York: Columbia University Press, 2005); Jurgen Habermas, *Between Facts and Norms: Contributions to a Discourse of Law and Democracy* (Cambridge, MA: MIT Press, 1996); and Chantal Mouffe, *The Democratic Paradox* (London: Verso, 2000).

23. Jason Frank, *Constituent Moments: Enacting the People in Postrevolutionary America* (Durham, NC: Duke University Press, 2010).

24. Edmund Burke, "Speech on Opening of Impeachment," in *W&S*, 6:276, 290.

25. Schmitt, *Nomos of the Earth*.

26. Giorgio Agamben, *Homo Sacer: Sovereign Power and Bare Life* (Stanford, CA: Stanford University Press, 1998); and Agamben, *State of Exception* (Chicago: University of Chicago Press, 2005).

27. For liberal thinkers, the picture was further complicated by normative commitments to juridical equality and contractual freedom. As we have seen, when confronted by colonial primitive accumulation, Locke, Burke, and Wakefield also invoked secular and immanent myths of concord for capturing this unruly political element and couching it in liberal terms: the universal tacit consent of mankind (Locke), imperial power as a trust from the governed (Burke), and the originary agreement of human beings to divide themselves into the capitalists and laborers (Wakefield).

28. Giovanni Arrighi, *The Long Twentieth Century: Money, Power, and the Origins of Our Times* (New York: Verso, 1994); Fraser, "Behind Marx's Hidden Abode"; David Harvey, *The New Imperialism* (Oxford: Oxford University Press, 2003).

29. Stefan Halper, *Beijing Consensus: How China's Authoritarian Model Will Dominate the Twenty-First Century* (New York: Basic, 2010).

30. Sassen, *Expulsions*; Annelies Zoomers, "Globalization and the Foreignization of Space: The Seven Processes Driving the Current Global Land Grab," *Journal of Peasant Studies* 37 (2010): 429–47.

INDEX

CPSIA information can be obtained
at www.ICGtesting.com
Printed in the USA
JSHW021340030120
3323JS00004B/13